I0755770

KEEP AWAY !—p. 139.

THE

PRAIRIE TRAVELER,

A HAND-BOOK

FOR

OVERLAND EXPEDITIONS.

WITH ILLUSTRATIONS, AND ITINERARIES OF THE PRINCIPAL ROUTES BETWEEN THE MISSISSIPPI AND THE PACIFIC, AND A MAP.

By RANDOLPH B. MARCY,

CAPTAIN U. S. ARMY.

(NOW GENERAL MARCY, CHIEF OF STAFF, ARMY OF THE POTOMAC.)

EDITED (WITH NOTES) BY

RICHARD F. BURTON, F.R.G.S.,

ETC.

PUBLISHED IN THE UNITED STATES BY AUTHORITY OF THE WAR DEPARTMENT.

LONDON:

TRÜBNER AND CO., 60, PATERNOSTER ROW.

1863.

LONDON
PRINTED BY WERTHEIMER AND CO.
FINSBURY CIRCUS.

CONTENTS.

CHAPTER I.

CHAPTER II.

CHAPTER III.

CHAPTER IV.

CHAPTER V.

CHAPTER VI.

CHAPTER VII.

LIST OF ILLUSTRATIONS.

PREFACE.

A QUARTER of a century's experience in frontier life, a great portion of which has been occupied in exploring the interior of our continent, and in long marches where I have been thrown exclusively upon my own resources, far beyond the bounds of the populated districts, and where the traveler must vary his expedients to surmount the numerous obstacles which the nature of the country continually reproduces, has shewn me under what great disadvantages the "*voyageur*" labors for want of a timely initiation into those minor details of prairie-craft, which, however apparently unimportant in the abstract, are sure, upon the plains, to turn the balance of success for or against an enterprise.

This information is so varied, and is derived from so many different sources, that I still find every new expedition adds substantially to my practical knowledge, and am satisfied that a good Prairie Manual will be for the young traveler an addition to his equipment of inappreciable value.

With such a book in his hand, he will be able, in difficult circumstances, to avail himself of the matured experience of veteran travelers, and thereby avoid many otherwise unforeseen disasters; while, during the ordinary routine of marching, he will greatly augment the sum of his comforts, avoid many serious losses, and enjoy a comparative exemption from doubts and anxieties. He will feel himself a master spirit in the wilderness he traverses, and not the victim of every *new* combination of circumstances which nature affords or fate allots, as if to try his skill and prowess.

I have waited for several years, with the confident expectation that some one more competent than myself would assume the task, and give the public the desired information; but it seems that no one has taken sufficient interest in the subject to disseminate the benefits of his experience in this way. Our frontier-men, although brave in council and action, and possessing an intelligence that quickens in the face of danger, are apt to feel shy of the pen. They shun the atmosphere of the student's closet; their sphere is in the free and open wilderness. It is not to be wondered at, therefore, that to our veteran borderer the field of literature should remain a "*terra incognita.*" It is our army that unites the chasm between the culture of civilization in the aspect of science, art, and social refinement, and the powerful simplicity of nature. On leaving the Military Academy, a majority of our officers are attached to the line of the army, and forthwith assigned to duty upon our remote and extended frontier, where the restless and warlike habits of the nomadic tribes, render the soldier's life almost as unsettled as that of the savages themselves.

A regiment is stationed to-day on the borders of tropical Mexico; to-morrow, the war whoop, borne on a gale from the northwest, compels its presence in the frozen latitudes of Puget's Sound. The very limited numerical strength of our army, scattered as it is over a vast area of territory, necessitates constant changes of station, long and toilsome marches, a promptitude of action, and a tireless energy and self-reliance, that can only be acquired through an intimate acquaintance with the sphere in which we act and move.

The education of our officers at the Military Academy is, doubtless, well adapted to the art of civilised warfare, but cannot familiarise them with the diversified details of border service; and they often, at the outset of their military career, find themselves compelled to improvise new expedients to meet novel emergencies.

The life of the wilderness is an *art* as well as that of the city or court, and every art subjects its votaries to discipline in preparing them for a successful career in its pursuit. The Military Art, as enlarged to meet all the requirements of border service—the savage in his wiles, or the elements in their caprices—embraces many other special arts which have hitherto been almost ignored; and results which experience and calculation should have guaranteed, have been improvidently staked upon favorable chances.

The main object at which I have aimed in the following pages, has been to explain and illustrate, as clearly and succinctly as possible, the best methods of performing the duties devolving upon the prairie traveler, so as to meet their contingencies under all circumstances, and thereby to endeavor to establish a more uniform system of marching and campaigning in the Indian country.

I have also furnished itineraries of most of the principal routes that have been traveled across the plains, taken from the best and most reliable authorities; and I have given some information concerning the habits of the Indians and wild animals that frequent the prairies, with the secrets of the hunter's and warrior's strategy, which I have endeavoured to impress more forcibly upon the reader by introducing illustrative anecdote.

I take great pleasure in acknowledging my indebtedness to several officers of the Topographical Engineers, and of other corps of the army, for the valuable information I have obtained from their official reports regarding the different routes embraced in the itineraries; and to these gentlemen I beg leave very respectfully to dedicate my book.

EDITOR'S PREFACE.

The object of this little Volume, as the author has explained, is to initiate the novice into the mysteries of Prairie-craft. I have been induced to re-edit it, at the instance of my friend Mr. Trübner—not by the vain expectation of improving upon "a quarter of a century's experience in (American) frontier life," and the work of an accomplished woodsman—but with the humble hope that a little collateral knowledge gathered in other lands, may add variety, and perhaps something of value to what is at present our best Handbook of Western Field Sports. When that "late lamented institution," the once United States, shall have passed away, and when, after this detestable and fratricidal war—the most disgraceful to human nature that civilization ever witnessed,—the New World shall be restored to order and tranquility, our shikaris will not forget, that a single fortnight of comfortable travel suffices to transport them from fallow-deer and pheasant-shooting to the haunts of the bison and the grizzly bear. There is little chance of these animals being "improved off" the Prairies, or even of their becoming rare during the life-time of the present generation; those who love noble game may thus save themselves a journey to monotonous India or to pestilential Africa.

The English reader will be disposed to criticise a book which tells so much of what has been already told, and well told too, in the "Art of Travel," by Mr. Francis Galton. My belief is, that the more publications of the kind the better. Sad experience in the Crimea, proves that were the subject compulsorily rendered a part of military studies, it would contribute not a little to the efficiency of the service. Men would not then pine over "green coffee," with tons of bones lying around them waiting to become bonfires. They would not starve upon half-rations, nor reduce them to a quarter by injudicious management and an ignorance touching soup.

I have not taken liberties with the gallant author's style or order of chapters. He has retained all such naïvétes as "traveler," "cantel," "canvas," "woolen," "wagon," "segar," and "give out,"—*Anglicè* "give in." He has been left to indulge in the "Ay-merican" as much as he pleases. My work has been confined to notes, which, for the reader's satisfaction, I have marked ED., and for which I am wholly responsible. They are mostly drawn from my last study—"The City of the Saints, and Across the Rocky Mountains to California."

I venture, however, to solicit attention to two points. The first is the improved form of carbine shell. The second is the organized pantomimic practice, by which the North American Aborigines express themselves. It is my hope, presently, to produce a system of hand-language, with which, assisted by some 100 words, any man of average abilities shall make himself understood in any country after a week's study. Such a contrivance would be most useful in Africa, where within fifty miles, one meets with four or five different dialects.

Nothing remains now but to make my salam to the reader, and to conclude with a quotation from Southey:—

"Go, little book, from this my solitude!
"I cast thee on the waters—go thy ways!"

FERNANDO PO.
1st June, 1862.

THE PRAIRIE TRAVELER.

CHAPTER I.

The different Routes to California and Oregon.—Their respective Advantages.—Organization of Companies.—Elections of Captains.—Wagons and Teams.—Relative Merits of Mules and Oxen.—Stores and Provisions.—How packed.—Desiccated and canned Vegetables.—Pemmican.—Anti-scorbutics.—Cold Flour.—Substitutes in case of Necessity.—Amount of Supplies.—Clothing.—Camp Equipage.—Arms.

ROUTES TO CALIFORNIA AND OREGON.

Emigrants or others desiring to make the overland journey to the Pacific should bear in mind, that there are several different routes which may be traveled with wagons, each having its advocates in persons directly or indirectly interested in attracting the tide of emigration and travel over them.

Information concerning these routes coming from strangers living or owning property near them, from agents of steam-boats or railways, or from other persons connected with transportation companies, should be received with great caution, and never without corroborating evidence from disinterested sources.

There is no doubt that each one of these roads has its advantages and disadvantages; but a judicious selection must depend chiefly upon the following considerations, namely, the locality from whence the individual is to take his departure, the season of the year when he desires to commence his journey, the character of his means of transportation, and the point upon the Pacific coast that he wishes to reach.

Persons living in the Northeastern States can, with about equal facility and dispatch, reach the eastern terminus of any one of the routes they may select by means of public transport. And, as animals are much cheaper upon the frontier than in the Eastern States, they should purchase their teams at or near the point where the overland journey is to commence.

Those living in the Northwestern States having their own teams, and wishing to go to any point north of San Francisco, will of course make choice of the route which takes its departure from the Missouri River.

Those who live in the middle Western States, having their own means of transportation, and going to any point upon the Pacific coast, should take one of the middle routes.*

Others, who reside in the extreme Southwest, and whose destination is south of San Francisco, should travel the southern road running through Texas, which is the only one practicable for comfortable winter travel. The grass upon a great portion of this route is green during the entire winter, and snow seldom covers it. This road leaves the Gulf coast at *Powder-horn,* on Montagorda Bay, which point is difficult of access by land from the north, but may be reached by steamers from New Orleans five times a week.

There are stores at Powder-horn and Indianola where the traveler can obtain most of the articles necessary for his journey, but I would recommend him to supply himself before leaving New Orleans with everything he requires with the exception of animals, which he will find cheaper in Texas.

This road has received a large amount of travel since 1849, is well tracked and defined, and, excepting about twenty miles of "*Hog-wallow Prairie*" near Powder-horn,

* In a detailed account of these routes I must refer the reader to Chap. ii., City of the Saints; and for an Itinerary, to No. iv. in the list at the end of this volume.—Ed.

it is an excellent road for carriages and wagons. It passes through a settled country for 250 miles, and within this section supplies can be had at reasonable rates.

At Victoria and San Antonio many fine stores will be found, well supplied with large stocks of goods, embracing all the articles the traveler will require.

The next route to the north is that over which the semi-weekly mail to California passes, and which, for a great portion of the way to New Mexico, I traveled and recommended in 1849. This road leaves the Arkansas River at Fort Smith, to which point steamers run during the seasons of high water in the winter and spring.

Supplies of all descriptions necessary for the overland journey may be procured at Fort Smith, or at Van Buren on the opposite side of the Arkansas. Horses and cattle are cheap here. The road, on leaving Fort Smith, passes through the Choctaw and Chickasaw country for 180 miles, then crosses Red River by ferry-boat at Preston, and runs through the border settlements of northern Texas for 150 miles, within which distances supplies may be procured at moderate prices.

This road is accessible to persons desiring to make the entire journey with their own transportation from Tennessee or Mississippi, by crossing the Mississippi River at Memphis or Helena, passing Little Rock, and thence through Washington Country, intersecting the road at Preston. It may also be reached by taking steamers up Red River to Shreveport or Jefferson, from either of which places there are roads running through a populated country, and intersecting the Fort Smith road near Preston.

This road also unites with the San Antonio road at El Paso, and from that point they pass together over the mountains to Fort Yuma and to San Francisco in California.

Another road leaves Fort Smith and runs up the south side of the Canadian River to Santa Fé and Albuquerque in New Mexico.

This route is set down upon most of the maps of the present day as having been discovered and explored by various persons, but my own name seems to have been carefully excluded from the list. Whether this omission has been intentional or not, I leave for the authors to determine. I shall merely remark, that I had the command and entire direction of an expedition which in 1849 discovered, explored, located, and marked out this identical wagon road from Fort Smith, Arkansas, to Santa Fé, New Mexico, and that this road, for the greater portion of the distance, is the same that has been since recommended for a Pacific railway.

This road, near Albuquerque, unites with Captain Whipple's and Lieutenant Beall's roads to California.

Another road, which takes its departure from Fort Smith and passes through the Cherokee country, is called the "Cherokee Trail." It crosses Grand River at Fort Gibson, and runs a little north of west to the Verdigris River, thence up the valley of this stream on the north side for 80 miles, when it crosses the river, and, taking a northwest course, strikes the Arkansas river near old Fort Mann, on the Santa Fé trace; thence it passes near the base of Pike's Peak, and follows down Cherry Creek from its source to its confluence with the South Platte, and from thence over the mountains into Utah, and on to California *via* Fort Bridger and Salt Lake City.

For persons who desire to go from the Southern States to the gold diggings in the vicinity of Cherry Creek, this route is shorter by some 300 miles than that from Fort Smith *via* Fort Leavenworth. It is said to be an excellent road, and well supplied with the requisites for encamping. It has been traveled by large parties of California emigrants for several years, and is well tracked and defined.

The grass upon all the roads leaving Fort Smith is sufficiently advanced to afford sustenance to animals by the first of April, and from this time until winter sets in it is abundant. The next route on the north leaves the Missouri River at Westport, Leavenworth City, Atcheson, or from other towns above, between either of which points and St. Louis steamers ply during the entire summer season.

The necessary outfit of supplies can always be procured at any of the starting-points on the Missouri River at moderate rates.

This is the great emigrant route from Missouri to California and Oregon, over which so many thousands have traveled within the past few years. The track is broad, well worn, and cannot be mistaken. It has received the major part of the Mormon emigration, and was traversed by the army in its march to Utah in 1857.

At the point where this road crosses the South Platte River, Lieutenant Bryan's road branches off to the left, leading through Bridger's Pass, and thence to Fort Bridger. The Fort Kearney route to the golden region near Pike's Peak also leaves the emigrant road at this place and runs up the South Platte.

From Fort Bridger there are two roads that may be traveled with wagons in the direction of California; one passing Salt Lake City, and the other running down Bear River to Soda Springs, intersecting the Salt Lake City road at the *City of Rocks*. Near Soda Springs the Oregon road turns to the right, passing Fort Hall, and thence down Snake River to Fort Wallah-Wallah. Unless travelers have business in Salt Lake Valley, I would advise them to take the Bear River route, as it is much shorter, and better in every respect. The road, on leaving the Missouri River, passes for 150 miles through a settled country where grain can be purchased cheap, and there are several stores in this section where most of the articles required by travelers can be obtained.

Many persons who have had much experience in prairie-traveling prefer leaving the Missouri River in March or April, and giving grain to their animals until the new grass appears. The roads become muddy and heavy after the spring rains set in, and by starting out early the worst part of the road will be passed over before the ground becomes wet and soft. This plan, however, should never be attempted unless the animals are well supplied with grain, and kept in good condition. They will eat the old grass in the spring, but it does not, in this climate, as in Utah and New Mexico, afford them sufficient sustenance.

The grass, after the first of May, is good and abundant upon this road as far as the South Pass, from whence there is a section of about fifty miles where it is scarce; there is also a scarcity upon the desert beyond the sink of the Humboldt. As large numbers of cattle pass over the road annually, they soon consume all the grass in these barren localities, and such as pass late in the season are likely to suffer greatly, and oftentimes perish from starvation. When I came over the road in August, 1858, I seldom found myself out of sight of dead cattle for 500 miles along the road, and this was an unusually favorable year for grass, and before the main body of animals had passed for that season.

Upon the head of the Sweetwater River, and west of the South Pass, alkaline springs are met with, which are exceedingly poisonous to cattle and horses. They can readily be detected by the yellowish-red color of the grass growing around them. Animals should never be allowed to graze near them or to drink the water.

ORGANIZATION OF COMPANIES.

After a particular route has been selected to make the journey across the plains, and the requisite number have arrived at the eastern terminus, their first business should be to organize themselves into a company and elect a commander. The company should be of sufficient magnitude to herd and guard animals, and for protection against Indians.

From fifty to seventy men, properly armed and equipped, will be enough for these purposes, and any greater number only makes the movements of the party more cumbersome and tardy.

In the selection of a captain, good judgment, integrity of purpose, and practical experience are the essential requisites, and these are indispensable to the harmony and consolidation of the association. His duty should be to direct the order of march, the time of starting and halting, to select the camps, detail and give orders to guards, and, indeed, to control and superintend all the movements of the company.

An obligation should then be drawn up and signed by all the members of the association, wherein each one should bind himself to abide in all cases by the orders and decisions of the captain, and to aid him by every means in his power in the execution of his duties; and they should also obligate themselves to aid each other, so as to make the individual interest of each member the common concern of the whole company. To ensure this, a fund should be raised for the purchase of extra animals to supply the place of those which may give out or die on the road; and if the wagon or team of a particular member should fail and have to be abandoned, the company should obligate themselves to transport his luggage, and the captain should see that he has his share of transportation equal with any other member. Thus it will be made the interest of every member of the company to watch over and protect the property of others as well as his own.

In case of failure on the part of any one to comply with the obligations imposed by the articles of agreement after they have been duly executed, the company should, of course, have the power to punish the delinquent member, and, if necessary, exclude him from all the benefits of the association.

On such a journey as this, there is much to interest and amuse one who is fond of picturesque scenery, and of wild life in its most primitive aspect, yet no one should attempt it without anticipating many rough knocks and much hard labor; every man must expect to do his share of duty faithfully and without a murmur.

On long and arduous expeditions, men are apt to become irritable and ill-natured, and oftentimes fancy they have more labor imposed upon them than their comrades, and that the person who directs their march is partial towards his favorites, etc. That man who exercises the greatest forbearance under such circumstances, who is cheerful, slow to take up quarrels, and endeavours to reconcile difficulties among his companions, is deserving of all praise, and will, without doubt, contribute largely to the success and comfort of an expedition.

The advantages of an association such as I have mentioned are manifestly numerous. The animals can be herded together and guarded by the different members of the company in rotation, thereby securing to all the opportunities of sleep and rest. Besides, this is the only way to resist depredations of the Indians, and to prevent their stampeding and driving off animals; and much more efficiency is secured in every respect, especially in crossing streams, repairing roads, etc.

Unless a systematic organization be adopted, it is impossible for a party of any magnitude to travel in company for any great length of time, and for all the members to agree upon the same arrangements in marching, camping, etc. I have several times observed, where this has been attempted, that discords and dissensions, sooner or later arose, which invariably resulted in breaking up and separating the company.

When a captain has once been chosen, he should be sustained in all his decisions, unless he commit some manifest outrage, when a majority of the company can always remove him, and put a more competent man in his place. Sometimes men may be selected, who, upon trial, do not come up to the anticipations of those who have placed them in power, and other men will exhibit, during the march, more capacity. Under these circumstances, it will not be unwise to make a change, the first election having been distinctly provisional.*

WAGONS AND TEAMS.

A company having been organized, its first interest is to procure a proper outfit of transportation, and supplies for the contemplated journey.

* Mr. W. Kelly's California presents by far the most life-like and instructive picture of an organized Caravan March across the Prairies.—Ed.

Wagons should be of the simplest possible construction —strong, light, and made of well-seasoned timber, especially the wheels, as the atmosphere, in the elevated and arid region over which they have to pass, is so exceedingly dry during the summer months, that unless the wood-work is thoroughly seasoned, they will require constant repairs to prevent them from falling to pieces.

Wheels made of the bois-d'arc, or Osage orange-wood, are the best for the plains, as they shrink but little, and seldom want repairing. As, however, this wood is not easily procured in the Northern States, white oak answers a very good purpose if well seasoned.

Spring wagons made in Concord, New Hampshire, are used to transport passengers and the mails upon some of the routes across the plains, and they are said, by those who have used them, to be much superior to any others. They are made of the close-grained oak that grows in a high northern latitude, and is well seasoned.

The pole of the wagon should have a joint where it enters the hounds, to prevent the weight from coming upon it and breaking the hounds in passing short and abrupt holes in the road.

The perch or coupling-pole should be shifting or movable, as, in the event of the loss of a wheel, an axle, or other accident rendering it necessary to abandon the wagon, a temporary cart may be constructed out of the remaining portion. The tires should be examined just before commencing the journey, and, if not perfectly snug, reset.

One of the chief causes of accidents to carriages upon the plain arises from the nuts coming off from the numerous bolts that secure the running gearing. To prevent this, the ends of all the bolts should be rivetted; it is seldom necessary to take them off, and when this is required the ends of the bolts may easily be filed away.

Wagons with six mules should never, on a long journey over the prairies, be loaded with over 2000 pounds, unless grain is transported, when an additional thousand pounds may be taken, provided it is fed out daily to the team.

When grass constitutes the only forage, 2000 pounds is deemed a sufficient load. I regard our government wagons as unnecessarily heavy for six mules. There is sufficient material in them to sustain a burden of 4000 pounds, but they are seldom loaded with more than half that weight. Every wagon should be furnished with substantial bows and double Osnaburg covers, to protect its contents from the sun and weather.

There has been much discussion regarding the relative merits of mules and oxen for prairie traveling, and the question is yet far from being settled. Upon good firm roads, in a populated country, where grain can be procured, I should unquestionably give the preference to mules, as they travel faster, and endure the heat of summer much better than oxen; and if the journey be not over 1000 miles, and the grass abundant, even without grain, I think mules would preferable. But when the march is to extend 1500 or 2000 miles, or over a rough sandy or muddy road, I believe young oxen will endure better than mules; they will, if properly managed, keep in better condition, and perform the journey in an equally brief space of time. Besides, they are much more economical, a team of six mules costing six hundred dollars, while an eight-ox team only costs upon the frontier about two hundred dollars. Oxen are much less liable to be stampeded and driven off by Indians, and can be pursued and overtaken by horsemen; and, finally, they can, if necessary, be used for beef.

In Africa oxen are used as saddle animals, and it is said that they perform good service in this way. This will probably be regarded by our people as a very undignified and singular method of locomotion, but, in the absence of any other means of transportation upon a long journey, a saddle-ox might be found serviceable.

Andersson, in his work on South-western Africa, says: "A short strong stick, of peculiar shape, is forced through the cartilage of the nose of the ox, and to either end of this stick is attached (in bridle fashion) a tough leathern thong. From the extreme tenderness of the nose he is now more easily managed." "Hans presented me with an ox called 'Spring,' which I afterwards rode upwards of 2000 miles. On the day of our departure he mounted us all on oxen; and a curious sight it was to see some of the men take their seats who had never before ridden on ox-back. It is impossible to guide an ox as one would guide a horse; for in the attempt to do so you would instantly jerk the stick out of his nose, which at once deprives you of every control over the beast; but by pulling *both* sides of the bridle at the same time, and toward the side you wish him to take, he is easily managed.* Your seat is not less awkward and difficult; for the skin of the ox, unlike that of the horse, is loose, and, notwithstanding your saddle may be tightly girthed, you keep rocking to and fro like a child in a cradle. A few days, however, enables a person to acquire a certain steadiness; and long habit will do the rest."

"Ox-traveling, when once a man becomes accustomed to it, is not so disagreeable as might be expected, particularly if one succeeds in obtaining a tractable animal. On emergencies, an ox can be made to proceed at a tolerably quick pace; for, though his walk is only about three miles an hour at an average, he may be made to perform double that distance in the same time. Mr. Galton once accomplished twenty-four miles in four hours, and that, too, through heavy sand!"

Cows will be found very useful upon long journeys when the rate of travel is slow, as they furnish milk, and in emergencies they may be worked in wagons. I once saw a small cow yoked beside a large ox, and driven about six hundred miles attached to a loaded wagon, and she performed her part equally well with the ox. It has been by no means an unusual thing for emigrant travelers to work cows in their teams.†

* A ring instead of the stick put through the cartilage of the nose, would obviate this difficulty.—AUTHOR.

In the use of this ring I perfectly disagree with the Author. It would often be torn away from the nose by the sage and other tough growths of the Prairies.—ED.

† Englishmen, as well as Americans, deride the working of cows

The inhabitants of Pembina, on Red River, work a single ox harnessed in shafts like a horse, and they transport a thousand pounds in a rude cart made entirely of wood, without a particle of iron. One man drives and takes the entire charge of eight or ten of these teams upon long journeys. This is certainly a very economical method of transportation.

STORES AND PROVISIONS.

Supplies for a march should be put up in the most secure, compact, and portable shape.

Bacon should be packed in strong sacks of a hundred pounds to each; or, in very hot climates, put in boxes and surrounded with bran, which in a great measure prevents the fat from melting away.

If pork be used, in order to avoid transporting about forty per cent. of useless weight, it should be taken out of the barrels and packed like the bacon; then so placed in the bottom of the wagons as to keep it cool. The pork, if well cured, will keep several months in this way, but bacon is preferable.

Flour should be packed in stout double canvas sacks well sewed, a hundred pounds in each sack.

Butter may be preserved by boiling it thoroughly, and skimming off the scum as it rises to the top until it is quite clear like oil.* It is then placed in tin canisters and soldered up. This mode of preserving butter has been adopted in the hot climate of southern Texas, and it is

---

in trains; and they are wrong. Cows, like mares and she-camels get through hard journeys; they also supply milk—no small advantage to the Prairie Traveller. In Africa, I used "Jennies" for the purpose, as the natives would not touch their milk, whilst they never allowed me the use of a cow.—Ed.

* This is the Ghi of India, the Raughan of Persia, the Samn of Arabia, and the "one sauce" of the East. It is preserved for any length of time in leather bottles; and habit soon makes it as palatable as butter.—Ed.

found to keep sweet for a great length of time, and its flavor is but little impaired by the process.

Sugar may be well secured in India-rubber or gutta-percha sacks, or so placed in the wagon as not to risk getting wet.

Desiccated or dried vegetables are almost equal to the fresh, and are put up in such a compact and portable form as easily to be transported over the plains. They have been extensively used in the Crimean war, and by our own army in Utah, and have been very generally approved. They are prepared by cutting the fresh vegetables into thin slices and subjecting them to a very powerful press, which removes the juice and leaves a solid cake, which, after having been thoroughly dried in an oven, becomes almost as hard as a rock. A small piece of this, about half the size of a man's hand, when boiled, swells up so as to fill a vegetable dish, and is sufficient for four men. It is believed that the antiscorbutic properties of vegetables are not impaired by desiccation; and they will keep for years if not exposed to dampness. Canned vegetables are very good for campaigning, but are not so portable as when put up in the other form. The desiccated vegetables used in our army have been prepared by Chollet and Co., 46, Rue Richer, Paris. There is an agency for them in New York. I regard these compressed vegetables as the best preparation for prairie traveling that has yet been discovered. A single ration weighs, before being boiled, only an ounce, and a cubic yard contains 16,000 rations. In making up their outfit for the plains, men are very prone to overload their teams with a great variety of useless articles. It is a good rule to carry nothing more than is absolutely necessary for use upon the journey. One cannot expect, with the limited allowance of transportation that emigrants usually have, to indulge in luxuries upon such expeditions, and articles for use in California can be purchased there at less cost than that of overland transport.

The allowance of provisions for men in marching should be much greater than when they take no exercise. The army ration I have always found insufficient for soldiers who perform hard service, yet it is ample for them when in quarters.

The following table shows the amount of subsistence consumed per day by each man of Dr. Rae's party, in his spring journey to the Arctic regions of North America in 1854:

Pemmican	1.25 lbs.
Biscuit	0.25 „
Edward's preserved potatoes	0.10 „
Flour	0.33 „
Tea	0.03 „
Sugar	0.14 „
Grease or alcohol, for cooking	0.25 „
	2.35 lbs.

This allowance of a little over two pounds of the most nutritious food was found barely sufficient to subsist the men in that cold climate.

The pemmican, which constitutes almost the entire diet of the Fur Company's men in the north-west, is prepared as follows: the buffalo meat is cut into thin flakes, and hung up to dry in the sun, or before a slow fire; it is then pounded between two stones and reduced to a powder; this powder is placed in a bag of the animal's hide, with the hair on the outside; melted grease is then poured into it, and the bag sewn up. It can be eaten raw, and many prefer it so. Mixed with a little flour and boiled, it is a very wholesome and exceedingly nutritious food, and will keep fresh for a long time.

I would advise all persons who travel for any considerable time through a country where they can procure no vegetables to carry with them some antiscorbutics; and if they cannot transport desiccated or canned vegetables, citric acid answers a good purpose, and is very portable. When mixed with sugar and water, with a few drops of the essence of lemon, it is difficult to distinguish it from lemonade. Wild onions are excellent as antiscorbutics; also wild grapes and greens. An infusion of hemlock leaves is also said to be an antidote to scurvy.

The most portable and simple preparation of subsistence that I know of, and which is used extensively by the Mexicans and Indians, is called "*cold flour*." It is made by parching corn, and pounding it in a mortar to the consistency of coarse meal; a little sugar and cinnamon added makes it quite palatable. When the traveler becomes hungry or thirsty, a little of the flour is mixed with water and drunk. It is an excellent article for a traveler who desires to go the greatest length of time upon the smallest amount of transportation. It is said that half a bushel is sufficient to subsist a man thirty days.

Persons undergoing severe labor, and driven to great extremities for food, will derive sustenance from various sources that would never occur to them under ordinary circumstances. In passing over the Rocky Mountains during the winter of 1857-8, our supplies of provisions were entirely consumed eighteen days before reaching the first settlements in New Mexico, and we were obliged to resort to a variety of expedients to supply the deficiency. Our poor mules were fast failing and dropping down from exhaustion in the deep snows, and our only dependence for the means of sustaining life was upon these starved animals as they became unserviceable and could go no further. We had no salt, sugar, coffee, or tobacco, which, at a time when men are performing the severest labour that the human system is capable of enduring, was a great privation. In this destitute condition we found a substitute for tobacco in the bark of the red willow, which grows upon many of the mountain streams in that vicinity. The outer bark is first removed with a knife, after which the inner bark is scraped up into ridges around the sticks, and held in the fire until it is thoroughly roasted, when it is taken off the stick, pulverized in the hand, and is ready for smoking. It has the narcotic properties of the tobacco, and is quite agreeable to the taste and smell. The sumach leaf is also used by the Indians in the same way, and has a similar taste to the willow bark.* A decoction of the

* Ample details concerning this "kinnikinik" and other succedanea for tobacco used by the Western tribes are given in the "City

dried wild or horse mint, which we found abundant under the snow, was quite palatable, and answered instead of coffee. It dries up in that climate, but does not lose its flavor. We suffered greatly for the want of salt; but, by burning the outside of our mule steaks, and sprinkling a little gunpowder upon them, it did not require a very extensive stretch of the imagination to fancy the presence of both salt and pepper. We tried the meat of horse, colt, and mules, all of which were in a starved condition, and of course not very tender, juicy, or nutritious. We consumed the enormous amount of from five to six pounds of this meat per man daily, but continued to grow weak and thin, until, at the expiration of twelve days, we were able to perform but little labor, and were continually craving for fat meat.

The allowance of provisions for each grown person, to make the journey from the Missouri River to California, should suffice for 110 days. The following is deemed requisite, viz.: 150 lbs. of flour, or its equivalent in hard bread; 25 lbs. of bacon or pork, and enough fresh beef to be driven on the hoof to make up the meat component of the ration; 15 lbs. of coffee, and 25 lbs. of sugar; also a quantity of saleratus or yeast powders for making bread,* and salt, and pepper.

These are the chief articles of subsistence necessary for the trip, and they should be used with economy, reserving a good portion for the western half of the journey. Heretofore many of the California emigrants have improvidently exhausted their stocks of provision before reaching their journey's end, and have, in many cases, been obliged to pay the most exorbitant prices in making up the deficiency.

---

of the Saints," chapter ii. Tobacco and green tea are the prairie traveller's soothers and stimulants. Wine and spirits should be regarded as remedial agents.—Ed.

* Many of these are quasi-poisonous. I am practically acquainted with only one preparation that resists an African climate: "Borwick's General Baking Powder;" There are, however, doubtless many other equally valuable recipes.—Ed.

It is true, that if persons choose to pass through Salt Lake City, and the Mormons *happen* to be in an amiable mood, supplies may sometimes be procured from them; but those who have visited them well know how little reliance is to be placed upon their hospitality or spirit of accommodation.*

I once traveled with a party of New Yorkers *en route* for California. They were perfectly ignorant of every thing relating to this kind of campaigning, and had overloaded their wagons with almost every thing except the very articles most important and necessary; the consequence was, that they exhausted their teams, and were obliged to throw away the greater part of their loading. They soon learned that Champagne, East India sweetmeats, olives, etc., etc., were not the most useful articles for a prairie tour.

CLOTHING.

A suitable dress for prairie traveling is of great import to health and comfort. Cotton or linen fabrics do not sufficiently protect the body against the direct rays of the sun at mid-day, nor against rains or sudden changes of temperature. Wool, being a non-conductor, is the best material for this mode of locomotion, and should always be adopted for the plains. The coats should be short and stout, the shirt of red or blue flannel, such as can be found in almost all the shops on the frontier; this, in warm weather, answers for an outside garment. The pants should be of thick and soft woolen material, and it is well to have them re-inforced on the inside, where they come in contact with the saddle, with soft buckskin, which makes them more durable and comfortable.

Woolen socks and stout boots, coming up well at the knees, and made large, so as to admit the pants, will be

* Here also my experience differs *toto cœlo* from that of the gallant author. I found supplies at the Great Salt Lake City plentiful, and by no means exorbitantly dear. Perhaps, however, such was not the case to the Federal Officer.—Ed.

found the best for horsemen, and they guard against rattlesnake bites.

In traveling through deep snow during very cold weather in winter, moccasins are preferable to boots or shoes, as being more pliable, and allowing a freer circulation of blood. In crossing the Rocky Mountains in winter, the weather being intensely cold, I wore two pairs of woolen socks, and a square piece of thick blanket sufficient to cover the feet and ankles, over which were drawn a pair of thick buckskin moccasins, and the whole enveloped in a pair of buffalo-skin boots with the hair inside, made open in the front and tied with buckskin strings. At the same time I wore a pair of elkskin pants, which most effectually prevented the air from penetrating to the skin, and made an excellent defence against brush and thorns.

My men, who were dressed in the regulation-clothing, wore out their pants and shoes before we reached the summit of the mountains, and many of them had their feet badly frozen in consequence. They mended their shoes with pieces of leather cut from the saddle-skirts as long as they lasted, and, when this material was gone, they covered the entire shoe with green beeve or mule-hide, drawn together and sewed upon the top, with the hair inside, which protected the upper as well as the sole leather. The sewing was done with an awl and buckskin strings. These simple expedients contributed greatly to the comfort of the party; and, indeed, I am by no means sure that they did not, in our straitened condition, without the transportation necessary for carrying disabled men, save the lives of some of them. Without the awl and buckskins we should have been unable to have repaired the shoes. They should never be forgotten in making up the outfit for a prairie expedition.

We also experienced great inconvenience and pain, by the reflection of the sun's rays from the snow upon our eyes, and some of the party became nearly snow-blind. Green and blue glasses, inclosed in a wire net-work, are an effectual protection to the eyes; but, in the absence of these, the skin around the eyes and upon the nose should be blackened with wet powder or charcoal, which will afford great relief.*

In the summer season shoes are much better for footmen than boots, as they are lighter, and do not cramp the ankles; the soles should be broad, so as to allow a square, firm tread, without distorting or pinching the feet.

The following list of articles is deemed a sufficient outfit for one man upon a three months' expedition, viz.:

2 blue or red flannel overshirts, open in front, with buttons.
2 woolen undershirts.
2 pairs thick cotton drawers.
4 pairs woolen socks.
2 pairs cotton socks.
4 colored silk handkerchiefs.
2 pairs stout shoes, for footmen.
1 pair boots, for horsemen.
1 pair shoes, for horsemen.
3 towels.
1 gutta percha poncho.
1 broad-brimmed hat of soft felt.
1 comb and brush.
2 tooth-brushes.
1 pound Castile soap.
3 pounds bar soap for washing clothes.
1 belt-knife and small whetstone.
Stout linen thread, large needles, a bit of beeswax, a few buttons, paper of pins, and a thimble, all contained in a small buckskin or stout cloth bag.

The foregoing articles, with the coat and overcoat, complete the wardrobe.

CAMP EQUIPAGE.

The bedding for each person should consist of two blankets, a comforter, and a pillow, and a gutta percha or painted canvas cloth to spread beneath the bed upon the ground, and to contain it when rolled up for transportation.

Every mess of six or eight persons will require a wrought-iron camp kettle, large enough for boiling meat and making soup; a coffee-pot and cups of heavy tin, with the handles riveted on; tin plates, frying and bake pans of wrought-iron, the latter for baking bread and roasting

* Those who know how to use the Oriental Kohl or Surma will do well to take some with them.

I deprecate the use of *red* shirts, if sporting be the traveller's object, and I advise a double broad-brim of soft felt, one being fitted inside the other.—Ed.

coffee. Also a mess pan of heavy tin or wrought-iron for mixing bread and other culinary purposes; knives, forks, and spoons; an extra camp kettle; tin or gutta percha bucket for water—wood, being liable to shrink and fall to pieces, is not deemed suitable; an axe, hatchet, and spade will also be needed, with a mallet for driving picket-pins. Matches should be carried in bottles and corked tight, so as to exclude the moisture.

A little blue mass, quinine, opium, and some cathartic medicine, put up in doses for adults, will suffice for the medicine-chest.*

* The diseases to be guarded against in Prairie travelling are ophthalmia, fever and ague, and dysenteric affections, proceeding from liver complaint. A man can hardly expect to escape scathless from a sudden change of London life to that of the Far West, and he should be prepared to doctor himself rather than trust to the faculty as represented in the Far West.

For ophthalmia, the best treatment is a self-adhering blister affixed to the temples till inflammation disappears. The eyes must be washed with warm water, *coupé*, if possible, with milk, and the cure should be assisted by the usual drop of nitrate of silver or sulphate of zinc.

For fevers, calomel—not the blue pill, which easily becomes rancid—Epsom salts or castor oil capsules, and quinine, will be found sufficient. In very dangerous places, I always travel with a few phials of tinctura Warburgii or Warburg's drops, a patent medicine which may be bought of Sanger and Co., chemists, 150, Oxford Street.

The best, and indeed the only remedy for the legion of dysenteric diseases, arising from hepatic derangements, is nitro-muriatic acid. I copy from the City of the Saints (chap. 6), the proportions for internal administration. ℞—Acid nit. . ℥j.
Acid mur. . ʒij Misce.
Of this mixture, fifteen drops in a tumbler of water, twice a day before meals, form the dose.

The local bath may be taken either by compress or by placing the feet in a basin half filled with a quart of hot water and 1 oz. of the nitro-muriatic acid, wrapping at the same time a blanket round the lower extremities to confine the chlorine.

Nitro-muriatic acid is by no means convenient to carry; but its essential value should render the labour light. Above all things let the traveler avoid using, in dysentery and diarrhœa, opium, laudanum, and morphia or catechu, and similar astringents. Half the deaths from those diseases which occurred in the Crimea, were caused, I believe, by the injudicious use of opiates.

When the malady is not complicated by hepatic affections, it is

Each ox-wagon should be provided with a covered tar-bucket, filled with a mixture of tar or resin and grease, two bows extra, six S's, and six open links for repairing chains. Every set of six wagons should have a tongue, coupling pole, king-bolt, and pair of hounds extra.

Every set of six-mule wagons should be furnished with five pairs of hames, two double trees, four whipple-trees, and two pairs of lead bars extra.

Two lariats will be needed for every horse and mule, as one generally wears out before reaching the end of a long journey. They will be found useful in crossing deep streams, and in letting wagons down steep hills and mountains; also in repairing broken wagons. Lariats made of hemp* are the best.

One of the most indispensable articles to the outfit of the prairie traveler is buckskin. For repairing harness, saddles, bridles, and numerous other purposes of daily necessity, the awl and buckskin will be found in constant requisition.

ARMS.

Every man who goes into the Indian country should be armed with a rifle and revolver, and he should never, either in camp or out of it, lose sight of them. When not on the march, they should be placed in such a position that they can be seized at an instant's warning; and when moving about outside the camp, the revolver should invariably be worn in the belt, as the person does not know at what moment he may have to use it.

A great diversity of opinion obtains regarding the kind of rifle that is the most efficient and best adapted to Indian warfare; and the question is perhaps as yet very far from being settled to the satisfaction of all. A large

---

easily removed by simple measures. The best, I believe, is a large spoonful of iron-rust in a small coffee-cup of rum, or cognac burnt down till the spirit has almost evaporated, and a diet of gruel or hominy mixed with common or prepared chalk.—Ed.

* The hemp should be Russian, not Manilla.—Ed.

majority of men prefer the breech-loading arm; but there are those who still adhere tenaciously to the old-fashioned muzzle-loading rifle as preferable to any of the modern inventions. Among these may be mentioned the border hunters and mountaineers, who cannot be persuaded to use any other than the Hawkin's rifle, for the reason that they know nothing about the merits of any others. My own experience has forced me to the conclusion, that the breech-loading arm possesses great advantages over the muzzle-loading, for the reason that it can be charged and fired with much greater rapidity.

Colt's revolving pistol is very generally admitted, both in Europe and America, to be the most efficient arm of its kind known at the present day. As the same principles are involved in the fabrication of his breech-loading rifle as are found in the pistol, the conviction to me is irresistible that, if one arm is worthy of consideration, the other is equally so. For my own part, I look upon Colt's new patent rifle as a most excellent arm for border service. It gives six shots in more rapid succession than any other rifle I know of, and these, if properly expended, are oftentimes sufficient to decide a contest. Moreover, it is the most reliable and certain weapon to fire that I have ever used; and I cannot resist the force of my conviction that, if I were alone upon the prairies, and expected an attack from a body of Indians, I am not acquainted with any arm I would not as soon have in my hands as this.

The army and navy revolvers have both been used in our army; but the officers are not united in opinion in regard to their relative merits. I prefer the large army size, for reasons which will be given hereafter.*

* After some experience, I still prefer the "Colt," especially the new edition, with the improved plan of removing the cylinder. The army (dragoon or largest) size is best fitted for holsters, the navy, or medium, for the belt.

Few men would, in these days, be mad enough to prefer the muzzle-loader to the breech-loader, except in places like Central Africa, where, in long travel, the simplest lock lasts the longest; where the flint is better than the percussion cap, and where, perhaps, the matchlock is superior to the flint. The remotest corners of the American States, however, are so closely connected with civilization, that in case of accidents by fire or flood, a fresh supply of cartridges could readily be procured. Besides which, a breech-loader should always be convertible into a muzzle-loader.

When I visited the Prairies in the summer of 1860, the Maynard breech-loader was incomparably "the cheese." Since that time, the exigencies of the so-called "Secession" have produced new and improved forms. Of the English, I prefer Cooper, of Birmingham, as being more simple than the well-known "Terry."

Against so dangerous and powerful an animal as the grizzly bear of the Rocky Mountains, I should be disposed, though some may deem the proceeding unsportsmanlike, to use detonating shells, six to the pound. Thrown from a double-barrelled rifle, made short, heavy, and handy, and carrying, without kicking, four drachms of powder. The "shells" now mostly in use are those invented by the late Gen. Jacob, of Jacobadad, Sindh, and perpetuated in the Blakeley gun. They are objectionable, because they require a peculiar ramrod, and cautious loading. Moreover, they are not wholly free from danger in case of violent falls or other shocks.

My own system is to cast the leaden cone in two separate pieces, which can be connected by a male and female screw, thus :—

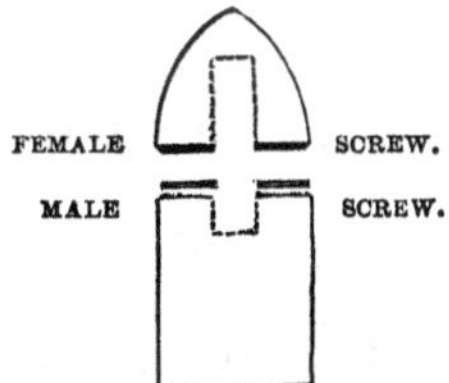

The fulminating powder, carefully proportioned to the weight of metal, is contained in an air-proof cap of thin copper tube, and this is inserted into the hollow left for it in the length of the missile. The dotted line in the diagram represents the plan of the detonating agent. Such cones can be carried about without risk. They keep for ever—they require no change of ramrod, nor care in loading; and they are not liable to explode, even when forcibly thrown against a stone.

Those who object to shells, will, of course, remember that there are such things as steel tips, and that they were successfully used by M. Jules Gérard, against that king of kings, the lion of Kabylie. And the many who prefer in such encounters, when rapid loading may save life, a smooth-bore to a rifle, will hardly think encountering "Ole Cuffy," except with a heavy weapon throwing balls of 3 oz. in weight, hardened with zinc, spelter, or quicksilver.—Ed.

CHAPTER II.

Marching.—Treatment of Animals.—Water.— Different methods of finding and purifying it.—Journadas.—Methods of crossing them. —Advance and Rear Guards.—Selection of Camp.—Sanitary Considerations.—Dr. Jackson's Report.—Picket Guards.—Stampedes. —How to prevent them.—Corraling Wagons.

MARCHING.

The success of a long expedition through an unpopulated country depends mainly on the care taken of the animals, and the manner in which they are driven, herded, and guarded. If they are broken down or lost, everything must be sacrificed, and the party becomes perfectly helpless.

The great error into which inexperienced travellers are liable to fall, and which probably occasions more suffering and disaster than almost anything else, lies in overworking their cattle at the commencement of the journey. To obviate this, short and easy drives should be made until the teams become habituated to their work, and gradually inured to this particular method of traveling. If animals are overloaded and overworked when they first start out into the prairies, especially if they have been recently taken from grain, they soon fall away, and give out before reaching the end of the journey.

Grass and water are abundant and good upon the eastern portions of all the different overland routes; animals should not, therefore, with proper care, fall away in the least before reaching the mountains, as, west of them, are long stretches were grass and water are scarce, and it requires the full amount of strength and vigor of animals in good condition to endure the fatigues and hard labor attendant upon the passage of these deserts. Drivers should be closely watched, and never, unless absolutely necessary, permitted to beat their animals or to force them out of a walk, as this will soon break down the best teams. Those teamsters who make the least use of the whip invariably keep their animals in the best condition. Unless the drivers are checked at the outset, they are very apt to fall into the habit of flogging their teams. It is not only wholly unnecessary, but cruel, and should never be tolerated.

In traveling with ox teams in the summer season, great benefit will be derived from making early marches; starting with the dawn, and making a "nooning" during the heat of the day, as oxen suffer much from the heat of the sun in midsummer. These noon halts should, if possible, be so arranged as to be near grass and water, where the animals can improve their time in grazing. When it gets cool, they may be hitched to the wagons again, and the journey continued in the afternoon. Sixteen or eighteen miles a day may thus be made without injury to the beasts, and longer drives can never be expedient, unless in order to reach grass or water. When the requisites for encamping cannot be found at the desired intervals, it is better for the animals to make a very long drive than to encamp without water or grass. The noon halt in such cases may be made without water, and the evening drive lengthened.

WATER.

The scarcity of water upon some of the routes across the plains occasionally exposes the traveler to intense suffering, and renders it a matter of much importance for him to learn the best methods of guarding against the disasters liable to occur to men and animals in the absence of this most necessary element.

In mountainous districts, water can generally be found either in springs, the dry beds of streams, or in holes in the rocks, where they are sheltered from rapid evaporation. For example, in the Hueco tanks, thirty miles east of El

Paso, New Mexico, upon the Fort Smith road, where there is an immense reservoir in a cave, water can always be found. This reservoir receives the drainage of a mountain.

During a season of the year when there are occasional showers, water will generally be found iu low places where there is a substratum of clay ; but after the dry season has set in these pools evaporate, and it is necessary to dig wells. The lowest spots should be selected for this purpose, where the grass is green and the surface earth moist.

In searching for water along the dry sandy beds of streams, it is well to try the earth with a stick or ramrod, and if this indicates moisture, water will generally be obtained by excavation. Streams often sink in light and porous sand, and sometimes make their appearance again lower down, where the bed is more tenacious ; but it is a rule with prairie travelers, in searching for water in a sandy country, to ascend the streams, and, the nearer their sources are approached, the more water will be found in a dry season.

Where it becomes necessary to sink a well in a stream, the bed of which is quicksand, a flour barrel perforated with small holes, should be used as a curb, to prevent the sand from caving in. The barrel must be forced down as the sand is removed ; and when, as is often the case, there is an under current through the sand, the well will be continually filled with water.

There are many indications of water known to old campaigners, although none of them are absolutely infallible. The most certain of them are deep green cottonwood or willow trees growing in depressed localities ; also flags, water-rushes, tall green grass, etc.

The fresh tracks and trails of animals converging toward a common centre, and the flight of birds and water-fowl toward the same points, will also lead to water. In a section frequented by deer or mustangs, it may be certain that water is not far distant, as these animals drink daily, and they will not remain long in a locality after the water has dried up. Deer generally go to water during the middle of the day, but birds toward evening.

A supply of drinking water may be obtained during a shower from the drippings of a tent, or by suspending a cloth or blanket by the four corners and hanging a small weight to the centre, so as to allow all the rain to run toward one point, from whence it drops into a vessel beneath. India-rubber, gutta-percha, or painted canvas cloths answer a very good purpose for catching water during a rain, but they should be previously well washed, to prevent them from imparting a bad taste.

When there are heavy dews, water may be collected by spreading out a blanket with a stick attached to one end, tying a rope to it, dragging it over the grass, and wringing out the water as it accumulates. In some parts of Australia this method is practised.

In traversing the country upon the head waters of Red River, during the summer of 1852, we suffered most severely from thirst, having nothing but the acrid and bitter waters from the river, which, issuing from a gypsum formation, was highly charged with salts, and, when taken into the stomach, did not quench thirst in the slightest degree, but, on the contrary, produced a most painful and burning sensation, accompanied with diarrhœa. During the four days that we were compelled to drink this water, the thermometer rose to 104° in the shade; and the only relief we found was from bathing in the river.

The use of water is a matter of habit, very much within our control, as by practice we may discipline ourselves so as to require but a small amount. Some persons for example, who place no restraint upon their appetites, will, if they can get it, drink water twenty times a day, while others will not perhaps drink more than once or twice during the same time. I have found a very effectual preventive to thirst by drinking a large quantity of water before breakfast, and, on feeling thirsty on the march, chewing a small green twig or leaf.

Water taken from stagnant pools, charged with putrid vegetable matter and animalculæ, would be very likely to generate fevers and dysenteries if taken into the stomach without purification. It should, therefore, be thoroughly boiled, and all the scum removed from the surface as it rises; this clarifies it, and by mixing powdered charcoal with it the disinfecting process is perfected. Water may also be purified by placing a piece of alum in the end of a stick that has been split, and stirring it round in a bucket of water. Charcoal and the leaves of the prickly pear are also used for the same purpose. I have recently seen a compact and portable filter, made of charcoal, which clarifies the water very effectually, and draws it off on the siphon principle. It can be obtained at 85, West Street, New York, for one dollar and a half. Water may be partially filtered in a muddy pond by taking a barrel and boring the lower half full of holes, then filling it up with grass or moss above the upper holes, after which it is placed in the pond with the top above the surface. The water filters through the grass or moss, and rises in the barrel to a level with the pond. Travelers frequently drink muddy water by placing a cloth or handkerchief over the mouth of a cup to catch the larger particles of dirt and animalculæ.

Water may be cooled so as to be quite palatable by wrapping cloths around the vessels containing it, wetting them, and hanging them in the air, when a rapid evaporation will be produced. Some of the frontier-men use a leathern sack for carrying water: this is porous, and allows the necessary evaporation without wetting.

The Arabs also use a leathern bottle, which they call *zemzemiyah.* When they are *en route* they hang it on the shady side of a camel, where the evaporation keeps the water continually cool.

No expedition should ever set out into the plains without being supplied with the means for carrying water, especially in an unknown region. If wooden kegs are used they must frequently be looked after, and soaked, in order that they may not shrink and fall to pieces. Men, in marching in a hot climate, throw off a great amount of perspiration from the skin, and require a corresponding quantity of water to supply the deficiency; and, unless they get this, they suffer greatly. When a party makes an expedition into a desert section, where there is a probability of finding no water, and intends to return over the same track, it is well to carry water as far as convenient, and bury it in the ground for use on the return trip.

"Captain Stuart, when he explored Australia, took a tank in his cart, which burst, and, besides that, he carried casks of water. By these he was enabled to face a desert country with a success which no traveler had ever attained to. For instance, when returning homeward, the water was found to be drying up from the country on all sides of him. He was at a pool, and the next stage was 118 miles, at the end of which it was doubtful if there remained any water. It was necessary to send to reconnoitre, and to furnish the messenger with means of returning should the pool be found dry. He killed a bullock, skinned it, and, filling the skin with water (which held 150 gallons), sent it by an ox dray thirty miles, with orders to bury it and to return. Shortly after, he dispatched a light one-horse cart, carrying thirty-six gallons to supply them for a journey of 476 miles, or six days at thirty miles a day, at the close of which they would return to the ox hide—sleeping, in fact, five nights on thirty-six gallons of water. This a hardy, well-driven horse could do, even in the hottest climate."*

JOURNADAS.

In some localities 50 or 60 miles, and even greater distances, are frequently traversed without water; these long stretches are called by the Mexicans "*journadas*," or day's journeys. There is one in New Mexico called *Journada del Muerto*, which is 78½ miles in length, where, in a dry season, there is not a drop of water; yet, with proper care, this drive can be made with ox or mule teams, and without loss or injury to the animals.

* F. Galton's *Art of Travel*, p. 17 and 18.—AUTHOR. The English traveler will not neglect to make a companion of the Second Edition of this most useful Manual. I would rather examine officers in the Art of Travel than "put them through" Roman History, or even Latin.—ED.

On arriving at the last camping-ground before entering upon the journada, all the animals should be as well rested and refreshed as possible. To insure this, they must be turned out upon the best grass that can be found, and allowed to eat and drink as much as they desire during the entire halt. Should the weather be very warm, and the teams composed of oxen, the march should not be resumed until it begins to cool in the afternoon. They should be carefully watered just previous to being hitched up and started out upon the journada, the water-kegs having been previously filled. The drive is then commenced, and continued during the entire night, with ten or fifteen minutes rest every two hours. About daylight a halt should be made, and the animals immediately turned out to graze for two hours, during which time, especially if there is dew upon the grass, they will have become considerably refreshed, and may be put to the wagons again, and driven until the heat becomes oppressive toward noon, when they are again turned out upon a spot where the grass is good, and, if possible, where there are shade-trees. About four o'clock P.M. they are again started, and the march continued into the night, and as long as they can be driven without suffering. If, however, there should be dew, which is seldom the case on the plains, it would be well to turn out the animals several times during the second night, and by morning, if they are in good condition, the journada of seventy or eighty miles will have been passed without any great amount of suffering. I am supposing, in this case, that the road is firm and free from sand.

Many persons have been under the impression that animals, in traversing the plains, would perform better, and keep in better condition, by allowing them to graze in the morning before commencing the day's march, which involves the necessity of making late starts, and driving during the heat of the day. The same persons have been of the opinion that animals will graze only at particular hours; that the remainder of the day must be allowed them for rest and sleep, and that, unless these rules be observed, they would not thrive. This opinion is, however, erroneous, as animals will in a few days adapt themselves to any circumstances, so far as regards their hours of labor, rest, and refreshment. If they have been accustomed to work at particular periods of the day, and the order of things is suddenly reversed, the working hours changed into hours of rest, and *vice versa,* they may not do as well for a short time; but they will soon accustom themselves to the change, and eat and rest as well as before. By making early drives during the summer months the heat of the day is avoided, whereas, I repeat, if allowed to graze before starting, the march can not commence until it grows warm, when animals, especially oxen, will suffer greatly from the heat of the sun, and will not do as well as when the other plan is pursued.

Oxen upon a long journey will sometimes wear down their hoofs and become lame. When this occurs, a thick piece of raw hide wrapped around the foot and tied firmly to the leg will obviate the difficulty, provided the weather is not wet; for if so, the shoe soon wears out. Mexican and Indian horses and mules will make long journeys without being shod, as their hoofs are tough and elastic, and wear away very gradually; they will, however, in time became very smooth, making it difficult for them to travel upon grass.

A train of wagons should always be kept closed upon a march; and if, as often happens, a particular wagon gets out of order and is obliged to halt, it should be turned out of the road, to let the others pass while the injury is being repaired. As soon as the broken wagon is in order, it should fall into the line wherever it happens to be. In the event of a wagon breaking down so as to require important repairs, men should be immediately dispatched with the necessary tools and materials, which should be placed in the train where they can readily be got at, and a guard should be left to escort the wagon to camp after having been repaired. If, however, the damage be so serious as to require any great length of time to repair it, the load should be transferred to other wagons, so that the team which is left behind will be able to travel rapidly and overtake the train.

If the broken wagon is a poor one, and there be abundance of better ones, the accident being such as to involve much delay for its repair, it may be wise to abandon it, taking from it such parts as may possibly be wanted in repairing other wagons.

ADVANCE AND REAR GUARDS.

A few men, well mounted, should constitute the advance and rear guards for each train of wagons passing through the Indian country. Their duty will be to keep a vigilant look-out in all directions, and to reconnoitre places where Indians would be likely to lie in ambush. Should hostile Indians be discovered, the fact should be at once reported to the commander, who (if he anticipates an attack) will rapidly form his wagons into a circle or "*corral,*" with the animals toward the centre, and the men on the inside, with their arms in readiness to repel an attack from without. If these arrangements be properly attended to, few parties of Indians will venture to make an attack, as they are well aware that some of their warriors might pay with their lives the forfeit of such indiscretion.

I know an instance where one resolute man, pursued for several days by a large party of Comanches on the Santa Fé trace, defended himself by dismounting and pointing his rifle at the foremost whenever they came near him, which always had the effect of turning them back. This was repeated so often that the Indians finally abandoned the pursuit, and left the traveler to pursue his journey without further molestation. During all this time he did not discharge his rifle; had he done so he would doubtless have been killed.

SELECTION OF CAMPS.

The security of animals, and, indeed, the general safety of a party, in traveling through a country occupied by hostile Indians, depends greatly upon the judicious selection of camps. One of the most important considerations that should influence the choice of a locality is its capability for defence. If the camp be pitched beside a stream, a concave bend, where the water is deep, with a soft alluvial bed inclosed by high and abrupt banks, will be the most defensible, and all the more should the concavity form a peninsula. The advantages of such a position are obvious to a soldier's eye, as that part of the encampment inclosed by the stream is naturally secure, and leaves only one side to be defended. The concavity of the bend will enable the defending party to cross its fire in case of attack from the exposed side. The bend of the stream will also form an excellent corral in which to secure animals from a stampede, and thereby diminish the number of sentinels needful around the camp. In herding animals at night within the bend of a stream, a spot should be selected where no clumps of brush grow on the side where the animals are posted. If thickets of brush can not be avoided, sentinels should be placed near them, to guard against Indians, who might take advantage of this cover to steal animals, or shoot them down with arrows, before their presence was known.

In camping away from streams, it is advisable to select a position in which one or more sides of the encampment shall rest upon the crest of an abrupt hill or bluff. The prairie Indians make their camps upon the summits of the hills, whence they can see in all directions, and thus avoid a surprise.*

The line of tents should be pitched on that side of the camp most exposed to attack, and sentinels so posted that they may give alarm in time for the main body to rally and prepare for defence.

SANITARY CONSIDERATIONS.

When camping near rivers and lakes surrounded by

* Captain Sturt, and other Australian explorers, successfully adopted this plan.—ED.

large bodies of timber and a luxuriant vegetation, which produces a great amount of decomposition and consequent exhalations of malaria, it is important to ascertain what localities will be the least likely to generate disease, and to affect the sanitary condition of men occupying them.

This subject has been thoroughly examined by Dr. Robert Johnson, Inspector General of Hospitals in the English army in 1845;* and, as his conclusions are deduced from enlarged experience and extended research, they should have great weight. I shall, therefore, make no apology for introducing here a few extracts from his interesting report touching upon this subject:—

"It is consonant with the experience of military people, in all ages and in all countries, that camp-diseases most abound near the muddy banks of large rivers, near swamps and ponds, and on grounds which have been recently stripped of their woods. The fact is precise, but it has been set aside to make way for an opinion. It was assumed, about half a century since, by a celebrated army-physician, that camp diseases originated from causes of putrefaction, and that putrefaction is connected radically with a stagnant condition of the air.

"As streams of air usually proceed along rivers with more certainty and force than in other places, and as there is evidently a more certain movement of air, that is, more wind on open grounds than among woods and thickets, this sole consideration, without any regard to experience, influenced opinion, gave currency to the destructive maxim that the banks of rivers, open grounds, and exposed heights are the most eligible situations for the encampment of troops. They are the best ventilated; they must, if the theory be true, be the most healthy.

"The fact is the reverse; but, demonstrative as the fact may be, fashion has more influence than multiplied examples of facts experimentally proved. Encampments are still formed in the vicinity of swamps, or on grounds

* And later still by Sir Ranald Martin, K.C.B., whose well-digested opinions touching sanitaria in tropical climates will, I hope, presently change the map of British India.—Ed.

which are newly cleared of their woods, in obedience to theory, and contrary to fact.

"It is prudent, as now said, in *selecting ground for encampment*, to avoid the immediate vicinity of swamps and rivers. The air is there noxious; but, as its influence thence originating does not extend beyond a certain limit, it is a matter of some importance to ascertain to what distance it does extend; because, if circumstances do not permit that the encampment be removed out of its reach, prudence directs that remedies be applied to weaken the force of its pernicious impressions.

"The remedies consist in the interposition of rising grounds, woods, or such other impediments as serve to break the current in its progress from the noxious source. It is an obvious fact, that the noxious cause, or the exhalations in which it is enveloped, ascends as it traverses the adjacent plain, and that its impression is augmented by the adventitious force with which it strikes upon the subject of its action.

"It is thus that a position of three hundred paces from the margin of a swamp, or on a level with the swamp itself, or but moderately elevated, is less unhealthy than one at six hundred on the same line of direction on an exposed height.* The cause here strikes fully in its ascent; and as the atmosphere has a more varied temperature, and the successions of the air are more irregular on the height than on the plain, the impression is more forcible, and the noxious effect more strongly marked. In accord with this principle, it is almost uniformly true, *cæteris paribus*, that diseases are more common, at least more violent, in broken, irregular, and hilly countries, where the temperature is liable to sudden changes, and where blasts descend with fury from the mountains, than in large and extensive inclined plains under the action of equal and gentle breezes only.

* Hence it is, that in British India the hills were always held to be the least wholesome sites, until some enterprizing men bethought themselves of ascending above the mean level of malaria—from 2,500 to 4,000 feet.—Ed.

"From this fact it becomes an object of the first consideration, in selecting ground for encampment, to guard against the impression of strong winds on their own account, independently of their proceeding from swamps, rivers, and noxious soils.

"It is proved by experience, in armies as in civil life, that injury does not often result from simple wetting with rain when the person is fairly exposed in the open air, and habitually inured to the contingencies of weather. Irregular troops, which act in the advanced line of armies, and which have no other shelter from weather than a hedge or tree, rarely experience sickness—never, at least, the sickness which proceeds from contagion; hence it is inferred that the shelter of tents is not necessary for the preservation of health. Irregular troops, with contingent shelter only, are comparatively healthy, while sickness often rages with violence in the same scenes, among those who have all the protection against the inclemencies of weather which can be furnished by canvas. The fact is verified by experience, and the cause of it is not of difficult explanation. When the earth is damp, the action of heat on its surface occasions the interior moisture to ascend. The heat of the bodies of a given number of men, confined within a tent of a given dimension, raises the temperature within the tent beyond the temperature of the common air outside the tent. The ascent of moisture is thus encouraged, generally by a change of temperature in the tent, and more particularly by the immediate or near contact of the heated bodies of the men with the surface of the earth. Moisture, as exhaled from the earth, is considered by observers of fact to be a cause which acts injuriously on health. Produced artificially by the accumulation of individuals in close tents, it may reasonably be supposed to produce its usual effects on armies. A cause of contagious influence, of fatal effect, is thus generated by accumulating soldiers in close and crowded tents, under the pretext of defending them from the inclemencies of the weather; and hence it is that the means which are provided for the preservation of health are actually the causes of destruction of life.*

"There are two causes which more evidently act upon the health of troops in the field than any other, namely, moisture exhaled direct from the surface of the earth in undue quantity, and emanations of a peculiar character arising from diseased action in the animal system in a mass of men crowded together. These are principal, and they are important. The noxious effects may be obviated, or rather the noxious cause will not be generated, under the following arrangement, namely, a carpet of painted canvas for the floor of the tent; a tent with a light roof, as defence against perpendicular rain or the rays of a vertical sun; and with side walls of moderate height, to be employed only against driving rains. To the first, there can be no objection: it is useful, as preventing the exhalations of moisture from the surface of the earth; it is convenient, as always ready; and it is economical, as less expensive than straw. It requires to be fresh painted only once a year."

The effect of crowding men together in close quarters, badly ventilated, was shown in the prisons of Hindostan, where at one time, when the English held sway, they had, on an average, 40,000 natives in confinement; and this unfortunate population was every year liberated by death in proportions varying from 4,000 to 10,000. The annual average mortality by crowded and unventilated barracks in the English army has sometimes been enormous, as at Barrackpore, where it seldom fell far short of one-tenth; that is to say, its garrisons were every year decimated by fever or cholera, while the officers and other inhabitants, who lived in well-ventilated houses, did not find the place particularly unhealthy.

The same fact of general exemption among the officers, and complete exemption among their wives, was observed in the marching regiments, which lost by cholera from

* The author here omits one well-known fomes of malarious disease in tropical lands—turning up or digging into virgin ground. Fresh clearings in bush or jungle are also dangerous.—Ed.

one tenth to one sixth of the enlisted men, who were packed together at night ten and twelve in a tent, with the thermometer at 96°. The dimensions of the celebrated Black Hole of Calcutta — where in 1756, 123 prisoners out of 140 died by carbonic acid in one night — was but eighteen feet square, and with but two small windows. Most of the twenty-three who survived until morning were seized with putrid fever and died very soon afterward.

On the first of December, 1848, 150 deck passengers of the steamer Londonderry were ordered below by the captain and the hatches closed upon them: seventy were found dead the next morning.

The streams which intersect our great prairies have but a very sparse growth of wood or vegetation upon their banks, so that one of the fundamental causes for the generation of noxious malaria does not, to any great extent, exist here; and I believe that persons may encamp with impunity directly upon their banks.*

PICKET GUARDS.

When a party is sufficiently strong, a picket guard should be stationed during the night some two or three hundred yards in advance of the point which is most open to assault, and on low ground, so that an enemy approaching over the surrounding higher country can be seen against the sky, while the sentinel himself is screened from observation. These sentinels should not be allowed to keep fires, unless they are so placed that they cannot be seen from a distance.

During the day the pickets should be posted on the summits of the highest eminences in the vicinity of camp, with instructions to keep a vigilant look-out in all direc-

* There are exceptions—the line of the Platte River, for instance, is notorious for "chills." As a rule the Prairie Traveller should prefer a Northern aspect, defended in rear by a curtain of high ground from the miasmatic South winds that sweep up from the Gulf of Mexico.—Ed.

tions; and, if not within hailing distance, they should be instructed to give some well-understood telegraphic signals to inform those in camp when there is danger. For example, should Indians be discovered approaching at a great distance, they may raise their caps upon the muzzles of their pieces, and at the same time walk around in a circle; while, if the Indians are near and moving rapidly, the sentinel may swing his cap and run around rapidly in a circle. To indicate the direction from which the Indians are approaching, he may direct his piece toward them, and walk in the same line of direction.

Should the pickets suddenly discover a party of Indians very near, and with the apparent intention of making an attack, they should fire their pieces to give the alarm to the camp.

These telegraphic signals, when well understood and enforced, will tend greatly to facilitate the communication of intelligence throughout the camp, and conduce much to its security.

The picket guards should receive minute and strict orders regarding their duties under all circumstances; and these orders should be distinctly understood by every one in the camp, so that no false alarms will be created. All persons, with the exception of the guards and herders, should after dark be confined to the limits of the chain of sentinels, so that, if any one is seen approaching from without these limits, it will be known that they are strangers.

As there will not often be occasion for any one to pass the chain of pickets during the night, it is a good rule (especially if the party is small), when a picket sentinel discovers any one lurking about his post from without, if he has not himself been seen, to quietly withdraw and report the fact to the commander, who can collect his men and make his arrangements to repel an attack and protect his animals. If, however, the man upon the picket has been seen, he should distinctly challenge the approaching party, and if he receives no answer, fire, and retreat to camp to report the fact.

It is of the utmost importance that picket guards should be wide awake, and allow nothing to escape their observation, as the safety of the whole camp is involved. During a dark night a man can see better himself, and is less exposed to the view of others, when in a sitting posture than when standing up or moving about. I would, therefore, recommend this practice for night pickets.*

Horses and mules (especially the latter), whose senses of hearing and smelling are probably more acute than those of almost any other animals, will discover anything strange or unusual about camp much sooner than a man. They indicate this by turning in the direction from whence the object is approaching, holding their heads erect, projecting their ears forward, and standing in a fixed and attentive attitude. They exhibit the same signs of alarm when a wolf or other wild animal approaches the camp; but it is always wise, when they show fear in this manner, to be on the alert till the cause is ascertained.

Mules are very keenly sensitive to danger, and, in passing along over the prairies, they will often detect the proximity of strangers long before they are discovered by their riders. Nothing seems to escape their observation; and I have heard of several instances where they have given timely notice of the approach of hostile Indians, and thus prevented stampedes.

Dogs are sometimes good sentinels, but they often sleep sound, and are not easily awakened on the approach of an enemy.

In marching with a large force, unless there is a guide who knows the country, a small party should always be sent in advance to search for good camping-places, and these parties should be dispatched early enough to return and meet the main command in the event of not finding a a camping-place within the limits of the day's march. A regiment should average upon the prairies, where the

* In this position the danger is sleep—few raw men can resist the temptation, especially about the "small hours" which North American Indians, like Africans and Australians, always choose for onslaught.—Ed.

roads are good, about eighteen miles a day, but, if necessary, it can make twenty-five or even thirty miles. The advance party should, therefore, go as far as the command can march, provided the requisites for camping are not found within that distance. The article of first importance in campaigning is grass, the next water, and the last fuel.*

It is the practice of most persons traveling with large ox-trains to select their camps upon the summit of a hill, where the surrounding country in all directions can be seen. Their cattle are then continually within view from the camp, and can be guarded easily.

When a halt is made the wagons are "corraled," as it is called, by bringing the two front ones near and parallel to each other. The two next are then driven up on the outside of these, with the front wheels of the former touching the rear wheels of the latter, the rear of the wagons turned out upon the circumference of the circle that is being formed, and so on, until one-half the circle is made, when the rear of the wagons are turned in to complete the circle. An opening of about twenty yards should be left between the last two wagons for animals to pass in and out of the corral, and this may be closed with two ropes stretched between the wagons. Such a corral forms an excellent and secure barricade against Indian attacks, and a good inclosure for cattle while they are being yoked: indeed, it is indispensable.

STAMPEDES.

Inclosures are made in the same manner for horses and mules, and, in case of an attempt to stampede them, they should be driven with all possible dispatch into the corral, where they will be perfectly secure. A "stampede" is more to be dreaded upon the plains than almost any disaster that can happen. It not unfrequently occurs that very many animals are irretrievably lost in this way, and the objects of an expedition thus defeated.

The Indians are perfectly familiar with the habits and

* I should say water first and grass second.—Ed.

dispositions of horses and mules, and with the most effectual methods of terrifying them. Previous to attempting a stampede, they provide themselves with rattles and other means for making frightful noises; thus prepared, they approach as near the herds as possible without being seen, and suddenly, with their horses at full speed, rush in among them, making the most hideous and unearthly screams and noises to terrify them, and drive them off before their astonished owners are able to rally and secure them.

As soon as the animals are started, the Indians divide their party, leaving a portion to hurry them off rapidly, while the rest linger some distance in the rear, to resist those who may pursue them. Horses and mules, will sometimes, especially in the night, become frightened and stampeded from very slight causes. A wolf or a deer passing through a herd will often alarm them, and cause them to break away in the most frantic manner. Upon one occasion, in the Choctaw country, my entire herd of two hundred horses and mules all stampeded in the night, and scattered over the country for many miles, and it was several days before I succeeded in collecting them together. The alarm occurred while the herders were walking among the animals, and without any perceptible cause. The foregoing facts go to show how important it is at all times to keep a vigilant guard over animals. In the vicinity of hostile Indians, where an attack may be anticipated, several good horses should be secured in such positions that they will continually be in readiness for an emergency of this kind. The herdsmen should have their horses in hand, saddled and bridled, and ready at an instant's notice to spring upon their backs and drive the herds into camp. As soon as it is discovered that the animals have taken fright, the herdsmen should use their utmost endeavors to turn them in the direction of the camp, and this can generally be accomplished by riding the bell mare in front of the herd, and gradually turning her toward it, and slackening her speed as the familiar objects about the camp come in sight. This usually tends to quiet their alarm.

CHAPTER III.

Repairing broken Wagons.—Fording Rivers.—Quicksand.—Wagon Boats.—Bull Boats.—Crossing Packs.—Swimming Animals.—Marching with loose Horses.—Herding Mules.—Best Methods of Marching.—Herding and guarding Animals.—Descending Mountains.—Storms.—Northers.

REPAIRS OF ACCIDENTS.

THE accidents most liable to happen to wagons on the plains arise from the great dryness of the atmosphere, and the consequent shrinkage and contraction of the woodwork in the wheels, the tires working loose, and the wheels, in passing over sidling ground, oftentimes falling down and breaking all the spokes where they enter the hub. It therefore becomes a matter of absolute necessity for the prairie traveler to devise some means of repairing such damages, or of guarding against them by the use of timely expedients.

The wheels should be frequently and closely examined, and whenever a tire becomes at all loose it should at once be tightened with pieces of hoop-iron, or wooden wedges driven by twos, simultaneously, from opposite sides. Another remedy for the same thing is to take off the wheels after encamping, sink them in water, and allow them to remain over night. This swells the wood, but is only temporary, requiring frequent repetition; and, after a time, if the wheels have not been made of thoroughly seasoned timber, it becomes necessary to reset the tires, in order to guard against their destruction by falling to pieces and breaking the spokes.

If the tires run off near a blacksmith's shop, or if there

be a traveling forge with the train, they may be tied on with raw hide or ropes, and thus driven to the shop or camp. When a rear wheel breaks down upon a march, the best method I know of for taking the vehicle to a place where it can be repaired, is to take off the damaged wheel, and place a stout pole of three or four inches in diameter under the end of the axle, outside the wagon-bed, and extending forward above the front wheel, where it is firmly lashed with ropes, while the other end of the pole runs six or eight feet to the rear, and drags upon the ground. The pole must be of such length and inclination that the axle shall be raised and retained in its proper horizontal position, when it can be driven to any distance that may be desired. The wagon should be relieved as much as practicable of its loading, as the pole dragging upon the ground will cause it to run heavily.

When a front wheel breaks down, the expedient just mentioned cannot be applied to the front axle, but the two rear wheels may be taken off and placed upon this axle (they will always fit), while the sound front wheel can be substituted upon one side of the rear axle, after which the pole may be applied as before described. This plan I have adopted upon several different occasions, and I can vouch for its efficacy.

The foregoing facts may appear very simple and unimportant in themselves; but blacksmiths and wheelwrights are not met with at every turn of the road upon the prairies; and in the wilderness, where the traveler is dependant solely upon his own resources, this kind of information will be found highly useful.

When the spokes in a wheel shrink more than the felloes, they work loose in the hub, and cannot be tightened by wedging. The only remedy in such cases is to cut the felloe with a saw on opposite sides, taking out two pieces of such dimensions that the reduced circumference will draw back the spokes into their proper places, and make them snug. A thin wagon-bow, or barrel hoops, may then be wrapped around the outside of the felloe, and secured with small nails or tacks. This increases the diameter of the wheel, so that when the tire has been heated, put on, and cooled, it forces back the spokes into their true places, and makes the wheel as sound and strong as it ever was. This simple process can be executed in about half-an-hour, if there be fuel for heating, and obviates the necessity of cutting and welding the tire. I would recommend that the tires should be secured with bolts and nuts, which will prevent them from running off when they work loose, and, if they have been cut and reset, they should be well tried with a hammer where they are welded to make sure that the junction is sound.

FORDING RIVERS.

Many streams that intersect the different routes across our continent are broad and shallow, and flow over beds of quicksand, which, in seasons of high water, become boggy and unstable, and are then exceedingly difficult to cross. When these streams are on the rise, and, indeed, before any swelling is perceptible, their beds become surcharged with the sand loosened by the action of the under-current from the approaching flood; and from this time until the water subsides fording is difficult, requiring great precautions. On arriving upon the bank of a river of this character which has not recently been crossed, the condition of the quicksand may be ascertained by sending an intelligent man over the fording-place, and, should the sand not yield under his feet, it may be regarded as safe for animals or wagons. Should it, however, prove soft and yielding, it must be thoroughly examined, and the best track selected. This can be done by a man on foot, who will take a number of sharp sticks long enough, when driven into the bottom of the river, to stand above the surface of the water. He starts from the shore, and with one of the sticks and his feet tries the bottom, in the direction of the opposite bank, until he finds the firmest ground, where he plants one of the sticks to mark the track. A man incurs no danger in walking over quicksand, provided he step rapidly, and he will soon detect the safest ground. He then proceeds, planting his sticks as often as may be necessary to mark the way, until he reaches the opposite bank. The ford is thus ascertained, and, if there are footmen in the party, they should cross before the animals and wagons, as they pack the sand, and make the track more firm and secure.

If the sand is soft, horses should be led across, and not allowed to stop in the stream; and the better to ensure this, they should be watered before entering upon the ford; otherwise, as soon as they stand still, their feet sink in the sand, and soon it becomes difficult to extricate them. The same rule holds in the passage of wagons; they must be driven steadily across, and the animals never allowed to stop while in the river, as the wheels sink rapidly in quicksand. Mules will often stop from fear, and when once embarrassed in the sand, they lie down, and will not use the slightest exertion to regain their footing. The only alternative, then, is to drag them out with ropes. I have even known some mules refuse to put forth the least exertion to get up after being pulled out upon firm ground, and it was necessary to set them upon their feet before they were restored to a consciousness of their own powers.

In crossing rivers where the water is so high as to come into the wagon-beds, but is not above a fording stage, the contents of the wagons may be kept dry by raising the beds between the uprights, and retaining them in that position with blocks of wood placed at each corner, between the rockers and the bottom of the wagon-beds. The blocks must be squared at each end, and their length, of course, should vary with the depth of water, which can be determined before cutting them. This is a very common and simple method of passing streams among emigrant travelers.

When streams are deep, with a very rapid current, it is difficult for the drivers to direct their teams to the proper coming-out places, as the current has a tendency to carry them too far down. This difficulty may be obviated by attaching a lariat rope to the leading animals, and having a mounted man ride in front with the rope in his hand, to assist the team in stemming the current, and direct it toward the point of egress. It is also a wise precaution, if the ford be at all hazardous, to place a mounted man on the lower side of the team with a whip, to urge forward any animal that may not work properly.

When rivers are wide, with a swift current, they should always, if possible, be forded obliquely down stream, as the action of the water against the wagons, assists very materially in carrying them across. In crossing the North Platte upon the Cherokee trail at a season when the water was high and very rapid, we were obliged to take the only practicable ford, which ran diagonally up the stream. The consequence was, that the heavy current, coming down with great force against the wagons, offered such powerful resistance to the efforts of the mules, that it was with difficulty they could retain their footing; and several were drowned. Had the ford crossed obliquely down the river, there would have been no difficulty.

When it becomes necessary, with loaded wagons, to cross a stream of this character against the current, I would recommend that the teams be doubled, the leading animals led, a horseman placed on each side with whips to assist the driver, and that, before the first wagon enters the water, a man should be sent in advance to ascertain the best ford.

During seasons of high water, men, in traversing the plains, often encounter rivers which rise above a fording stage, and remain in that condition for many days, and to await the falling of the water might involve a great loss of time. If the traveler be alone, his only way is to swim his horse; but if he retains the seat on his saddle, his weight presses the animal down into the water, and cramps his movements very sensibly. It is a much better plan to attach a cord to the bridle-bit, and drive him into the stream; then, seizing his tail, allow him to tow you across. If he turns out of the course, or attempts to turn back, he can be checked with the cord, or by splashing water at his head. If the rider remains in the saddle, he should allow the horse to have a loose rein, and never pull upon it except when necessary to guide. If he wishes to steady himself, he can lay hold upon the mane.

In travelling with large parties, the following expedients for crossing rivers have been successfully resorted to within my own experience; and they are attended with no risk to life or property.

A rapid and deep stream, with high, abrupt, and soft banks, probably presents the most formidable array of unfavorable circumstances that can be found. Streams of this character are occasionally met with, and it is important to know how to cross them with the greatest promptitude and safety.

A train of wagons having arrived upon the bank of such a stream, first select the best point for the passage, where the banks upon both sides require the least excavation for a place of ingress and egress to and from the river. As I have before remarked, the place of entering the river should be above the coming-out place on the opposite bank, as the current will then assist in carrying wagons and

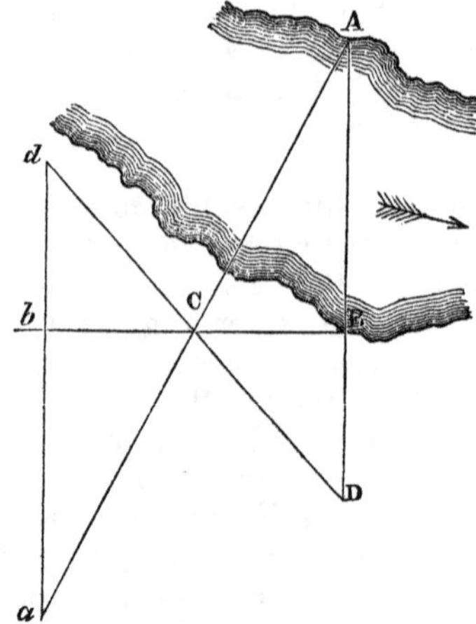

The line AB (the distance to be measured) is extended upon the bank to D, from which point, after having marked it, lay off equal distances, DC and C*d*; produce BC to *b*, making CB=C*b*; then extend the line *db* until it intersects the prolongation of the line through CA at *a*. The distance between *ab* is equal to AB, or the width of the crossing.

animals across. A spot should be sought where the bed of the stream is firm at the place where the animals are to get out on the opposite bank. If, however, no such place can be found, brush and earth should be thrown in to make a foundation sufficient to support the animals, and to prevent them from bogging. After the place for crossing has been selected, it will be important to determine the breadth of the river between the points of ingress and egress, in order to show the length of rope necessary to reach across. A very simple practical method of doing this without instruments, is found in the French "Manuel du Génie." This is shewn in the accompanying Diagram.

A man who is an expert swimmer then takes the end of a fishing-line or a small cord in his mouth, and carries it across, leaving the other end fixed upon the opposite bank, after which a lariat is attached to the cord, and one end of it pulled across and made fast to a tree; but if there is nothing convenient to which the lariat can be attached, an extra axle or coupling-pole can be pulled over by the man who has crossed, firmly planted in the ground, and the rope tied to it. The rope must be long enough to extend twice across the stream, so that one end may always be left on each shore. A very good substitute for a ferry-boat may be made with a wagon-bed by filling it with empty water-casks, stopped tight and secured in the wagon with ropes, with a cask lashed opposite the centre of each outside. It is then placed in the water bottom upwards, and the rope that has been stretched across the stream attached to one end of it, while another rope is made fast to the other end, after which it is loaded, the shore-end loosened, and the men on the opposite bank pull it across to the landing, where it is discharged and returned for another load, and so on until all the baggage and men are passed over.

The wagons can be taken across by fastening them down to the axles, attaching a rope to the end of the tongue, and another to the rear of each to steady it and hold it from drifting below the landing. It is then pushed into the stream, and the men on the opposite bank pull it over.

I have passed a large train of wagons in this way across a rapid stream fifteen feet deep without any difficulty. I took, at the same time, a six-pounder cannon, which was separated from its carriage, and ferried over upon the wagon-boat; after which the carriage was pulled over in the same way as described for the wagons.

There are not always a sufficient number of air-tight water-casks to fill a wagon-bed, but a tent-fly, paulin, or wagon-cover can generally be had. In this event, the wagon-bed may be placed in the centre of one of these, the cloth brought up around the ends and sides, and secured firmly with ropes tied around transversely, and another rope fastened lengthwise around under the rim. This holds the cloth in its place, and the wagon may then be placed in the water right side upward, and managed in the same manner as in the other case. If the cloth be made of cotton, it will soon swell so as to leak but very little, and answers a very good purpose.

Another method of ferrying streams is by means of what is called by the mountaineers a "*bull-boat,*" the frame-work of which is made of willows bent in the shape of a short and wide skiff, with a flat bottom. Willows grow upon the banks of almost all the streams on the prairies, and can be bent into any shape desired. To make a boat with but one hide, a number of straight willows are cut about an inch in diameter, the ends sharpened and driven into the ground, forming a frame-work in the shape of a half egg-shell cut through the longitudinal axis. Where these rods cross, they are firmly secured with strings. A stout rod is then heated and bent around the frame in such a position, that the edges of the hide, when laid over it and drawn tight, will just reach it. This rod forms the gunwale, which is secured by strings to the ribs. Small rods are then wattled in so as to make it symmetrical and strong. After which the green or soaked hide is thrown over the edges, sewed to the gunwales, and left to dry. The rods are then cut off even with the gunwale, and the boat is ready for use.

To build a boat with two or more hides; a stout pole

of the desired length is placed upon the ground for a keel, the ends turned up and secured by a lariat; willow rods of the required dimensions are then cut, heated, and bent into the proper shape for knees, after which their centres are placed at equal distances upon the keel, and firmly tied with cords. The knees are retained in their proper curvature by cords around the ends. After a sufficient number of them have been placed upon the keel, two poles of suitable dimensions are heated, bent around the ends for a gunwale, and firmly lashed to each knee. Smaller willows are then interwoven, so as to model the frame.

Green or soaked hides are cut into the proper shape to fit the frame, and sewed together with buckskin strings; then the frame of the boat is placed in the middle, the hide drawn up snug around the sides, and secured with raw-hide thongs to the gunwale. The boat is then turned bottom upwards and left to dry, after which the seams where they have been sewed are covered with a mixture of melted tallow and pitch: the craft is now ready for launching.

A boat of this kind is very light and serviceable, but after a while becomes water-soaked, and should always be turned bottom upward to dry whenever it is not in the water. Two men can easily build a *bull-boat* of three hides in two days which will carry ten men with perfect safety.*

* A boat has been invented by Colonel R. C. Buchanan, of the army, which has been used in several expeditions in Oregon and in Washington Territory, and has been highly commended by several experienced officers who have had the opportunity of giving its merits a practical service test.

It consists of an exceedingly light framework of thin and narrow boards, in lengths suitable for packing, connected by hinges, the different sections folding into so small a compass as to be conveniently carried upon mules. The frame is covered with a sheet of stout cotton canvas, or duck, secured to the gunwales with a cord running diagonally back and forth through eyelet-holes in the upper edge.

When first placed in the water, the boat leaks a little; but the canvas soon swells so as to make it sufficiently tight for all practical purposes. The great advantage to be derived from the use of this boat is, that it is so compact and portable as to be admirably adapted

A small party traveling with a pack train, and arriving upon the banks of a deep stream, will not always have the time to stop or the means to make any of the boats that have been described. Should their luggage be such as to become seriously injured by a wetting, and there be an India-rubber or gutta percha cloth disposable, or if even a green beef or buffalo-hide can be procured, it may be spread out upon the ground, and the articles of baggage placed in the centre, in a square or rectangular form; the ends and sides are then brought up so as entirely to envelop the package, and the whole secured with ropes or raw hide. It is then placed in the water with a rope attached to one end, and towed across by men in the same manner as the boats before described. If hides be used, they will require greasing occasionally, to prevent their becoming water-soaked.

When a mounted party with pack animals arrives upon the borders of a rapid stream, too deep to ford, and where the banks are high and abrupt, with perhaps but one place where the beasts can get out upon the opposite shore, it would not be safe to drive or ride them in, calculating that all will make the desired landing. Some of them will probably be carried by the swift current too far down the stream, and thereby endanger not only their own lives, but the lives of their riders. I have seen the experiment tried repeatedly, and have known several animals to be carried by the current below the point of egress, and thus drowned. Here is a simple, safe, and expeditious method of taking animals over such a stream. Suppose, for

---

to the requirements of campaigning in a country where the streams are liable to rise above a fording stage, and where the allowance of transportation is small.

It may be put together or taken apart and packed in a very few minutes; and one mule suffices to transport a boat, with all its appurtenances, capable of sustaining ten men.

Should the canvas become torn, it is easily repaired by putting on a patch, and it does not rot or crack like India-rubber or gutta percha; moreover, it is not affected by changes of climate or temperature.

example, a party of mounted men arrive upon the bank of the stream. There will always be some good swimmers in the party, and probably others who cannot swim at all. Three or four of the most expert of these are selected, and sent across with one end of a rope made of lariats tied together, while the other end is retained upon the first bank, and made fast to the neck of a gentle and good swimming horse; after which another gentle horse is brought up and made fast by a lariat around his neck to the tail of the first, and so on until all the horses are thus tied together. The men who cannot swim are then mounted upon the best swimming horses and tied on, otherwise they are liable to become frightened, lose their balance, and be carried away in a rapid current; or a horse may stumble and throw his rider. After the horses have been strung out in a single line by their riders, and everything is in readiness, the first horse is led carefully into the water, while the men on the opposite bank, pulling upon the rope, thus direct him across, and, if necessary, aid him in stemming the current. As soon as this horse strikes the bottom he pulls upon those behind him, and thereby assists in making the landing; and in this manner, all are passed over in perfect safety.*

DRIVING LOOSE HORSES.

In traveling with loose horses across the plains, some persons are in the habit of attaching them in pairs by their halters to a long stout rope, stretched between two wagons drawn by mules, each wagon being about half loaded. The principal object of the rear wagon being to hold back and keep the rope stretched, not more than two stout mules are required, as the horses aid a good deal with their heads in pulling this wagon. From thirty to

* For finding fords, crossing streams, making rafts, ferries, and coracles, and determining the breadth of rivers, the reader will consult the "Art of Travel," and "What to Observe," an excellent work by the late Col. J. R. Jackson, F.R.S., etc. Third edition. Revised and edited by Dr. Norton Shaw, M.D., etc., Acting Secretary to the Royal Geographical Society of London.—Ed.

forty horses may be driven very well in this manner, and, if they are wild, it is perhaps the safest method, except that of leading them with halters held by men riding beside them. The rope to which the horses are attached should be about an inch and a quarter in diameter, with loops or rings inserted at intervals sufficient to admit the horses without allowing them to kick each other, and the halter straps tied to these loops. The horses, on first starting, should have men by their sides, to accustom them to this manner of being led. The wagons should be so driven as to keep the rope continually stretched. Good drivers must be assigned to these wagons, who will constantly watch the movements of the horses attached, as well as their own teams.

I have had 150 loose horses driven by ten mounted herdsmen. This requires great care for some considerable time, until the horses become gentle and accustomed to their herders. It is important to ascertain, as soon as possible after starting, which horses are wild, and may be likely to stampede and lead off the herd; such should be led, and never suffered to run loose, either on the march or in camp. Animals of this character will soon indicate their propensities, and can be secured during the first days of the march. It is desirable that all animals that will not stampede when not working should run loose on a march, as they pick up a good deal of grass along the road when traveling, and the success of an expedition, when animals get no other forage but grass, depends in a great degree upon the time given them for grazing. They will thrive much better when allowed a free range than when picketed, as they then are at liberty to select such grass as suits them. It may, therefore, be set down as an infallible rule never to be departed from, that all animals, excepting such as will be likely to stampede, should be turned loose for grazing immediately after arriving at the camping-place; but it is equally important that they should be carefully herded as near the camp as good grass will admit; and those that it is necessary to picket should be placed upon the best grass, and their places changed often. The ropes to which they are attached should be about forty feet long; the picket-pins, of iron, fifteen inches long, with ring and swivel at top, so that the rope shall not twist as the animal feeds around it; and the pins must be firmly driven into tenacious earth.

Animals should be herded during the day at such distances as to leave sufficient grass undisturbed around and near the camp for grazing through the night.

METHOD OF MARCHING.

Among men of limited experience in frontier-life will be found a great diversity of opinion regarding the best methods of marching, and of treating animals in expeditions upon the prairies. Some will make late starts and travel during the heat of the day, without nooning, while others will start early and make two marches, lying by during the middle of the day; some will picket their animals continually in camp, while others will herd them day and night, etc., etc. For mounted troops, or, indeed, for any body of men traveling with horses and mules, a few general rules may be specified which have the sanction of mature experience; and a deviation from them will inevitably result in consequences highly detrimental to the best interests of an expedition.

In ordinary marches through a country where grass and water are abundant and good, animals receiving proper attention should not fall away, even if they receive no grain; and, as I said before, they should not be made to travel faster than a walk, unless absolutely necessary; neither should they be taken off the road for the purpose of hunting or chasing buffalo, as one buffalo-chase injures them more than a week of moderate riding. In the vicinity of hostile Indians, the animals must be carefully herded and guarded, within protection of the camp, while those picketed should be changed as often as the grass is eaten off within the circle described by the tether-rope. At night they should be brought within the chain of sentinels and picketed as compactly as is consistent with the space needed for grazing, and, under no circumstances unless the Indians are known to be near and an attack is to be expected, should they be tied up to a picket line where they can get no grass. Unless allowed to graze at night, they will fall away rapidly, and soon become unserviceable. It is much better to march after nightfall, turn some distance off the road, and to encamp without fires in a depressed locality, where the Indians cannot track the party, and the animals may be picketed without danger.

In descending abrupt hills and mountains, one wheel of a wagon should always be locked, as this relieves the wheel animals, and makes everything more secure. When the declivity is great, both rear wheels should be locked; and, if very abrupt, requiring great effort on the wheel animals to hold the wagon, the wheels should be rough-locked by lengthening the lock-chains, so that the part which goes around the wheels will come directly upon the ground, and thus create more friction. Occasionally, however, hills are met with so nearly perpendicular, that it becomes necessary to attach ropes to the rear axle, and to station men to hold back upon them and steady the vehicle down the descent. Rough-locking is a very safe method of passing heavy artillery down abrupt declivities. There are several mountains between the Missouri River and California, where it is necessary to resort to one of the two last-mentioned methods in order to descend with security. If there are no lock-chains upon wagons, the front and rear wheels on the same side may be tied together with ropes, so as to lock them very firmly.

It is an old and well-established custom among men experienced in frontier life, always to cross a stream upon which it is intended to encamp for the night, and this rule should never be departed from where a stream is to be forded, as a rise during the night might detain the traveler for several days in awaiting the fall of the waters.*

* The hint is notably useful for Indian and African travellers. And, generally, it is well to surmount an obstacle at the end of a march, rather than reserve it for the next day, when precious time may be wasted.—Ed.

STORMS.

In Western Texas, during the autumn and winter months, storms arise very suddenly, and, when accompanied by a north wind, are very severe upon men and animals; indeed, they are sometimes so terrific as to make it necessary for travelers to hasten to the nearest sheltered place to save the lives of their animals. When these storms come from the north, they are called "*northers*;" and as, during the winter season, the temperature often undergoes a sudden change of many degrees at the time the storm sets in, the perspiration is checked, and the system receives an instantaneous shock, against which it requires great vital energy to bear up. Men and animals are not, in this mild climate, prepared for these capricious meteoric revolutions, and they not unfrequently perish under their effects.

While passing near the head waters of the Colorado in October, 1849, I left one of my camps at an early hour in the morning under a mild and soft atmosphere, with a gentle breeze from the south, but had marched only a short distance when the wind suddenly whipped round into the north, bringing with it a furious chilling rain, and in a short time the road became so soft and heavy as to make the labor of pulling the wagons over it very exhausting upon the mules, and they came into camp in a profuse sweat, with the rain pouring down in torrents upon them.

They were turned out of harness into the most sheltered place that could be found; but, instead of eating, as was their custom, they turned their heads from the wind, and remained in that position, chilled and trembling, without making the least effort to move. The rain continued with unabated fury during the entire day and night, and, on the following morning, thirty-five out of 110 mules had perished, while those remaining could hardly be said to have had a spark of vitality left. They were drawn up with the cold, and could with difficulty walk. Tents and wagon-covers were cut up to protect them, and they were then driven about for some time, until a little vital energy was restored, after which they commenced eating grass; but it was three or four days before they recovered sufficiently to resume the march.

The mistake I made was in driving the mules after the "norther" had commenced. Had I gone immediately into camp, before they became heated and wearied, they would probably have eaten the grass, and this, I have no doubt, would have saved them; but, as it was, their blood became heated from overwork, and the sudden chill brought on a reaction which proved fatal. If an animal will eat his forage plentifully, there is but little danger of his perishing with cold. This I assert with much confidence, as I once, when traveling with about 1500 horses and mules, encountered the most terrific snow-storm that has been known within the memory of the oldest mountaineers. It commenced on the last day of April, and continued without cessation for sixty consecutive hours. The day had been mild and pleasant; the green grass was about six inches high; the trees had put on their new leaves, and nature conspired to show, that the sombre garb of winter had been permanently superseded by the smiling attire of spring. About dark, however, the wind turned into the north; it commenced to snow violently, and increased until it became a frightful tempest, filling the atmosphere with a dense cloud of driving snow, against which it was impossible to ride or walk. Soon after the storm set in, one herd of 300 horses and mules broke away from the herdsmen who were around them, and in spite of all their efforts, ran at full speed, directly with the wind and snow, for fifty miles before they stopped.

Three of the herdsmen followed them as far as they were able, but soon became exhausted and lost on the prairie. One of them found his way back to camp in a state of great prostration and suffering. One of the others was found dead, and the third crawling about upon his hands and knees, after the storm had ceased.

It happened, fortunately, that I had reserved a quantity of corn to be used in the event of finding a scarcity of grass, and as soon as the ground became covered with snow, so that the animals could not get at the grass, I fed out the corn, which I am induced to believe saved their lives. Indeed, they did not seem at all affected by this prolonged and unseasonable tempest. This occurred upon the summit of the elevated ridge dividing the waters of the Arkansas and South Platte Rivers, where storms are said to be of frequent occurrence.

The greater part of the animals that stampeded were recovered after the storm; and, although they had traveled a hundred miles at a very rapid pace, they did not seem to be much affected by it.

CHAPTER IV.

Packing.—Saddles.—Mexican Method.—Madrina, or Bell-mare.—Attachment of the Mule illustrated.—Best Method of Packing.—Hobbling Animals.—Selecting Horses and Mules.—Grama and Bunch Grass.—European Saddles.—Californian Saddle.—Saddle Wounds.—Alkali.—Flies.—Colic.—Rattlesnake Bites.—Cures for the Bite.

PACKING AND DRIVING.

WITH a train of pack animals properly organized and equipped, a party may travel with much comfort and celerity. It is enabled to take short cuts, and move over the country in almost any direction without regard to roads. Mountains and broken ground may easily be traversed, and exemption is gained from many of the troubles and detentions attendant upon the transit of cumbersome wagon-trains.*

One of the most essential requisites to the outfit of a pack train is a good pack-saddle. Various patterns are in use, many of which are mere instruments of torture upon the backs of the poor brutes, lacerating them cruelly, and causing continued pain.

The Mexicans use a leathern pack-saddle without a tree. It is stuffed with hay, and is very large, covering almost the entire back, and extending far down the sides. It is secured with a broad hair girth, and the load is kept in position by a lash-rope drawn by two men so tight as to give the unfortunate beast intense suffering.

* For information touching saddles of various sorts, packing animals, tethering, hobbling, and knee-haltering, the English reader will refer to Mr. Galton.—ED.

A pack-saddle is made by T. Grimsley, No. 41, Main Street, St. Louis, Mo. It is open at the top, with a light, compact, and strong tree, which fits the animal's back well, and is covered with raw hide, put on green, and drawn tight by the contraction in drying. It has a leathern breast-strap, breeching, and lash-strap, with a broad hair girth fastened in the Mexican fashion. Of sixty-five of these saddles that I used in crossing the Rocky Mountains, over an exceedingly rough and broken section, not one of them wounded a mule's back, and I regard them as the best saddles I have ever seen.

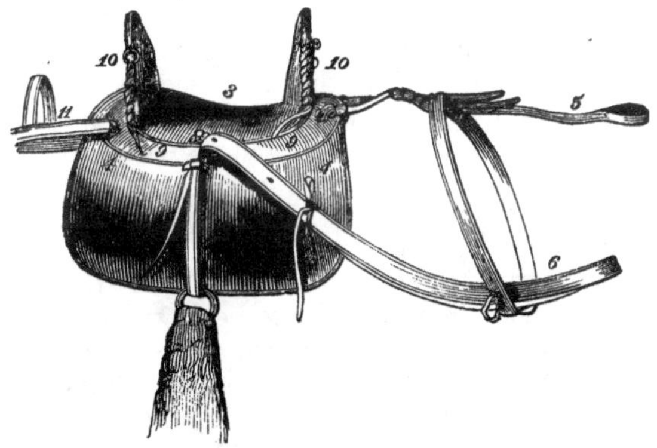

GRIMSLEY'S PACK-SADDLE.

No people, probably, are more familiar with the art of packing than the Mexicans. They understand the habits, disposition, and powers of the mule perfectly, and will get more work out of him than any other men I have ever seen. The mule and the donkey are to them as the camel to the Arab—their porters over deserts and mountains where no other means of transportation can be used to advantage. The Spanish Mexicans are, however, cruel masters, having no mercy upon their beasts, and it is no uncommon thing for them to load their mules with the enormous burden of 300 or 400 lbs.

These muleteers believe, that, when the pack is firmly

lashed, the animal supports his burden better, and travels with greater ease, which seems quite probable, as the tension forms, as it were, an external sheath supporting and bracing the muscles.* It also has a tendency to prevent the saddle from slipping and chafing the mule's back. With such huge *cargas* as the Mexicans load upon their mules, it is impossible, by any precautions, to prevent their backs and withers from becoming horribly mangled, and it is common to see them working their animals day after day in this miserable plight. This heavy packing causes the scars that so often mark Mexican mules.

The animal, in starting out from camp in the morning, groaning under the weight of his heavy burden, seems hardly able to move; but the pack soon settles, and so loosens the lashing that after a short time he moves along with more ease. Constant care and vigilance on the part of the muleteers are necessary to prevent the packs from working loose and falling off. The adjustment of a *carga* upon a mule does not, however, detain the caravan, as the others move on while it is being righted. If the mules are suffered to halt, they are apt to lie down, and it is very difficult for them, with their loads, to rise; besides, they are likely to strain themselves in their efforts to do so. The Mexicans, in traveling with large caravans, usually make the day's march without nooning, as too much time would be consumed in unloading and packing up again.

Packs, when taken off in camp, should be piled in a row upon the ground, and, if there be a prospect of rain, the saddles should be placed over them, and the whole covered with the saddle-blankets or canvas.

The muleteers and herders should be mounted upon well-trained horses, and be careful to keep the animals of the caravan from wandering or scattering along the road.

* The art of packing is, firstly, a proper balance and adjustment of packs; secondly, a firm lashing of loads. For long journeys, however, a strong mule should not carry more than 120 lbs., and asses about half. Mr. Galton gives for the ass 65 lbs.; the small mule 90 lbs.; the horse 100 lbs.; and the ox 120 lbs. But he, probably, never saw the Mexican or Californian mule.—ED.

This can easily be done by having some of the men riding upon each side, and others in rear of the caravan.

In herding mules, it is customary among prairie travelers to have a bell-mare, to which the mules soon become so attached, that they will follow her wherever she goes. By keeping her in charge of one of the herdsmen, the herds are easily controlled ; and during a stampede, if the herdsman mounts her, and rushes ahead toward camp, they will generally follow.

In crossing rivers the bell-mare should pass first, after which the mules are easily induced to take to the water and pass over, even if they have to swim. Mules are good swimmers unless they happen, by plunging off a high bank, to get water in their ears, when they are often drowned. Whenever a mule in the water drops his ears, it is a sure indication that he has water in them, and he should be taken out as soon as possible. To prevent accidents of this nature, where the water is deep and the banks abrupt, the mule-herds should be allowed to enter slowly, and without crowding, as otherwise they are not only likely to get their heads under water, but to throw each other over and get injured.

The *madrina*, or bell-mare, acts a most important part in a herd of mules, and is regarded by experienced campaigners as indispensable to their security. She is selected for her quiet and regular habits. She will not wander far from the camp. If she happen to have a colt by her side, this is no objection, as the mules soon form the most devoted attachment to it. I have often seen them leave their grazing when very hungry, and flock around a small colt, manifesting their delight by rubbing it with their noses, licking it with their tongues, kicking up their heels, and making a variety of other grotesque demonstrations of affection, while the poor little colt, perfectly unconscious of the cause of these ungainly caresses, stood trembling with fear, but unable to make his escape from the compact circle of his mulish admirers. Horses and asses are also used as bell-animals, and the mules soon become accustomed to following them. If a man leads or rides a bell-animal in advance, the mules follow, like so many dogs, in the most orderly procession.

"After traveling about fourteen miles," says Bayard Taylor, "we were joined by three miners, and our mules, taking a sudden liking for their horses, jogged on at a more brisk pace. The instincts of the mulish heart form an interesting study to the traveler in the mountains. I would (were the comparison not too ungallant) liken it to a woman's, for it is quite as uncertain in its sympathies, bestowing its affections when least expected, and, when bestowed, quite as constant, so long as the object is not taken away. Sometimes a horse, sometimes an ass, captivates the fancy of a whole drove of mules, but often an animal nowise akin. Lieutenant Beale told me that his whole train of mules once galloped off suddenly, on the plains of the Cimarone, and ran half a mile, when they halted in apparent satisfaction. The cause of their freak was found to be a buffalo calf which had strayed from the herd. They were frisking around it in the greatest delight, rubbing their noses against it, throwing up their heels, and making themselves ridiculous by abortive attempts to neigh and bray, while the calf, unconscious of its attractive qualities, stood trembling in their midst."

"If several large troops," says Charles Darwin, "are turned into one field to graze in the morning, the muleteer has only to lead the *madrinas* a little apart and tinkle their bells, and, although there may be 200 or 300 mules together, each immediately knows its own bell, and separates itself from the rest. The affection of these animals for their madrina saves infinite trouble. It is nearly impossible to lose an old mule, for, if detained several hours by force, she will, by the power of smell, like a dog, track out her companions, or rather the madrina; for, according, to the muleteer, she is the chief object of affection. The feeling, however, is not of an individual nature; for I believe I am right in saying that any animal with a bell will serve as a madrina."

Of the attachment that a mule will form for a horse, I will cite an instance from my own observation, which struck me at the time as being one of the most remarkable and touching evidences of devotion that I have ever known among the brute creation.

On leaving Fort Leavenworth with the army for Utah in 1857, one of the officers rode a small mule, whose kind and gentle disposition soon caused him to become a favorite among the soldiers, and they named him "Billy." As this officer and myself were often thrown together upon the march, the mule, in the course of a few days, evinced a growing attachment for a mare that I rode. The sentiment was not, however, reciprocated on her part, and she intimated as much by the reversed position of her ears, and the free exercise of her feet and teeth whenever Billy came within her reach; but these signal marks of displeasure, instead of discouraging, rather seemed to increase his devotion, and whenever at liberty he invariably sought to get near her, and appeared much distressed when not permitted to follow her.

On leaving Camp Scott for New Mexico, Billy was among the number of mules selected for the expedition. During the march I was in the habit, when starting out from camp in the morning, of leading off the party, and directing the packmen to hold the mule until I should get so far in advance with the mare that he could not see us; but the moment he was released, he would, in spite of all the efforts of the packers, start off at a most furious pace, and never stop or cease braying until he reached the mare's side. We soon found it impossible to keep him with the other mules, and he was finally permitted to have his own way.

In the course of time we encountered the deep snows in the Rocky Mountains, where the animals could get no forage, and Billy, in common with the others, at length became so weak and jaded that he was unable any longer to leave his place in the caravan and break a track through the snow around to the front. He made frequent attempts to turn out and force his way ahead, but after numerous unsuccessful efforts he would fall down exhausted, and set up a most mournful braying.

The other mules soon began to fail, and to be left, worn out and famished, to die by the wayside; it was not, however, for some time that Billy showed symptoms of becoming one of the victims, until one evening after our arrival at camp I was informed that he had dropped down and been left upon the road during the day. The men all deplored his loss exceedingly, as his devotion to the mare had touched their kind hearts, and many expressions of sympathy were uttered around their bivouac fires on that evening.

Much to our surprise, however, about ten o'clock, just as we were about going to sleep, we heard a mule braying about half a mile to the rear upon our trail. Sure enough, it proved to be Billy, who, after having rested, had followed upon our track and overtaken us. As soon as he reached the side of the mare he lay down and seemed perfectly contented.

The next day I relieved him from his pack, and allowed him to run loose; but during the march he gave out, and was again abandoned to his fate, and this time we certainly never expected to see him more. To our great astonishment, however, about twelve o'clock that night the sonorous but not very musical notes of Billy in the distance aroused us from our slumbers, and again announced his approach. In an instant the men were upon their feet, gave three hearty cheers, and rushed out in a body to meet and escort him into camp.

But this well-meant ovation elicited no response from him. He came reeling and floundering along through the deep snow, perfectly regardless of these honors, pushing aside all those who occupied the trail or interrupted his progress in the least, wandered about until he found the mare, dropped down by her side, and remained until morning.

When we resumed our march on the following day he made another desperate effort to proceed, but soon fell down exhausted, when we reluctantly abandoned him, and saw him no more.

The articles to be transported should be made up into

two packages of precisely equal weight, and as nearly equal in bulk as practicable, otherwise they will sway the saddle over to one side, and cause it to chafe the animal's back.

The packages made, two ropes about six feet long are fastened around the ends by a slip-knot, and if the packages contain corn or other articles that will shift about, small sticks should be placed between the sacks and the ropes, which equalizes the pressure and keeps the packages snug. The ropes are then looped at the ends, and made precisely of the same length, so that the packs will balance and come up well toward the top of the saddle. Two men, then, each taking a pack, go upon opposite sides of the mule, that has been previously saddled, and, raising the packs simultaneously, place the loops over the pommel and cantel, settling them well down into their places. The lashing-strap is then thrown over the top, brought through the rings upon each side, and drawn as tight at every turn as the two men on the sides can pull it, and, after having been carried back and forth diagonally across the packs as often as its length admits (generally three or four times), it is made fast to one of the rings, and securely tied in a slip-knot.

The breast-strap and breeching must not be buckled so close as to chafe the skin; the girth should be broad and soft where it comes opposite the fore-legs, to prevent cutting them. Leather girths should be wrapped with cloth or bound with soft material. The hair girth, being soft and elastic, is much better than leather.

The crupper should never be dispensed with in a mountainous country, but it must be soft, round, and about an inch in diameter where it comes in contact with the tail, otherwise it will wound the animal in making long and abrupt descents.

In Norway they use a short round stick, about ten inches long, which passes under the tail, and from each end of this a cord connects with the saddle.*

* This is an excellent "wrinkle" (borrowed from the "Art of Travel,") to prevent chafing, which, in hot damp climates, soon disables the pluckiest animals."—Ed.

Camp-kettles, tin vessels, and other articles that will rattle and be likely to frighten animals, should be firmly lashed to the packs. When the packs work loose, the lash-straps should be untied, and a man upon each side draw it up again and make it fast. When ropes are used for lashing, they may be tightened by twisting them with a short stick and making the stick fast.

One hundred and twenty-five pounds is a sufficient load for a mule upon a long journey.

In traveling over a rocky country, and upon all long journeys, horses and mules should be shod, to prevent their hoofs wearing out or breaking. The mountaineers contend that beasts travel better without shoeing, but I have several times had occasion to regret the omission of this very necessary precaution. A few extra shoes and nails, with a small hammer, will enable travelers to keep their animals shod.

In turning out pack animals to graze, it is well either to keep the lariat ropes upon them with the ends trailing upon the ground, or to hopple them, as no corral can be made into which they may be driven in order to catch them. A very good way to catch an animal without driving him into an inclosure is for two men to take a long rope and stretch it out at the height of the animal's neck; some men then drive him slowly up against it, when one of the men with the rope runs round behind the animal and back to the front again, thus taking a turn with the rope round his neck and holding him secure.

To prevent an animal from kicking, take a forked stick and make the forked part fast to the bridle-bit, bringing the two ends above the head, and securing them there, leaving the part of the stick below the fork of sufficient length to reach near the ground when the animal's head is in its natural position. He cannot kick up unless he lowers his head, and the stick effectually prevents that.

Tether-ropes should be so attached to the neck of the animal as not to slip and choke him, and the picket-pins never be left on the ropes except when in the ground, as, in the event of a stampede, they are very likely to swing round and injure the animals.

Many experienced travelers were formerly in the habit of securing their animals with a strap or iron ring fastened around the fetlock of one fore foot, and this attached to the tether-rope. This method holds the animal very securely to the picket-pin, but when the rope is first put on, and before he becomes accustomed to it, he is liable to throw himself down and get hurt; so that I think the plan of tethering by the neck or halter is the safest, and, so far as I have observed, is now universally practised.

The mountaineers and Indians seldom tether their animals, but prefer the plan of hoppling, as this gives them more latitude for ranging and selecting the choicest grass.

Two methods of hoppling are practised among the Indians and hunters of the West: one with a strap about two feet long buckling around the fore legs above the fetlock joints; the other is what they term the "*side hopple*," which is made by buckling a strap around a fore and rear leg upon the same side. In both cases care should be taken not to buckle the strap so tight as to chafe the legs. The latter plan is the best, because the animal, side-hoppled, is able to go but little faster than a walk, while the front hopple permits him, after a little practice, to gallop off at considerable speed. If the hopples are made of iron connected with chains, like handcuffs, with locks and keys, it will be impossible for the Indians, without files, to cut them; but the parts that come in contact with the legs should be covered with soft leather.

"A horse," says Mr. Galton, "may be hoppled* with a stirrup-leather by placing the middle around one leg, then twisting it several times and buckling it round the other leg. When you wish to picket horses in the middle of a sandy plain, dig a hole two or three feet deep, and, tying your rope to a fagot of sticks or brushwood, or even to a bag filled with sand, bury this in it."

* The Englishman, however, spells the word "hobbled."—ED.

For prairie service, horses which have been raised exclusively upon grass, and never been fed upon grain—or "*range horses*," as they are called in the West—are decidedly the best, and will perform more hard labor than those that have been stabled and groomed. The large, stout ponies found among some of our frontier settlements are well adapted to this service, and endure admirably. The same remarks hold good in the choice of mules; and it will be found that the square-built, big-bellied, and short-legged Mexican mule will endure far more hard service, on short allowance of forage, than the larger American mule which has been accustomed to grain.*

* In traveling through deep snow, horses will be found much better than mules, as the latter soon become discouraged, lie down, and refuse to put forth the least exertion, while the former will work as long as their strength holds out.

When the snow is dry, and not deeper than 2½ feet, horses in good condition will walk through it without much difficulty, and throw aside the snow so as to open quite a track. If there are several horses they should be changed frequently, as the labour upon the leading one is very severe. When the snow is deeper than 2½ feet, it becomes very difficult for animals to wade through it, and they soon weary and give out. The best plan, under such circumstances (and it is the one I adopted in crossing the Rocky Mountains, where the snow was from two to five feet upon the ground), is to place all the disposable men in advance of the animals to break the track, requiring them to alternate from front to rear at regular intervals of time. In this manner a track is beaten, over which animals pass with comparative ease.

When the snow increases to about four feet, it is impossible for the leading men to walk erect through it, and two or three of them are compelled to crawl upon their hands and knees, all being careful to place their hands and feet in the same holes that have been made by those in advance. This packs the snow so that it will sustain the others walking erect, and after 20 or 30 have passed it becomes sufficiently firm to bear up the animals. This, of course, is an exceedingly laborious and slow process, but it is the only alternative when a party finds itself in the midst of very deep snows in a wilderness. Animals, in walking over such a track as has been mentioned, will soon acquire the habit of placing their feet in the holes that have been made by the men; and, indeed, if they lose the step or miss the holes, they will fall down or sink to their bellies.

Early in the winter, when the snow first falls in the Rocky Mountains, it is so light and dry that snow-shoes cannot be used to advan-

In our trip across the Rocky Mountains, we had both the American and Mexican mules; and improved a good opportunity of giving their relative powers of endurance a thorough service-trial. For many days they were reduced to a meagre allowance of dry grass, and at length got nothing but pine leaves, while their work in the deep snow was exceedingly severe. This soon told upon the American mules, and all of them, with the exception of two, died, while most of the Mexican mules went through. The result was perfectly conclusive.

We found that, where the snow was not more than two

---

tage. We tried the experiment when we crossed the mountains in December and January, but found it impossible to walk upon them.

Should a party, in a country where the snow is deep, have the misfortune to lose its animals by freezing, the journey cannot be continued for any great length of time without devising some method of transporting subsistence besides that of carrying it upon the backs of men, as they are unable to break a track through deep snow when loaded down in this way.

The following plan has suggested itself to me as being the most feasible, and it is the one I resolved to adopt in the event of losing our mules faster than we required them for subsistence when we passed the Mountains.

Take willow, or other flexible rods, and make long sleds, less in width than the track, securing the cross-pieces with raw-hide thongs. Skin the animals, and cut the hides into pieces to fit the bottom of the sleds, and make them fast, with the hair on the upper side. Attach a raw-hide thong to the front for drawing it, and it is complete. In a very cold climate the hide soon freezes, becomes very solid, and slips easily over the snow. The meat and other articles to be transported are then placed upon the sled so as not to project over the sides, and lashed firmly. Lieutenant Cresswell, who was detached from Captain M'Clure's ship in the Arctic regions in 1853, says his men dragged 200 pounds each upon sledges over the ice. They could not, of course, pull as much over deep snow; but it is believed that they would have no difficulty in transporting half this amount, which would be sufficient to keep them from starvation at least fifty days.

I am quite confident, that a party of men who find themselves involved in deep snow, dependent solely upon their own physical powers, and without beasts of burden, can prolong their lives for a greater time, travel farther, and perform more labour by adopting the foregoing suggestions than in any other way.

feet deep, the animals soon learned to paw it away and get at the grass. Of course they do not get sufficient in this way; but they do much better than one would suppose.

In Utah and New Mexico, the autumn is so dry that the grass does not lose its nutritious properties by being washed with rains. It gradually dries and cures like hay, so that animals eat it freely, and will fatten upon it even in mid-winter. It is seldom that any grain is fed to stock in either of these territories.*

Several of the varieties of grass growing upon the slopes of the Rocky Mountains are of excellent quality; among these may be mentioned the Gramma and bunch grasses. Horses and mules turned out to graze always prefer the grass upon the mountain sides to grass of the valleys.

We left New Mexico about the 1st of March, six weeks before the new grass appeared, with 1500 animals, many of them low in flesh, yet they improved upon the journey, and on their arrival in Utah were all, with very few exceptions, in fine working condition. Had this march been made at the same season in the country bordering upon the Missouri River, where there are heavy autumnal rains, the animals would probably have become very poor.

In this journey, the herds were allowed to range over the best grass that could be found, but were guarded both night and day with great care, whereas, if they had been corraled or picketed at night, I dare say they would have lost flesh.†

* I brought home a specimen of "bunch-grass" for trial in the sandy *landes* about Aldershott.—Ed.

† Some curious and interesting experiments are said to have been recently made at the veterinary school at Alfort, near Paris, by order of the minister of war, to ascertain the powers of endurance of horses. It appears, that a horse will live on water alone five-and-twenty days; seventeen days without eating or drinking; only five days if fed and unwatered; ten days, if fed and insufficiently watered. A horse kept without water for three days, drank 104 lbs. of water in three minutes. It was found, that a horse taken immediately after feed, and kept in the active exercise of the squadron school, completely digested its food in three hours; in the same time, in the conscript's school, its food was two-thirds digested; and, if kept perfectly quiet in the stable, its digestion was scarcely commenced in three hours.—Author.

SADDLES.

Great diversity of opinion exists regarding the best equipment for horses, and the long-mooted question is as yet very far from being definitely settled.

I do not regard the opinions of Europeans as having a more direct bearing upon this question, or as tending to establish any more definite and positive conclusions regarding it than have been developed by the experience of our own border citizens, the major part of whose lives has been spent in the saddle ; yet I am confident, that the following brief description of the horse equipments used in different parts of Europe, the substance of which I have extracted from Captain M'Clellan's interesting report, will be read with interest and instruction. The saddle used by the African chasseurs consists of a plain wooden tree, with a pad upon the top, but without skirts, and is somewhat similar to our own military saddle, but lower in the pommel and cantle. The girth and surcingle are of leather, with an ordinary woollen saddle blanket. Their bridle has a single head-stall, with the Spanish bit buckled to it.

A new saddle has recently been introduced into the French service by Captain Cogent, the tree of which is cut out of a single piece of wood, the cantle only being glued on, and a piece of walnut let into the pommel, with a thin strip veneered upon the front ends of the bars. The pommel and cantle are lower than in the old model ; the whole is covered with a wet raw hide, glued on and sewed at the edges. The great advantage this saddle possesses, is in being so arranged that it may be used for horses of all sizes and conditions. The saddle-blanket is made of thick felt cloth, and is attached to the pommel by a small strap passing through holes in the blanket, which is thus prevented from slipping, and at the same time it raises the saddle so as to admit a free circulation of air over the horse's spine.

The Hungarian saddle is made of hard wood, entirely uncovered, with a raised pommel and cantle. The seat is formed with a leather strap four inches wide, nailed to the forks on the front and rear, and secured to the side-boards by leather thongs, thus giving an elastic and easy saddle-seat. This is also the form of the saddle-tree used by the Russian and Austrian cavalry. The Russians have a leather girth fastened by three small buckles: it passes over the tree, and is tied to the side boards. The saddle-blanket is of stout felt cloth, in four thicknesses, and a layer of black leather over it, and the whole held together by leather thongs passing through and through. When the horse falls off in flesh, more thicknesses are added, and *vice versa.* This saddle-blanket is regarded by the Russian officers as the best possible arrangement. The Russians use the curb and snaffle-bits made of steel.

The Cossack-saddle has a thick padding under the side-boards, and on the seat, which raises the rider very high on his horse, so that his feet are above the bottom of the belly. Their bridle has but a simple snaffle-bit, and no martingale.

The Prussian cuirassiers have a heavy saddle with a low pommel and cantle, covered with leather; but it is not thought by Captain M'Clellan to present anything worthy of imitation.

The other Prussian cavalry ride the Hungarian saddle, of a heavier model than the one in the Austrian service. The surcingle is of leather, and fastens in the Mexican style; the girth is also of leather, three and a half inches wide, with a large buckle. It is in two parts, attached to the bars by raw hide thongs. The curb and snaffle steel bits are used, and attached to a single head-stall.

The English cavalry use a saddle which has a lower cantle and pommel than our *Grimsley* saddle, covered with leather. The snaffle-bit is attached to the halter head-stall by a chain and T; the curb has a separate head-stall, which, on a march is occasionally taken off and hung on the carbine stock.

The Sardinian saddle has a bare wooden tree very similar to the Hungarian. A common blanket, folded in twelve thicknesses, is placed under it. The girth and surcingle are of leather.

Without expressing any opinion as to the comparative merits of these different saddles, I may be permitted to give a few general principles, which I regard as infallible in the choice of a saddle.

The side-boards should be large, and made to conform to the shape of the horse's back, thereby distributing the burden over a large surface. It should stand up well above the spine, so as to admit a free circulation of air under it.

For long journeys, the crupper, where it comes in contact with the tail, should be made of soft leather. It should be drawn back only far enough to hold the saddle from the withers. Some horses require much more tension upon the crupper than others. The girth should be made broad, of a soft and elastic material. Those made of hair, in use among the Mexicans, fulfil the pre-cited conditions.

A light and easy bit, which will not fret or chafe the horse, is recommended.

The saddle-blanket must be folded even and smooth, and placed on so as to cover every part of the back that comes in contact with the saddle, and in warm weather it is well to place a gunny bag under the blanket, as it is cooler than the wool.

It will have been observed, that, in the French service, the folded saddle-blanket is tied to the pommel to prevent it slipping back. This is well, if the blanket be taken off and thoroughly dried whenever the horse is unsaddled.

A saddle-blanket made of moss is used in some of the South-western States, which is regarded by many as the perfection of this article of horse equipment. It is a mat woven into the proper shape and size from the beaten fibres of moss that hangs from the trees in our Southern States.* It is cheap, durable, is not in any way affected by sweat, and does not chafe or heat the horse's spine like the woolen blanket. Its open texture allows a rapid

* The well-known Tillandsia Usneoides of the Southern States, popularly called "Absalom's Hair."—Ed.

evaporation, which tends to keep the back cool, and obviates the danger of stripping and sudden exposure of the heated parts to the sun and air.

The experience of some of our officers, who have used this mat for years in Mexico and Texas, corroborates all I have said in its favor; and they are unanimous in the opinion, that a horse will never get a sore back when it is placed under a good saddle.

A saddle made by the Mexicans in California is called the *California saddle.* This is extensively used upon the Pacific slope of the mountains, and is believed to possess, at least, as many advantages for rough frontier service as any other pattern that has been invented. Those hardy and experienced veterans, the mountaineers, could not be persuaded to ride on any other saddle, and their ripened knowledge of such matters certainly gives weight to their conclusions.

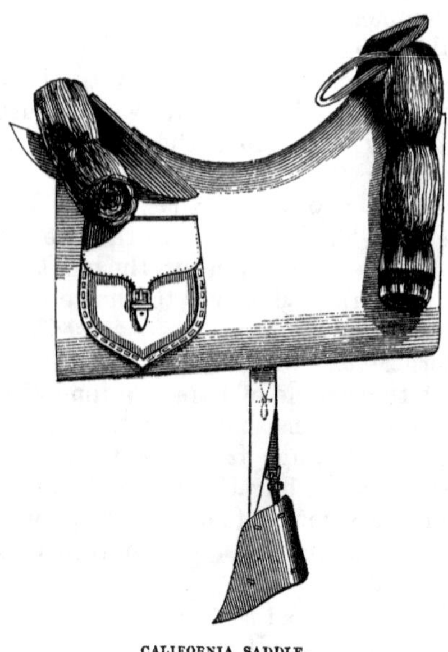

CALIFORNIA SADDLE.

The merits of the California saddle consist in its being light, strong, and compact, and conforming well to the shape of the horse. When strapped on, it rests so firmly in position that the strongest pull of a horse upon a lariat attached to the pommel cannot displace it. Its shape is such, that the rider is compelled to sit nearly erect, with his legs on the continuation of the line of the body, which makes his seat more secure, and at the same time, gives him a better control over his arms and horse. This position is attained by setting the stirrup-leathers farther back than on the old-fashioned saddle. The pommel is high, like the Mexican saddle, and prevents the rider from being thrown forward. The tree is covered with raw hide, put on green, and sewed; when this dries and contracts, it gives it great strength. It has no iron in its composition, but is kept together by buckskin strings, and can easily be taken to pieces for mending or cleaning. It has a hair girth about five inches wide.

The whole saddle is covered with a large and thick sheet of sole-leather, having a hole to lay over the pommel; it extends back over the horse's hips, and protects them from rain; and, when taken off in camp, it furnishes a good security against dampness when placed under the traveler's bed.

The California saddle-tree is regarded by many as the best of all others for the horse's back, and as having an easier seat than the Mexican.*

General Comte de la Roche-Aymon, in his treatise upon "Light Troops," published in Paris in 1856, says:—

"In nearly all the European armies, the equipment of the horse is not in harmony with the new tactics — with those tactics in which, during nearly all of a campaign, the cavalry remains in bivouac. Have we reflected upon the kind of saddle which, under these circumstances,

I have given my opinion of the California Saddle in the City of the Saints, chap. i. It has many advantages for a prairie country; none for rough ground, except the facility with which it it injures the rider. And, finally, it is too expensive for general use.—Ed.

would cover the horse best without incommoding him during the short periods that he is permitted to repose? Have we reflected upon the kind of saddle which, offering the least fragility, exposes the horse to the least danger of sore back? All the cuirassiers and the dragoons of Europe have saddles which they call *French saddles*, the weight of which is a load for the horse.* The interior mechanism of these saddles is complicated and filled with weak bands of iron, which become deranged, bend, and sometimes break. The rider does not perceive these accidents, or he does not wish to perceive them, for fear of being left behind or of having to go on foot; he continues on, and, at the end of a day's march, his horse has a sore back, and in a few days is absolutely unserviceable. We may satisfy ourselves of the truth of these observations, by comparing the lists of horses sent to the rear during the course of a campaign by the cuirassiers and dragoons who use the French saddle, and by the hussars with the Hungarian saddle. The number sent to the rear by the latter is infinitely less, although employed in a service much more active and severe; and it might be still less by making some slight improvements in their manner of fixing the saddle upon the horse.

"It is a long time since Marshal Saxe said, there was but one kind of saddle fit for cavalry, which was the hussar saddle: this combined all advantages, lightness, solidity, and economy. It is astonishing that the system of actual war had not led to the employment of the kind of saddle in use among the Tartars, the Cossacks, the Hungarians, and, indeed, among all horsemen and nomads. This saddle has the incontestable advantage of permitting the horse to

* During the Napoleonic landing in Egypt, a French dragoon was made prisoner, and his arms and accoutrements were forwarded to the Head Quarters of the Mameluke Beys, who, calling together their followers, drew the happiest augury from the ridiculous spectacle that lay on the ground before them. For long and hard riding, especially when the exercise is not habitual, nothing equals the Arab or Eastern pad, covered with leather and furnished with shovel iron stirrups.—Ed.

lie down and rest himself without inconvenience. If, notwithstanding the folded blanket which they place under the Hungarian saddle, this saddle will still wound the animal's back sometimes, this only proceeds from the friction occasioned by the motion of the horse and the movement of the rider upon the saddle; a friction which it will be nearly impossible to avoid, inasmuch as the saddle-bow is held in its place only by a surcingle, the ends of which are united by a leathern band: these bands always relax more or less, and the saddle becomes loose. To remedy this, I propose to attach to the saddle bow itself a double girth, one end of which shall be made fast to the arch in front, and the other end to the rear of the arch upon the right side, to unite in a single girth, which would buckle to a strap attached upon the left side in the usual manner. This buckle will hold the saddle firmly in its place.

"Notwithstanding all these precautions, however, there were still some inconveniences resulting from the nature of the blanket placed under the saddle, which I sought to remedy, and I easily accomplished it. The woolen nap of the cavalry saddle-blanket, not being carefully attended to, soon wears off, and leaves only the rough, coarse threads of the fabric; this absorbs the sweat from the horse, and, after it has dried and become hard, it acts like a rasp upon the withers, first taking off the hair, next the skin, and then the flesh, and finally, the beast is rendered unserviceable.

"I sought, during the campaign of 1807, a means to remedy this evil; and I soon succeeded by a process as simple as it was cheap. I distributed among a great number of cavalry soldiers pieces of linen cloth folded double, two feet square, and previously dipped in melted tallow. This cloth was laid next to the horse's back, under the saddle-blanket, and it prevented all the bad effects of the woolen blanket. No horses, after this appliance, were afflicted with sore backs. Such are the slight changes which I believe should be made in the use of the Hungarian saddle. The remainder of the equipment should remain (as it always has been) composed of a breast-strap, crupper, and martingale, etc."

The improvements of the present age do not appear to have developed any thing advantageous to the saddle; on the contrary, after experimenting upon numerous modifications and inventions, public sentiment has at length given the preference to the saddle-tree of the natives in Asia and America, which is very similar to that of the Hungarians.

SORES AND DISEASES.

If a horse be sweating at the time he is unsaddled, it is well to strap the folded saddle-blanket upon his back with the surcingle, where it is allowed to remain until he is perfectly dry. This causes the back to cool gradually, and prevents scalding or swelling. Some persons are in the habit of washing their horses' backs while heated and sweating with cold water; but this is pernicious, and often produces sores. It is well enough to wash the back after it cools, but not before. After horses' backs or shoulders once become chafed and sore, it is very difficult to heal them, particularly when they are continued at work. It is better, if practicable, to stop using them for a while, and wash the bruised parts often with Castile soap and water. Should it be necessary, however, to continue the animal in use, I have known very severe sores entirely healed by the free application of grease to the parts immediately after halting, and while the animal is warm and sweating. This seems to harden the skin and heal the wound, even when working with the collar in contact with it. A piece of bacon rind tied upon the collar over the wound, is also an excellent remedy.

In Texas, where the horse-flies are numerous, they attack animals without mercy, and where a contusion is found in the skin they deposit eggs, which speedily produce worms in great numbers. I have tried the effect of spirits of turpentine and several other remedies; but nothing seemed to have the desired effect but calomel blown into the wound, which destroyed the worms and soon effected a cure.

In the vicinity of the Pass upon the Humboldt River, and in some sections upon other routes to California, alkaline water is found, which is very poisonous to animals that drink it, and generates a disease known in California as "*alkali.*" This disease first makes it appearance by swellings upon the abdomen and between the fore legs, and is attended with a cough, which ultimately destroys the lungs and kills the animal. If taken at an early stage, this disease is curable, and the following treatment is generally considered as the most efficacious. The animal is first raked, after which a large dose of grease is poured down its throat; acids are said to have the same effect, and give immediate relief. When neither of these remedies can be procured, many of the emigrants have been in the habit of mixing starch or flour in a bucket of water, and allowing the animal to drink it. It is supposed that this forms a coating over the mucous membrane, and thus defeats the action of the poison.

Animals should never be allowed to graze in the vicinity of alkaline water, as the deposits upon the grass after floods are equally deleterious with the water itself.

In seasons when the water is low in the Humboldt River, there is much less danger of the alkali, as the running water in the river then comes from pure mountain springs, and is confined to the channel; whereas, during high water, when the banks are overflowed, the salts are dissolved, making the water more impure.

For *colic,* a good remedy is a mixture of two table-spoonfuls of brandy and two tea-spoonfuls of laudanum dissolved in a bottle of water and poured down the animal's throat. Another remedy, which has been recommended to me by an experienced officer as producing speedy relief, is a table-spoonful of chloride of lime dissolved in a bottle of water, and administered as in the other case.

RATTLE-SNAKE BITES.

Upon the southern routes to California rattle-snakes are

often met with, but it is seldom that any person is bitten by them. Yet this is a possible contingency, and it can never be amiss to have an antidote at hand.

Hartshorn applied externally to the wound, and drunk in small quantities diluted with water whenever the patient becomes faint or exhausted from the effects of the poison, is one of the most common remedies.

In the absence of all medicines, a string or ligature should at once be bound firmly above the puncture, then scarify deeply with a knife, suck out the poison, and spit out the saliva.

Andersson, in his book on South-western Africa, says: "In the Cape Colony the Dutch farmers resort to a cruel but apparently effective plan to counteract the bad effects of a serpent's bite. An incision having been made in the breast of a living fowl, the bitten part is applied to the wound. If the poison be very deadly, the bird soon evinces symptoms of distress, becomes drowsy, droops its head, and dies. It is replaced by a second, a third, and more if requisite. When, however, the bird no longer exhibits any of the signs just mentioned, the patient is considered out of danger. A frog similarly applied is supposed to be equally efficacious."

Haunberg, in his Travels in South Africa, mentions an antidote against the bite of serpents. He says: "The blood of the turtle was much cried up, which, on account of this extraordinary virtue, the inhabitants dry in the form of small scales or membranes, and carry about them when they travel in this country, which swarms with this most noxious vermin. Whenever any one is wounded by a serpent, he takes a couple of pinches of the dried blood internally, and applies a little of it to the wound."

I was present upon one occasion when an Indian child was struck in the fore-finger by a large rattle-snake. His mother, who was near at the time, seized him in her arms, and, placing the wounded finger in her mouth, sucked the poison from the puncture for some minutes, repeatedly spitting out the saliva; after which she chewed and mashed some plantain leaves and applied to the wound. Over this she sprinkled some finely-powdered tobacco, and wrapped the finger up in a rag. I did not observe that the child suffered afterward the least pain or inconvenience. The immediate application of the remedies probably saved his life.

Irritation from the bite of gnats and musquitoes, etc., may be relieved by chewing the plantain, and rubbing the spittle on the bite.

I knew of another instance near Fort Towson, in Northern Texas, where a small child was left upon the eastern floor of a cabin while its mother was washing at a spring near by. She heard a cry of distress; and, on going to the cabin, what was her horror on seeing a rattle-snake coiled around the child's arm, and striking it repeatedly with its fangs. After killing the snake, she hurried to her nearest neighbour, procured a bottle of brandy, and returned as soon as possible; but the poison had already so operated upon the arm, that it was as black as a negro's. She poured down the child's throat a huge draught of the liquor, which soon took effect, making it very drunk, and stopped the action of the poison. Although the child was relieved, it remained sick for a long time, but ultimately recovered.

A man was struck in the leg by a very large rattle-snake near Fort Belknap, Texas, in 1853. No other remedy being at hand, a small piece of indigo was pulverized, made into a poultice with water, and applied to the puncture. It seemed to draw out the poison, turning the indigo white; after which it was removed, and another poultice applied. These applications were repeated until the indigo ceased to change its colour. The man was then carried to the hospital at Fort Belknap, and soon recovered; and the surgeon of the post pronounced it a very satisfactory cure.

A Chickasaw woman, who was bitten upon the foot near Fort Washita by a ground rattle-snake (a very venomous species), drank a bottle of whisky and applied the indigo poultice, and when I saw her, three days afterwards, she was recovering, but the flesh around the wound sloughed away.

A Delaware remedy, which is said to be efficacious, is to burn powder upon the wound; but I have never known it to be tried excepting upon a horse. In this case it was successful; or, at all events, the animal recovered.

Of all the remedies known to me, I should decidedly prefer ardent spirits. It is considered a sovereign antidote among our Western frontier settlers, and I would make use of it with great confidence. It must be taken until the patient becomes very much intoxicated; and this requires a large quantity, as the action of the poison seems to counteract its effects.

Should the fangs of the snake penetrate deep enough to reach an artery, it is probable the person would die in a short time. I imagine, however, that it does not often occur.

The following remedial measures for the treatment of the bites of poisonous reptiles are recommended by Dr. Philip Weston in the London Lancet for July, 1859:—

1. The application of a ligature round the limb close to the wound, between it and the heart, to arrest the return of venous blood.

2. Excision of the bitten parts, or free incision through the wounds made by the poison-teeth, subsequently, encouraging the bleeding by warm solutions to favour the escape of the poison from the circulation.

3. Cauterization widely round the limb of the bite with a strong solution of nitrate of silver, one drachm to the ounce, to prevent the introduction of the poison into the system by the lymphatics.

4. As soon as indications of the absorption of the poison into the circulation begin to manifest themselves, the internal administration of ammonia in aërated or soda-water every quarter of an hour, to support the nervous energy and allay the distressing thirst.

"But," he continues, "there is yet wanting some remedy that shall rapidly counteract the poison introduced into the blood, and assist in expelling it from the system. The well-authenticated accounts of the success attending the internal use of arsenic in injuries arising from the bites of venomous reptiles in the East and West Indies, and also in Africa, and the well-known properties of this medicine as a powerful tonic and alterative in conditions of impaired vitality of the blood arising from absorption of certain blood-poisons, would lead me to include this agent in the treatment already mentioned. It should be administered in combination with ammonia, in full doses, frequently repeated, so as to neutralize quickly the poison circulating in the blood, before it can be eliminated from the system. This could readily be accomplished by adding ten to fifteen minims of Fowler's solution to the compound spirit of ammonia, to be given every quarter of an hour in aërated or soda-water, until the vomiting and the more urgent symptoms of collapse have subsided, subsequently repeating the dose at longer intervals, until reaction had become fully established, and the patient relieved by copious bilious dejections."

Cedron, which is a nut that grows on the Isthmus of Panama, and which is sold by the druggists in New York, is said to be an infallible antidote to serpent-bites. In the *Bullet. de l'Acad. de Méd.* for February, 1858, it is stated, that a man was bitten at Panama by a *coral snake*, the most poisonous species on the Isthmus. During the few seconds that it took him to take the cedron from his bag, he was seized with violent pains at the heart and throat; but he had scarcely chewed and swallowed a piece of the nut about the size of a small bean, when the pains ceased as by magic. He chewed a little more, and applied it externally to the wound, when the pains disappeared, and were followed by a copious evacuation of a substance like curdled milk. Many other cases are mentioned where the cedron proved an antidote.*

* In the absence of all remedies, even of fire and whiskey, the traveller will take two precautions: The first is to place a ligature—a string or rag will do—between the part bitten and the heart, thus preventing rapid absorption of the venom. The second is to suck the wound, poisons of this character being perfectly harmless when applied to a healthy mucous membrane.—Ed.

CHAPTER V.

Bivouacs.—Tente d'Abri.—Gutta-percha Knapsack Tent.—Comanche Lodge. — Sibley Tent.—Camp Furniture. — Litters. — Rapid Traveling.—Fuel.—Making Fires.—Fires on the Prairies,—Jerking Meat.—Making Lariats. — Making Caches.—Disposition of Fire-arms.—Colt's Revolvers.—Gun Accidents.—Trailing.—Indian Sagacity.

BIVOUACS AND TENTS.

In traveling with pack-animals, it is not always convenient or practicable to transport tents; and the traveler's ingenuity is often taxed in devising the most available means for making himself comfortable and secure against winds and storms. I have often been astonished to see how soon an experienced voyager, without any resources save those provided by nature, will erect a comfortable shelter in a place where a person having no knowledge of woodcraft would never think of such a thing.

Almost all people in different parts of the world have their own peculiar methods of bivouacking.

In the severe climate of Thibet, Dr. Hooker informs us that they encamp near large rocks, which absorb the heat during the day, and give it out slowly during the night. They form, as it were, reservoirs of caloric, the influence of which is exceedingly grateful during a cold night.

In the polar regions, the Esquimaux live and make themselves comfortable in huts of ice or snow, and with no other combustible but oil.

The natives of Australia bury their bodies in the sand, keeping their heads only above the surface, and thus sleep warm during the chilly nights of that climate.

Fortunately for the health and comfort of travelers upon the Plains, the atmosphere is pure and dry during the greater part of the year, and it is seldom that any rain or dew is seen; neither are there marshes, or ponds of stagnant water, to generate putrid exhalations and poisonous malaria. The night-air of the summer months is soft, exhilarating, and delightful. Persons may therefore sleep in it and inhale it with perfect impunity, and, indeed, many prefer this to breathing the confined atmosphere of a house or tent.

During the rainy season only is it necessary to seek shelter. In traveling with covered wagons one always has protection from storms, but with pack-trains it becomes necessary to improvise the best substitutes for tents.

A very secure protection against storms may be constructed by planting firmly in the ground two upright poles, with forks at their tops, and crossing them with a light pole laid in the forks. A gutta-percha cloth, or sheet of canvas, or, in the absence of either of these two, blankets, may be attached by one side to the horizontal pole, the opposite edge being stretched out to the windward, at an angle of about forty-five degrees to the ground, and there fastened with wooden pins, or with buckskin strings tied to the lower border of the cloth, and to pegs

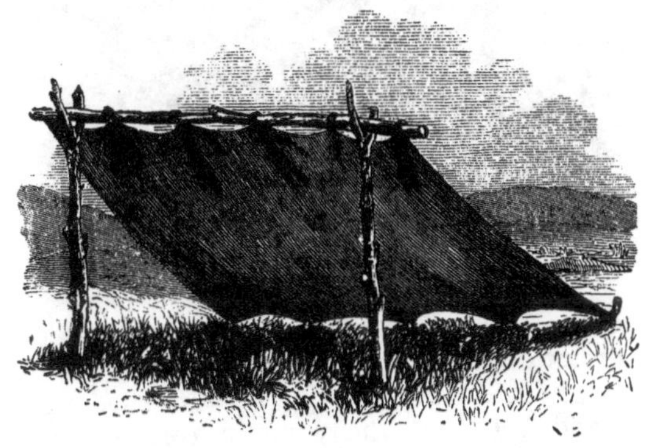

HALF-FACED CAMP.

driven firmly into the earth. This forms a shelter for three or four men, and is a good defence against winds and rains. If a fire be then made in front, the smoke will be carried away, so as not to incommode the occupants of the bivouac.

This is called a half-faced camp.*

Another method practised a great deal among mountain men and Indians, consists in placing several rough poles equidistant around in a half circle, and bringing the small ends together at the top, where they are bound with a thong. This forms the conical framework of the bivouac, which, when covered with a cloth stretched around it, makes a very good shelter, and is preferable to the half-faced camp, because the sides are covered.

CONICAL BIVOUAC.

When no cloths, blankets, or hides are at hand, to be placed over the poles of the lodge, it may be covered with green boughs laid on compactly, so as to shed a good deal of rain, and keep out the wind in cold weather. We

* And the "Break-wind" of Australian travellers. The Mpongwe of the Gaboon River call it "Olako."—Ed.

adopted this description of shelter in crossing the Rocky Mountains during the winter of 1857-8, and thus formed a very effectual protection against the bleak winds which sweep with great violence over those lofty and inhospitable *sierras*. We always selected a dense thicket for encampment, and covered the lodges with a heavy coating of pine boughs, wattling them together as compactly as possible, and piling snow upon the outside in such a manner as to make them quite impervious to the wind. The fires were then kindled at the mouths of the lodges, and our heads and bodies were completely sheltered, while our feet were kept warm by the fires.

The French troops, while serving in the Crimea, used what they call the *tente d'abri*, or shelter-tent, which seems to have been received with great favor in Europe. It is composed of two, four, or six square pieces of cloth, with buttons and button-holes adjusted upon the edges, and is pitched by planting two upright stakes in the ground at a distance corresponding with the length of the canvas when buttoned together. The two sticks are connected by a cord passed around the top of each, drawn tight, and the ends made fast to pins driven firmly into the ground. The canvas is then laid over the rope between the sticks, spread out at an angle about forty-five degrees, and the lower edges secured to the earth with wooden pins. This makes some defence against the weather, and was the only shelter enjoyed by the mass of the French army in the Crimea up to October, 1855. For a permanent camp, it is usual to excavate a shallow basement under the tent, and to bank up the earth on the outside in cold weather. It is designed that upon marches the *tente d'abri* shall be taken to pieces and carried by the soldiers.

A tent has recently been prepared by Mr. John Rider, 165, Broadway, New York, which is called the "*tent knapsack*." It has been examined by a board of army officers, and recommended for adoption in our military service.

This tent is somewhat similar to the *tente d'abri*, and is pitched in the same manner; but it has this advantage, that each separate piece may be converted into a water-proof knapsack.*

TENT KNAPSACK.

The following extracts from the Report of the Board go to show that this tent knapsack will be useful to parties traveling on the prairies with pack-trains:

"It is a piece of gutta-percha 5 feet 3 inches long, and 3 feet 8 inches wide, with double edges on one side, and brass studs and button-holes along two edges, and straps and buckles on the fourth edge; the whole weighing three pounds; two sticks, 3 feet 8 inches long

* It is the "Pál" which has been used for centuries in India.—Ed.

by $1\frac{1}{4}$ inches in diameter, and a small cord. When used as a knapsack, the clothing is packed in a cotton bag, and the gutta-percha sheet is folded round it, lapping at the ends. The clothing is thus protected by two or three thicknesses of gutta-percha, and in this respect there is a superiority over the knapsack now used by our troops. Other advantages are, that the tent knapsack has no seams, the parts at which those in use wear out soonest; it adapts itself to the size of the contents, so that a compact and portable bundle can be made, whether the kit be entire or not; and, with the cotton bag, it forms a convenient, commodious, and durable receptacle for all a soldier's clothing and necessaries.

"On a scout, a soldier usually carries only a blanket, overcoat, and at most a single shirt, pair of drawers, and a pair of socks, all of which can be packed in the tent knapsack in a small bundle, perfectly protected from rain, and capable of being suspended from the shoulders and carried with comfort and ease during a march.

"2d. As a shelter. The studs and eyelets along two edges of the tent knapsack are for the purpose of fastening a number of them together, and thus making a sheet of larger dimensions.

"A sheet formed by fastening together four knapsacks was exhibited to the Board, stretched upon a frame of wood. When used in service, the sheet is to be stretched on a rope supported by two poles, or by two rifles, muskets, or carbines, and pinned down at the sides with six pins, three on each side.

"The sheet of four knapsacks is 10 feet 6 inches long, and 7 feet 4 inches wide; and, when pitched on a rope 4 feet 4 inches above the ground, covers a horizontal space 6 feet 6 inches wide, and 7 feet 4 inches long, which will accommodate five men, and may be made to shelter seven. The sheet can also be used on the ground, and is a great protection from dampness, and as a shawl or talma; indeed, a variety of advantageous uses to which the gutta-percha sheet may be put, will suggest themselves to persons using it.

"The Board is satisfied with its merits in all the uses to which it is proposed to be put, and is of opinion that the gutta-percha tent knapsack may be adopted in the military service with advantage."

The usual tenement of the prairie tribes, and of the traders, trappers, and hunters who live among them, is the Comanche lodge, which is made of eight straight peeled poles about twenty feet long, covered with hides or cloth. The lodge is pitched by connecting the smaller extremities of three of the poles with one end of a long line. The three poles are then raised perpendicularly, and the larger extremities spread out in a tripod to the circumference of the circle that is to form the base of the lodge. The other poles are then raised, laid into the forks of the three first, and spread out equi-distant upon the circle, thus forming the conical framework of the structure. Nine or ten poles are generally used in one lodge.*

The long line attached to the tripod is then wound several times around the top, where the poles intersect, and the lower end made fast at the base of the lodge, thus securing the frame firmly in its position. The covering, made of buffalo hides, dressed without the hair, and cut and sewed together to fit the conical frame, is raised with a pole, spread out around the structure, and united at the edges with sharpened wooden pegs, leaving sufficient space open at the bottom for a doorway, which may be closed with a blanket spread out with two small sticks, and suspended over the opening.

The lower edge of the lodge is made fast to the ground with wooden pins. The apex is left open, with a triangular wing or flap on each side, and the windward flap constantly stretched out by means of a pole inserted into a pocket in the end of it, which causes it to draw like a sail, and thus occasions a draught from the fire built upon the ground in the centre of the lodge, and makes it warm

* The number of poles in a chief's lodge may reach twenty-four. I have described at some length, in the "City of the Saints," the tenement, and the mode of erecting it. The Comanche lodge is preferred to all other tents by the experienced trader.—Ed.

and comfortable in the coldest winter weather.* Canvas makes a very good substitute for the buffalo-skin covering.

SIBLEY TENT.

A tent has been invented by Major H. H. Sibley, of the army, which is known as the "*Sibley Tent.*" It is somewhat similar to the Comanche lodge; but in place of the conical frame-work of poles, it has but one upright standard, resting upon an iron tripod in the centre. The tripod can be used to suspend cooking utensils over the fire, and, when folded up, admits the wooden standard between the legs, thereby reducing the length one half, and making it more convenient for packing and traveling.

THE SIBLEY TENT.

This tent constituted the entire shelter of the army in Utah during the winter of 1857-8, and, notwithstanding

* The flap opens to windward when ventilation is wanted—to leeward when smoke is to be carried off.—Ed.

the severity of the climate in the elevated locality of Camp Scott, the troops were quite comfortable, and pleased with the tent.

In permanent camps the Sibley tents may be so pitched as to give more room by erecting a tripod upon the outside with three poles, high and stout enough to admit of the tent's being suspended by ropes attached to the apex. This method dispenses with the necessity of the central upright standard.

When the weather is very cold, the tent may be made warmer by excavating a basement about three feet deep, which also gives a wall to the tent, making it more roomy.

The tent used in the army will shelter comfortably twelve men.

Captain G. Rhodes, of the English army, in his recent work upon tents and tent-life, has given a description of most of the tents used in different armies in Europe; but, in my judgment, none of them, in point of convenience, comfort, and economy, will compare with the Sibley tent for compaigning in cold weather. One of its most important features, that of admitting of a fire within it and of causing a draught by the disposition of the wings, is not, that I am aware, possessed by any other tent. Moreover, it is exempt from the objections that are urged against some other tents on account of insalubrity from want of top ventilation to carry off the impure air during the night.*

CAMP FURNITURE.

The accompanying illustrations present some convenient articles of portable camp furniture.

Camp Chair No. 1 is of oak or other hard wood. Fig. 1 represents it opened for use; in Fig. 2 it is closed for transportation. *A* is a stout canvas, forming the back and seat; *b*, *b*, *b* are iron butt-hinges;† *c*, *c* are leather straps,

* Its main disadvantage is that of all conical tents,—waste of room, and more weight than accommodation.—Ed.

† All hinges are equally objectionable in rough travelling,—they are broken by the treatment they endure. The article furniture

one inch and a quarter wide, forming the arms; *d* is an iron rod, with nut and screw at one end.

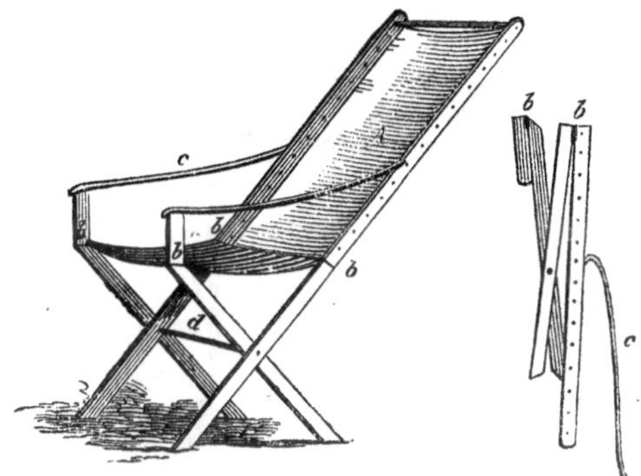

CAMP CHAIR. NO. 1.

CAMP CHAIRS. NOS. 2 AND 3.

---

is a prairie difficulty, and our Prairie Guide has by no means removed it.

CAMP CHAIR No. 2 is made of sticks tied together with thongs of buckskin or raw hide.

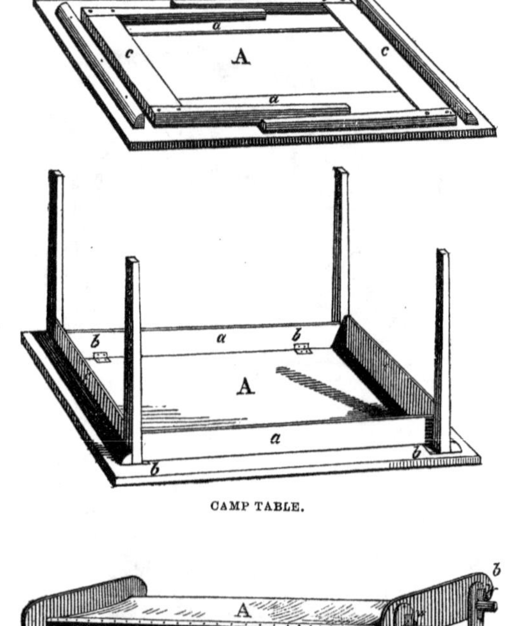

CAMP TABLE.

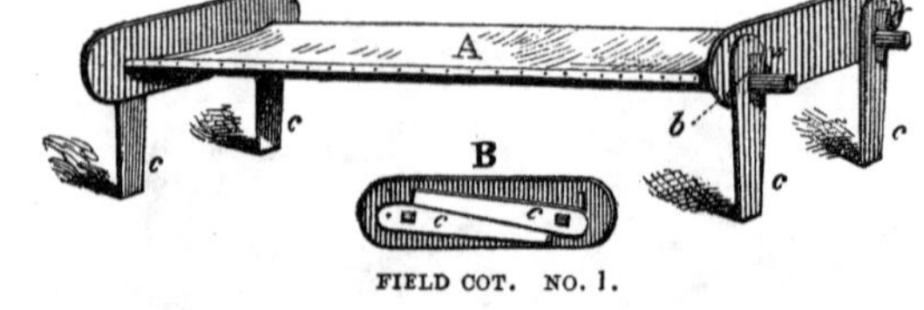

FIELD COT. NO. 1.

CAMP CHAIR No. 3 is a very comfortable seat, made of a barrel, the part forming the seat being filled with grass.

CAMP TABLE. Fig. 1 represents the table folded for transportation; in Fig. 2 it is spread out for use. *A* is the top of the table; *a, a* are side boards, and *c, c* are end boards, turning on butt-hinges,* *b, b, b*.

* Every man prefers, upon so uncertain a point, his own inven-

FIELD COTS. In No. 1, *A* represents the cot put up for use; *B*, the cot folded for transportation. The legs turn upon iron bolts running through the head and foot boards;

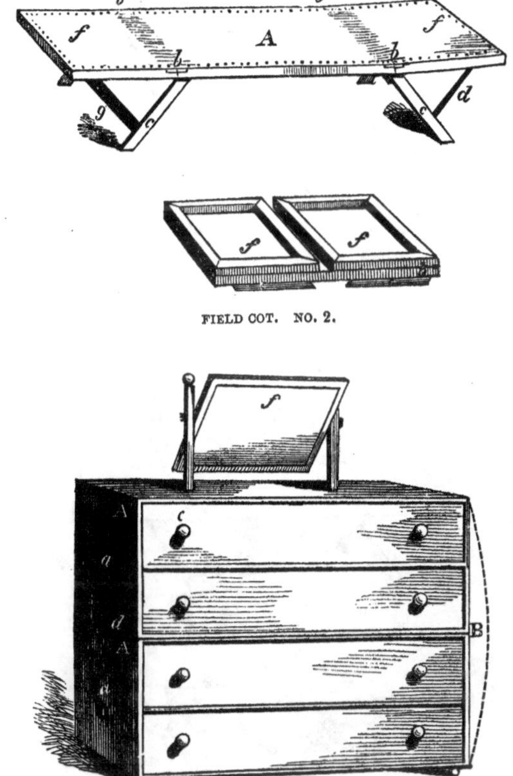

FIELD COT. NO. 2.

CAMP BUREAU.

---

tions. I hold to a pair of "bullock trunks," as made for the East Indian market. With a canvass stretched between them upon an iron frame, they form a cot; a table when one is placed upon the other; and chairs, when used singly. I make one of them answer for a canteen; the other acts wardrobe.—ED.

they are then placed upon the canvas, and the whole is rolled up around the side pieces. In No. 2, the upper figure represents the cot put up for use; the lower shows it folded for transportation. *A* is a stout canvas; *b, b* are iron butt-hinges; *c, c* the legs; *d, d* leather straps, with

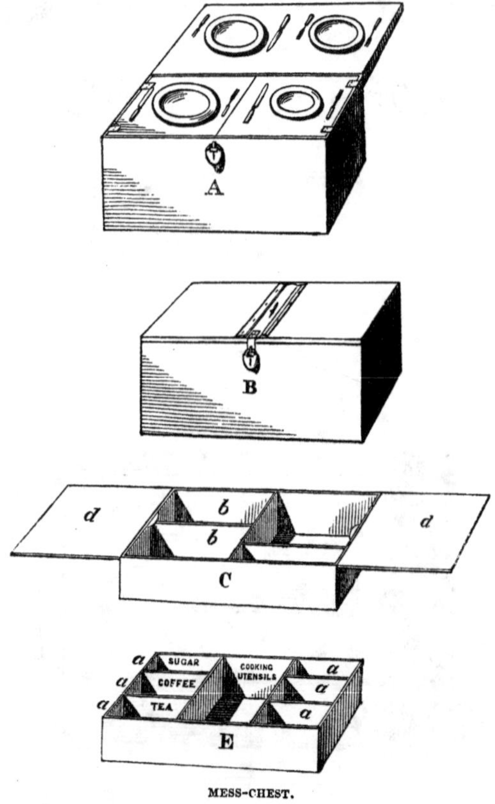

MESS-CHEST.

buckles, which hold the legs firm; *f, f,* ends, which fold upon hinges; *g, g,* cross-bars from leg to leg. This cot is strong, light, and portable.

CAMP BUREAU. This cut represents two chests, *A, A,*

with their handles, *a*, *a;* the covers taken off, they are placed one upon the other, and secured by the clamps, *B*, *B; d* shows the division between the two chests. When it is to be transported, the knobs, *c* are unscrewed from the drawers, the looking-glass *f* is removed, the drawers are filled with clothing, etc., and the lids are screwed on.

MESS-CHEST. *A* represents the chest open for the table; *B* is the same closed; *C* is the upper tray of tin, with compartments, *b*, *b; E* is the lower wooden tray, divided into compartments, *a*, *a*, for various purposes, and made fast to the bottom of the chest; *d*, *d*, are lids opening with hinges; *f* (in figure B) is a wooden leg, turning upon a hinge, and fitting snugly upon two pieces of wood screwed upon the cover.

LITTERS.

Should a party traveling with pack-animals, and without ambulance or wagons, have one of its members wounded or taken so sick as to be unable to walk or ride on horseback, a litter may be constructed by taking two polés about twenty feet in length, uniting them by two sticks three feet long lashed across the centre at six feet apart, and stretching a piece of stout canvas, a blanket, or hide between them to form the bed. Two steady horses or mules are then selected, placed between the poles in the front and rear of the litter, and the ends of the poles made fast to the sides of the animals, either by attachment to the stirrups or to the ends of straps secured over their backs.

The patient may then be placed upon the litter, and is ready for the march.

The elasticity of the long poles gives an easy motion to the conveyance, and makes this method of locomotion much more comfortable than might be supposed.

The prairie Indians have a way of transporting their sick and children upon a litter very similar in construction to the one just described, excepting that one animal is used instead of two. One end of the litter is made fast to the sides of the animal, while the other end is left to trail upon the ground. A projection is raised for the feet to rest against and prevent the patient from sliding down. Instead of canvas, the Indians sometimes lash a large willow basket across the poles, in which they place the person to be transported. The animals harnessed to the litter must be carefully conducted on the march, and caution used in passing over rough and broken ground.

A very convenient and comfortable method of packing a sick or wounded man when there are no animals disposable, and which is sometimes resorted to by the Indians, is to take two small poles, about ten feet long, and lash three cross-pieces to them, one in the centre, and the other two about eighteen inches from the ends. A blanket or hide is then secured firmly to this frame, and the patient placed upon it under the centre cross-piece, which prevents him from falling out. Two men act as carriers, walking between the ends of the long poles. The patient may be protected against the rain or sun by bending small willows over the frame, and covering them with a cloth.

RAPID TRAVELING.

Small parties with good animals, light vehicles, and little lading, may traverse the plains rapidly and comfortably, if the following injunctions be observed.

The day's drive should commence as soon as it is light, and, where the road is good, the animals kept upon a slow trot for about three hours, then immediately turned out upon the best grass that can be found for two hours, thus giving time for grazing and breakfast. After which, another drive of about three hours may be made, making the noon halt about three hours, when the animals are again harnessed, and the journey continued until night.

In passing through a country infested by hostile Indians, the evening drive should be prolonged until an hour or two after dark, turning off at a point where the ground is hard, going about half a mile from the road, and encamping without fires, in low ground, where the Indians will find it difficult to track or see the party.*

* This, in Prairie parlance, is called, "making a dark camp."—Ed.

These frequent halts serve to rest and recruit the animals, so that they will, without injury, make from thirty to forty miles a day for a long time. This, however, can only be done with very light loads and vehicles, such, for example, as an ambulance with four mules, only three or four persons, and a small amount of luggage.

FUEL AND FIRE.

There are long distances upon some of the routes to California where no other fuel is found but the dried dung of the buffalo, called by the mountaineers, "chips," and by the French, "bois de vache," the *argul* of the Tartary deserts.* It burns well when perfectly dry, answers a good purpose for cooking, and some men even prefer it to wood. As it will not burn when wet, it is well, in a country where no other fuel can be had, when it threatens to rain, for the traveler to collect a supply before the rain sets in, and carry it in wagons to the camp. When dry, the chips are easily lighted.

A great saving in fuel may be made by digging a trench about two feet long by eight inches in width and depth; the fires are made in the bottom of the trench, and the cooking utensils placed upon the top, where they receive all the heat. This plan is especially recommended for windy weather, and it is convenient at all times.† The wood should be cut short, and split into small pieces.

It is highly important that travelers should know the different methods that may be resorted to for kindling fires upon a march. The most simple and most expeditious of these is by using the lucifer-matches; but, unless they are kept in well-corked bottles, they are liable to become wet, and will then fail to ignite.

The most of those found in the shops easily imbibe dampness, and are of but little use in the prairies. Those marked "Van Duser, New York," and put up in flat

* And the East Indian "gobar."—Ed.

† By no means. The fireplace must, if possible, be raised above the ground for draught of air; three stones form a good base for pot or kettle, and act as screens against the wind.—Ed.

rectangular boxes, are the best I have met with, and were the only ones I saw which were not affected by the humid climate of Mexico. Wax lucifers are better than wooden, as they are impervious to moisture.

I have seen an Indian start a fire with flint and steel after others had failed to do it with matches. This was during a heavy rain, when almost all available fuel had become wet. On such occasions dry fuel may generally be obtained under logs, rocks, or leaning trees.

The inner bark of some dry trees, cedar for instance, is excellent to kindle a fire. The bark is rubbed in the hand until the fibres are made fine and loose, when it takes fire easily; dry grass or leaves are also good. After a sufficient quantity of small kindling fuel has been collected, a moistened rag is rubbed with powder, and a spark struck into it with a flint and steel, which will ignite it; this is then placed in the centre of the loose nest of inflammable material, and whirls around in the air until it bursts out into a flame. When it is raining, the blaze should be laid upon the driest spot that can be found, a blanket held over it to keep off the water, and it is fed with very small bits of dry wood and shavings until it has gained sufficient strength to burn the larger damp wood. When no dry place can be found, the fire may be started in a kettle or fryingpan, and afterwards transferred to the ground.*

Should there be no other means of starting a fire, it can always be made with a gun or pistol, by placing upon the ground a rag saturated with damp powder, and a little dry powder sprinkled over it. The gun or pistol is then (uncharged) placed with the cone directly over and near the rag, and a cap exploded, which will invariably ignite it. Another method is by placing about one-fourth of a charge of powder into a gun, pushing a rag down loosely upon it, and firing it out with the muzzle down near the ground, which ignites the rag.

* This useful "dodge" was first proposed, I believe, by D., 4, Albany, London in "The Lands of the Slave and the Free."—Ed.

The most difficult of all methods of making a fire, but one that is practised by some of the Western Indians, is by friction between two pieces of wood. I had often heard of this process, but never gave credit to its practicability until I saw the experiment successfully tried. It was done in the following manner: Two dried stalks of the Mexican soap plant, about three-fourths of a inch in diameter, were selected, and one of them made flat on one side; near the edge of this flat surface a very small indentation was made, to receive the end of the other stick, and a groove cut from this down the side. The other stick is cut with a rounded end, and placed upright upon the first. One man then holds the horizontal piece upon the ground, while another takes the vertical stick between the palms of his hands, and turns it back and forth as rapidly as possible, at the same time pressing forcibly down upon it. The point of the upright stick wears away the indentation into a fine powder, which runs off to the ground in the groove that has been cut; after a time it begins to smoke, and by continued friction it will at length take fire.

This is an operation that is difficult, and requires practice; but if a drill-stick is used with a cord placed around the centre of the upright stick, it can be turned much more rapidly than with the hands, and the fire produced more readily. The upright stick may be of any hard, dry wood, but the lower horizontal stick must be of a soft, inflammable nature, such as pine, cottonwood, or black walnut, and it must be perfectly dry. The Indians work the sticks with the palms of the hands, holding the lower piece between the feet; but it is better to have a man to hold the lower piece while another man works the drill-bow.

Inexperienced travelers are very liable, in kindling fires at their camp, to ignite the grass around them. Great caution should be taken to guard against the occurrence of such accidents, as they might prove excedingly disastrous. We were very near having our entire train of wagons and supplies destroyed, upon one occasion, by the carelessness of one of our party in setting fire to the grass, and it was only by the most strenuous and well-timed efforts of two hundred men in setting counter-fires, and burning around the train that it was saved. When the grass is dry, it will take fire like powder; and, if thick and tall, with a brisk wind, the flames run like a race-horse, sweeping everything before them. A lighted match, or the ashes from a segar or pipe, thrown carelessly into the dry grass, sometimes set it on fire; but the greatest danger lies in kindling camp fires.

To prevent accidents of this kind, before kindling the fire, a space should be cleared away sufficient to embrace the limits of the flame, and all combustibles removed therefrom, and while the fire is being made, men should be stationed around with blankets,* ready to put it out if it takes the grass.

When a fire is approaching, and escape from its track is impossible, it may be repelled in the following manner: The train and animals are parked compactly together; then several men, provided with blankets, set fire to the grass on the lee side, burning it away gradually from the train, and extinguishing it on the side next the train. This can easily be done, and the fire controlled with the blankets, or with dry sand thrown upon it, until an area large enough to give room for the train has been burned clear. Now the train moves on to this ground of safety, and the fire passes by harmless.

JERKING MEAT.

So pure is the atmosphere in the interior of our continent that fresh meat may be cured, or *jerked*, as it is termed in the language of the prairies,† by cutting it into strips about an inch thick, and hanging it in the sun,

* Or with hides, or, in wooded lands, with leafy boughs.—Ed.

† The word is originally "chaire cuite," corrupted by the Spaniards, to "charqui," and by the English to "jerked." Mr. Galton asserts, that jerked meat loses about one-half of its nourishing properties. I should say one-third, and less still if prepared with "ghi" (melted butter), like the Eastern "kavurmeh."—Ed.

where in a few days it will dry so well that it may be packed in sacks and transported over long journeys without putrefying.

When there is not time to jerk the meat by the slow process described, it may be done in a few hours by building an open framework of small sticks, about two feet above the ground, placing the strips of meat upon the top of it, and keeping up a slow fire beneath, which dries the meat rapidly.

The jerking process may be done upon the march without any loss of time, by stretching lines from front to rear upon the outside of loaded wagons, and suspending the meat upon them, where it is allowed to remain until sufficiently cured to be packed away. Salt is never used in this process, and is not required, as the meat, if kept dry, rarely putrefies.

If travelers have ample transportation, it will be a wise precaution, in passing through the buffalo range, to lay in a supply of jerked meat for future exigences.

LARIATS.

It frequently happens upon long journeys, that the lariat ropes wear out or are lost; and, if there were no means of replacing them, great inconvenience might result therefrom. A very good substitute may be made by taking the green hide of a buffalo, horse, mule, or ox, stretching it upon the ground, and pinning it down by the edges. After it has been well stretched, a circle is described with a piece of charcoal, embracing as much of the skin as practicable, and a strip about an inch wide cut from the outer edge of sufficient length to form the lariat. The strip is then wrapped round between two trees or stakes, drawn tight, and left to dry, after which it is subjected to a process of friction until it becomes pliable, when it is ready for use; but after it has been wet and dried again it becomes very hard and unyielding. This, however, may be obviated by boiling it in oil or grease until thoroughly saturated, after which it remains pliable.

The Indians make very good lariat ropes by dressed buffalo or buck-skins cut into narrow strips and braided; these, when oiled, slip much more freely than the hemp or cotton ropes, and are better for lassoing animals; but they are not as suitable for picketing as those made of other materials, because the wolves will eat them, and thus set free the animals to which they are attached.

CACHES.

It not unfrequently happens that travelers are compelled, for want of transportation, to abandon a portion of their luggage, and if it is exposed to the keen scrutiny of the thieving savages who often follow the trail of a party, and hunt over old camps for such things as may be left, it will be likely to be appropriated by them. Such contingencies have given rise to a method of secreting articles called by the old French Canadian voyagers "*caching*."

The proper places for making caches are in loose sandy soils, where the earth is dry and easily excavated. Near the bank of a river is the most convenient for this purpose, as the earth taken out can be thrown into the water, leaving no trace behind.

When the spot has been chosen, the turf is carefully cut and laid aside, after which a hole is dug in the shape of an egg, and of sufficient dimensions to contain the articles to be secreted, and the earth, as it is taken out, thrown upon a cloth or blanket, and carried to a stream or ravine, where it can be disposed of, being careful not to scatter any upon the ground near the cache. The hole is then lined with bushes or dry grass, the articles placed within, covered with grass, the hole filled up with earth, and the sods carefully placed back in their original position, and everything that would be likely to attract an Indian's attention removed from the locality. If an India-rubber or gutta-percha cloth is disposable, it should be used to envelop the articles in the cache.

Another plan of making the cache is to dig a hole inside

a tent, and occupy the tent for some days after the goods are deposited. This effaces the marks of excavation.*

The mountain traders were formerly in the habit of building fires over their caches; but the Indians have become familiar with this practice so that I should think it no longer safe.

Another method of caching which is sometimes resorted to is to place the articles in the top of an evergreen tree, such as the pine, hemlock, or spruce.† The thick boughs are so arranged around the packages that they cannot be seen from beneath, and they are tied to a limb to prevent them from being blown out by the wind. This will only answer for such articles as will not become injured by the weather.

Caves or holes in the rocks that are protected from the rains are also secure deposits for caching goods; but in every case care must be taken to obliterate all tracks or other indications of men having been near them. These caches will be more secure when made at some distance from roads or trails, and in places where Indians would not be likely to pass.

To find a cache again, the bearing and distance from the centre of it to some prominent object, such as a mound, rock, or tree, should be carefully determined and recorded, so that any one, on returning to the spot, would have no difficulty in ascertaining its position.‡

DISPOSITION OF FIRE-ARMS.

The mountaineers and trappers exercise a very wise precaution, on lying down for the night, by placing their

* Thus our dead officers were cached in Afghanistan, and the same was done with the corpse of General Braddock. But savages soon learn to suspect places where tents have been pitched.—Ed.

† This is the African mode. The hemlock is P. Canadensis; the spruce P. nigra and P. alba; and the pine is the white pine, P. strabus.—Ed.

‡ Carelessness or want of skill may lead to disastrous results, with an extreme readiness, as is proved by the melancholy fate of the late Australian expedition, under Mr. Burke.—Ed.

arms and ammunition by their sides, where they can be seized at a moment's notice. This rule is never departed from, and they are, therefore, seldom liable to be surprised. In Parkyns's "Abyssinia," I find the following remarks upon this subject:

"When getting sleepy, you return your rifle between your legs, roll over, and go to sleep. Some people may think this is a queer place for a rifle; but, on the contrary, it is the position of all others where utility and comfort are most combined. The butt rests on the arm,* and serves as a pillow for the head; the muzzle points towards the knees, and the arms encircle the lock and breech, so that you have a smooth pillow, and are always prepared to start up armed at a moment's notice."

I have never made the experiment of sleeping in this way; but I should imagine that a gun-stock would make rather a hard pillow.

Many of our experienced frontier officers prefer carrying their pistols in a belt at their sides to placing them in holsters attached to the saddle, as in the former case they are always at hand when they are dismounted; whereas, by the other plan, they become useless when a man is unhorsed, unless he has time to remove them from the saddle, which, during the excitement of an action, would seldom be the case.†

Nothwithstanding Colt's army and navy-sized revolvers have been in use for a long time in our army, officers are by no means of one mind as to their relative merits for frontier service. The navy pistol, being more light and portable, is more convenient for the belt; but it is very questionable, in my mind, whether these qualities counterbalance the advantages derived from the greater weight of powder and lead that can be fired from the larger pistol, and the consequent increased projectile force.

* How the gentleman prevents his arm becoming painfully numbed and can find comfort in this position—fit only for a Nottingham lamb—is a mystery of mysteries to me.—Ed.

† Colt's pocket pistol or a pair of Derringers, is the best weapon for carrying about the person, where it is advisable not to show arms.—Ed.

This point is illustrated by an incident which fell under my own observation. In passing near the "Medicine-Bow Butte" during the spring of 1858, I most unexpectedly encountered and fired at a full-sized grizzly bear; but, as my horse had become somewhat blown by the previous gallop, his breathing so much disturbed my aim that I missed the animal at the short distance of about fifty yards, and he ran off. Fearful, if I stopped to reload my rifle, the bear would make his escape, I resolved to drive him back to the advanced guard of our escort, which I could see approaching in the distance; this I succeeded in doing, when several mounted men, armed with the navy revolvers, set off in pursuit. They approached within a few paces, and discharged ten or twelve shots, the most of which entered the animal, but he still kept on, and his progress did not seem materially impeded by the wounds. After these men had exhausted their charges, another man rode up armed with the army revolver, and fired two shots, which brought the stalwart beast to the ground. Upon skinning him and making an examination of the wounds, it was discovered that none of the balls from the small pistols had, after passing through his thick and tough hide, penetrated deeper than about an inch into the flesh, but that the two balls from the large pistol had gone into the vitals and killed him. This test was, to my mind, a decisive one as to the relative efficiency of the two arms for frontier service, and I resolved thenceforth to carry the larger size.

Several different methods are practised in slinging and carrying fire-arms upon horseback. The shoulder-strap, with a swivel to hook into a ring behind the guard, with the muzzle resting downward in a leather cup attached by a strap to the same as the stirrup leather, is a very handy method for cavalry soldiers to sling their carbines; but, the gun being reversed, the jolting caused by the motion of the horse tends to move the charge and shake the powder out of the cone,* which renders it liable to burst the gun and to miss fire.

* The American "cone" is the English "nipple." Beg pardon for the indelicacy! Our "cousins," as we term them, so far from

An invention of the Namaquas, in Africa, described by Galton in his Art of Travel, is as follows:

"Sew a bag of canvas, leather, or hide, of such bigness as to admit of the butt of the gun pretty freely. The straps that support it buckle through a ring in the pommel, and the thongs by which its slope is adjusted fasten round the girth below. The exact adjustments may not be hit upon by an unpractised person for some little time, but, when they are once ascertained, the straps need never be shifted. The gun is perfectly safe, and never comes below the arm-pit, even in taking a drop leap; it is pulled out in an instant by bringing the elbow in front of the gun and close to the side, so as to throw the gun to the outside of the arm; then, lowering the hand, the gun is caught up. It is a bungling way to take out the gun while its barrel lies between the arm and the body. Any sized gun can be carried in this fashion. It offers no obstacle to mounting or dismounting."

This may be a convenient way of carrying the gun; I have never tried it. Of all methods I have used, I prefer, for hunting, a piece of leather about twelve inches by four, with a hole cut in each end; one of the ends is placed over the pommel of the saddle, and with a buckskin string made fast to it, where it remains a permanent fixture. When the rider is mounted, he places his gun across the strap upon the saddle, and carries the loose end forward over the pommel, the gun resting horizontally across his legs. It will now only be necessary occasionally to steady the gun with the hand. After a little practice, the rider will be able to control it with his knees, and it will be found a very easy and convenient method of carrying it.* When required for use, it is taken out in an instant by simply raising it with the hand, when the loose end of the strap comes off the pommel.

---

calling a spade, spade, explain a cock by "rooster," cockchafer by "chafer," and cockroach by "roach."—Ed.

* I have always carried my gun or rifle loose across the pommel, and I quite agree with Gen. Marcy, that practice soon makes it the handiest and readiest method.—Ed.

The chief causes of accidents from the use of fire-arms arise from carelessness; and I have always observed that those persons who are most familiar with their use are invariably the most careful. Many accidents have happened from carrying guns with the cock down upon the cap. When in this position, a blow upon the cock, and sometimes the concussion produced by the falling of the gun, will explode the cap; and, occasionally, when the cock catches a twig, or in the clothes, and lifts it from the cap, it will explode. With a gun at half-cock there is but little danger of such accidents; for, when the cock is drawn back, it either comes to the full-cock, and remains, or it returns to the half-cock, but does not go down upon the cone. Another source of very many sad and fatal accidents resulting from the most stupid and culpable carelessness is in persons standing before the muzzles of guns and attempting to pull them out of wagons, or to draw them through a fence or brush in the same position. If the cock encounters an obstacle in its passage, it will, of course, be drawn back and fall upon the cap. These accidents are of frequent occurrence, and the cause is well understood by all; yet men continue to disregard it, and their lives pay the penalty of their indiscretion. It is a wise maxim, which applies with especial force in campaigning on the prairies, "*Always look to your gun, but never let your gun look at you.*"

An equally important maxim might be added to this: *Never to point your gun at another, whether charged or uncharged, and never allow another to point his gun at you.* Young men, before they beome accustomed to the use of arms, are very apt to be careless, and a large percentage of gun accidents may be traced to this cause. That finished sportsman and wonderful shot, my friend Captain Martin Scott, than whom a more gallant soldier never fought a battle, was the most careful man with fire-arms I ever knew; and, up to the time he received his death-wound upon the bloody field of Molino del Rey, he never ceased his cautionary advice to young officers upon this subject. His extended experience and intimate acquaintance with the use of arms had fully impressed him with its importance, and no man ever lived whose opinions upon this subject should carry greater weight. As incomprehensible as it may appear to persons accustomed to the use of fire-arms, recruits are very prone, before they have been drilled at target practice with ball-cartridges, to place the ball below the powder in the piece. Officers conducting detachments through the Indian country, should, therefore, give their especial attention to this, and require the recruits to tear the cartridge and pour all the powder into the piece before the ball is inserted.

As accidents often occur in camp from the accidental discharge of fire-arms that have been capped, I would recommend that the arms be continually kept loaded in campaigning, but the caps not placed upon the cones until they are required for firing. This will cause but little delay in an action, and will conduce much to security from accidents.

When loaded fire-arms have been exposed for any considerable time to a moist atmosphere, they should be discharged, or the cartridges drawn, and the arms thoroughly cleaned, dried, and oiled.* Too much attention cannot be given to keeping arms in perfect firing order.

TRAILING.

I know of nothing in the woodman's education of so much importance, or so difficult to acquire, as the art of trailing or tracking men and animals. To become an adept in this art requires the constant practice of years, and with some men a lifetime does not suffice to learn it.†

* This I believe to be a "vulgar error." If the cartridge fit properly, and the nipple be defended by a waxed cap, powder will keep drier in the barrel than in the horn. I have often fired off a round of Colt that has remained loaded for months.—ED.

† I have met with but one man who could gallop over hard ground upon a "spoor"—hog or antelope—and he was of a genus soon likely to become extinct,—an "Indian officer." General Marcy, however, goes too far in asserting that the white man's perceptions are too blunt for good tracking. A few weeks of hard practice will tell wonderfully upon the progress of a man, whose organs of observation are well developed.—ED.

Almost all the Indians whom I have met with are proficient in this species of knowledge, the faculty for acquiring which appears to be innate with them. Exigencies of woodland and prairie-life stimulate the savage from childhood to develop faculties so important in the arts of war and of the chase.

I have seen very few white men who were good trailers, and practice did not seem very materially to improve their faculties in this regard; they have not the same acute perceptions for these things as the Indian or the Mexican. It is not apprehended that this difficult branch of woodcraft can be taught from books, as it pertains almost exclusively to the school of practice, yet I will give some facts relating to the habits of the Indians that will facilitate its acquirement.

A party of Indians, for example, starting out upon a war excursion, leave their families behind, and never transport their lodges; whereas, when they move with their families, they carry their lodges and other effects. If, therefore, an Indian trail is discovered with the marks of the lodge-poles upon it, it has certainly not been made by a war party; but if the track do not show the trace of lodge-poles, it will be equally certain that a war or hunting party has passed that way, and if it is not desired to come in conflict with them, their direction may be avoided. Mustangs or wild horses, when moving from place to place, leave a trail which is sometimes difficult to distinguish from that made by a mounted party of Indians, especially if the mustangs do not stop to graze. This may be determined by following upon the trail until some dung is found, and if this should lie in a single pile, it is a sure indication that a herd of mustangs has passed, as they always stop to relieve themselves, while a party of Indians would keep their horses in motion, and the ordure would be scattered along the road. If the trail pass through woodland, the mustangs will occasionally go under the limbs of trees too low to admit the passage of a man on horseback.

An Indian, on coming to a trail, will generally tell at a

glance its age, by what particular tribe it was made, the number of the party, and many other things connected with it astounding to the uninitiated.

I remember, upon one occasion, as I was riding with a Delaware upon the prairies, we crossed the trail of a large party of Indians traveling with lodges. The tracks appeared to me quite fresh, and I remarked to the Indian that we must be near the party. "Oh no," said he, "the trail was made two days before, in the morning," at the same time pointing with his finger to where the sun would be about 8 o'clock. Then seeing that my curiosity was excited to know by what means he arrived at this conclusion, he called my attention to the fact that there had been no dew for the last two nights; but that, on the previous morning, it had been heavy. He then pointed out to me some spears of grass that had been pressed down into the earth by the horse's hoofs, upon which the sand still adhered, having dried on, thus clearly showing that the grass was wet when the tracks were made.

At another time, as I was traveling with the same Indian, I discovered upon the ground what I took to be a bear-track, with a distinctly-marked impression of the heel and all the toes. I immediately called the Indian's attention to it, at the same time flattering myself that I had made quite an important discovery, which had escaped his observation. The fellow remarked with a smile, "Oh no, captain, may be so, he not bear-track." He then pointed with his gun-rod to some spears of grass that grew near the impression; but I did not comprehend the mystery until he dismounted and explained to me that, when the wind was blowing, the spears of grass would be bent over toward the ground, and the oscillating motion thereby produced would scoop out the loose sand into the shape I have described. The truth of this explanation was apparent, yet it occurred to me that its solution would have baffled the wits of most white men.

Fresh tracks generally show moisture where the earth has been turned up; but after a short exposure to the sun they become dry. If the tracks be very recent, the sand may sometimes, where it is very loose and dry, be seen running back into the tracks; and, by following them to a place where they cross water, the earth will be wet for some distance after they leave it. The droppings of the dung from animals are also good indications of the age of a trail. It is well to remember whether there have been any rains within a few days, as the age of a trail may sometimes be conjectured in this way. It is very easy to tell whether tracks have been made before or after a rain, as the water washes off all the sharp edges.

It is not a difficult matter to distinguish the tracks of American horses from those of Indian horses, as the latter are never shod; moreover, they are much smaller.

In trailing horses, there will be no trouble while the ground is soft, as the impressions they leave will then be deep and distinct; but when they pass over hard or rocky ground, it is sometimes a very slow and troublesome process to follow them. Where there is grass, the trace can be seen for a considerable time, as the grass will be trodden down and bent in the direction the party has moved; should the grass have returned to its upright position, the trail can often be distinguished by standing upon it and looking ahead for some distance in the direction it has been pursuing; the grass that has been turned over will show a different shade of green from that around it, and this often marks a trail for a long time.

Should all traces of the track be obliterated in certain localities, it is customary with the Indians to follow on in the direction it has been pursuing for a time, and it is quite probable that in some place where the ground is more favorable it will show itself again. Should the trail not be recovered in this way, they search for a place where the earth is soft, and make a careful examination, embracing the entire area where it is likely to run.

Indians who find themselves pursued, and wish to escape, scatter as much as possible, with an understanding that they are to meet again at some point in advance, so that, if the pursuing party follows any one of the tracks, it will invariably lead to the place of rendezvous. If, for example, the trail points in the direction of a mountain pass, or toward any other place which affords the only passage through a particular section of country, it would not be worth while to spend much time in hunting it, as it would probably be regained at the pass.

As it is important, in trailing Indians, to know at what gaits they are traveling, and as the appearance of the tracks of horses are not familiar to all, I have, in the following cut, represented the prints made by the hoofs at the ordinary speed of the walk, trot, and gallop, so that persons, in following the trail of Indians, may form an idea as to the probability of overtaking them, and regulate their movements accordingly.*

In traversing a district of unknown country where there are no prominent landmarks, and with the view of return- to the point of departure, a pocket compass should always be carried, and attached by a string to a button-hole of the coat, to prevent its being lost or mislaid; and on starting out, as well as frequently during the trip, to take the bearing, and examine the appearance of the country when facing toward the starting-point, as a landscape presents a very different aspect when viewing it from opposite directions.† There are few white men who can

* The "cut" is well worth study.—Ed.

† The traveller cannot pay too much attention to this direction. None but those endued with the highest development of locality can retrace a path with confidence, unless they have studied on the way, its bearings from the opposite direction. The best plan is to halt at times, and, turning round, to dwell upon some peculiar feature of the country which re-seen will be readily recognized. In the Prairie also, it is by no means easy to take a bee-line—to walk straight. The military man will readily march on a point to his front, by fixing his eye upon the distant objects,—clods, pebbles, grass tussocks, or shrubs,—in alignement.

I cannot agree with Mr. Galton, that there is any difficulty in steering oneself by the stars or the sun—a fortnight's work will conquer that. The author of the "Art of Travel" proposes, however, a good succedaneum, viz., a pocket compass without rhumbs, but showing the degrees round the rim by means of which true bearings can be ascertained. That traveller also proposes, very properly, that "the points of the compass, viz., North, North North-east, etc., should be used for none except true bearings, and the degrees, as

retrace their steps for any great distance, unless they take the above precautions in passing over an unknown country

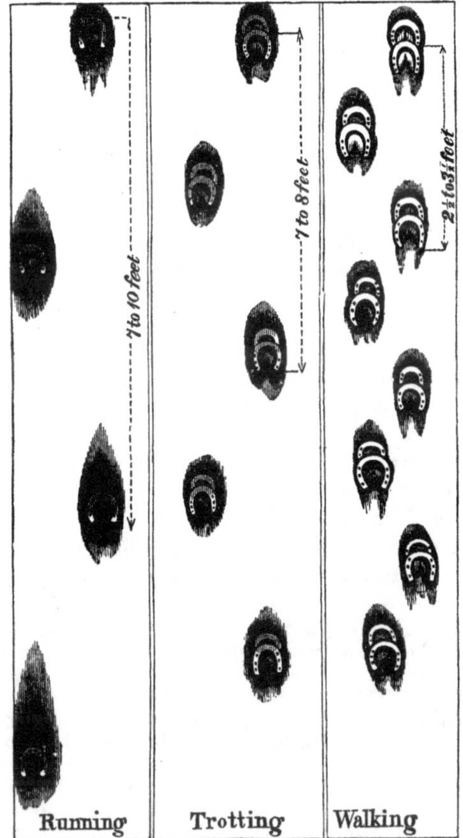

HORSE-TRACKS AT ORDINARY SPEED.

25°, for none except magnetic." Perhaps, however, the notation might be advantageously revised; it is easier, in mapping, to correct

for the first time ; but with the Indians it is different ; the sense of locality seems to be innate with them, and they do not require the aid of the magnetic needle to guide them.

Upon a certain occasion, when I made a long march over an unexplored section, and was returning upon an entirely different route without either road or trail, a Delaware, by the name of "Black Beaver," who was in my party, on arriving at a particular point, suddenly halted, and, turning to me, asked if I recognized the country before us. Seeing no familiar objects, I replied in the negative. He put the same question to the other white men of the party, all of whom gave the same answers, whereupon he smiled, and in his quaint vernacular said, "Injun he don't know nothing. Injun big fool. White man mighty smart ; he know heap." At the same time he pointed to a tree about two hundred yards from where we were then standing, and informed us that our outward trail ran directly by the side of it, which proved to be true.

Another time, as I was returning from the Comanche country over a route many miles distant from the one I had traveled in going out, one of my Delaware hunters, who had never visited the section before, on arriving upon the crest of an eminence in the prairie, pointed out to me

---

degrees than rhumbs; besides which, we more naturally say N.E. than 45°. The use of rhumbs and degrees mixed, *e.g.*, N. 25° E. (for simple 25°), is highly objectionable, and compasses should be graduated from 0° to 360°.

This is a long note ; but losing his way is one of the sorest accidents that can happen to the traveller. Such lately has twice been my fate in ascending unexplored African mountains ; and my feelings upon the subject are naturally enough acute. On the Prairies in Australia and in Northern Africa—*teste* Dr. Barth—such occurrences are very common, and terrible accidents have occurred from the frantic state of mind which is apt to be induced by losing one's way in the desert.

I have invariably found that coolness is the principal preservative, and that it is far better to sit or lie down awaiting rescue, than to waste strength by shouting, or by hastening to rejoin the party.—Ed.

a clump of trees in the distance, remarking that our outward track would be found there. I was not, however, disposed to credit his statement until we reached the locality and found the road passing the identical spot he had indicated.

This same Indian would start from any place to which he had gone by a sinuous route, through an unknown country, and keep a direct bearing back to the place of departure; and he assured me that he has never, even during the most cloudy or foggy weather, or in the darkest nights, lost the points of compass. There are very few white men who are endowed with these wonderful faculties, end those few are only tendered proficient by matured experience.

I have known several men, after they had become lost in the prairies, to wander about for days without exercising the least judgment, and finally exhibiting a state of mental aberration almost upon the verge of lunacy. Instead of reasoning upon their situation, they exhaust themselves running a-head at their utmost speed without any regard to direction. When a person is satisfied that he has lost his way, he should stop and reflect upon the course he has been traveling, the time that has elapsed since he left his camp, and the probable distance that he is from it; and if he is unable to retrace his steps, he should keep as nearly in the direction of them as possible; and, if he has a compass, this will be an easy matter; but, above all, he should guard against following his own track around in a circle with thc idea that he is in a beaten track.

When he is traveling with a train of wagons which leaves a plain trail, he can make the distance he has traveled from camp the radius of a circle in which to ride around, and, before the circle is described, he will strike the trail. If the person has no compass, it is always well to make an observation, and to remember the direction of the wind at the time of departure from camp; and as this would not generally change during the day, it would afford a means of keeping the points of the compass.

In the night, Ursa Major (the Great Bear) is not only useful to find the north star; but its position, when the pointers will be vertical in the heavens, may be estimated with sufficient accuracy to determine the north even when the north star cannot be seen. In tropical latitudes, the zodiacal stars, such as Orion and Antares, give the east and west bearing, and the Southern Cross the north and south, when Polaris and the Great Bear cannot be seen.

It is said that the moss upon the firs and other trees in Europe gives a certain indication of the points of compass in a forest country, the greatest amount accumulating upon the north side of the trees. But I have often observed the trees in our own forests, and have not been able to form any positive conclusions in this way.

CHAPTER VI.

Guides and Hunters.—Delawares and Shawnees.—Khebirs.—Black Beaver.—Anecdotes.—Domestic Troubles.—Lodges.—Similarity of Prairie Tribes to the Arabs.—Method of making War.—Tracking and pursuing Indians.—Method of attacking them.—Telegraphing by Smokes.

DELAWARES AND SHAWNEES.

It is highly important that parties making expeditions through an unexplored country should secure the services of the best guides and hunters; and I know of none who are superior to the Delawares and Shawnee Indians. They have been with me upon several different occasions, and I have invariably found them intelligent, brave, reliable, and in every respect well qualified to fill their pôsitions. They are endowed with those keen and wonderful powers in woodcraft which can only be acquired by instinct, practice, and necessity, and which are possessed by no other people that I have heard of, unless it be the khebirs or guides who escort the caravans across the great desert of Sahara.

General E. Dumas, in his treatise upon the "Great Desert," published in Paris, 1856, in speaking of these guides, says:—

"The khebir is always a man of intelligence, of tried probity, bravery, and skill. He knows how to determine his position from the appearance of the stars; by the experience of other journeys, he has learned all about the roads, wells, and pastures; the dangers of certain passes, and the means of avoiding them; all the chiefs whose territories it is necessary to pass through; the salubrity of the different localities; the remedies against diseases; the treatment of fractures, and the antidotes to the venom of snakes and scorpions.

"In these vast solitudes, where nothing seems to indicate the route, where the wind covers up all traces of the track with sand, the khebir has a thousand ways of directing himself in the right course. In the night, when there are no stars in sight, by the simple inspection of a handful of grass, which he examines with his fingers, which he smells and tastes, he informs himself of his locale without ever being lost or wandering.

"I saw with astonishment that our conductor, although he had but one eye, and that defective, recognized perfectly the route; and Leon, the African, states that the conductor of his caravan became blind upon the journey from ophthalmia, yet by feeling the grass and sand he could tell when we were approaching an inhabited place.

"Our guide had all the qualities which make a good khebir. He was young, large, and strong; he was a master of arms; his eye commanded respect, and his speech won the heart. But, if in the tent he was affable and winning, once *en route* he spoke only when it was necessary, and never smiled."

The Delawares are but a minute remnant of the great Algonquin family, whose early traditions declare them to be the parent stock from which the other numerous branches of the Algonquin tribes originated. And they are the same people whom the first white settlers found so numerous upon the banks of the Delaware.

When William Penn held his council with the Delawares upon the ground where the city of Philadelphia now stands, they were as peaceful and unwarlike in their habits as the Quakers themselves. They had been subjugated by the Five Nations, forced to take the appellation of squaws, and forego the use of arms; but after they moved west, beyond the influence of their former masters, their naturally independent spirit revived. They soon regained their lofty position as braves and warriors, and the male squaws of the Iroquois soon became formidable men and heroes, and so have continued to the present day. Their war-path has reached the shores of the Pacific Ocean on the west, Hudson's Bay on the north, and into the very heart of Mexico on the south.

They are not clannish in their dispositions like most other Indians, nor by their habits confined to any given locality, but are found as traders, trappers, or hunters among most of the Indian tribes inhabiting our continent. I even saw them living with the Mormons in Utah. They are among the Indians as the Jews among the whites, essentially wanderers.

The Shawnees have been associated with the Delawares 185 years. They intermarry and live as one people. Their present places of abode are upon the Missouri River, near Fort Leavenworth, and in the Choctaw Territory, upon the Canadian River, near Fort Arbuckle. They are familiar with many of the habits and customs of their pale-faced neighbours, and some of them speak the English language, yet many of their native characteristics tenaciously cling to them.

Upon one occasion, I endeavoured to teach a Delaware the use of the compass. He seemed much interested in its mechanism, and very attentively observed the oscillations of the needle. He would move away a short distance, then return, keeping his eyes continually fixed upon the needle, and the uniform position into which it settled. He did not, however, seem to comprehend it in the least, but regarded the entire proceeding as a species of necromantic performance got up for his especial benefit, and I was about putting away the instrument, when he motioned me to stop, and came walking toward it with a serious but incredulous countenance, remarking, as he pointed his finger toward it, "May-be so he tell lie sometime."

The ignorance evinced by this Indian regarding the uses of the compass, is less remarkable than that of some white men who are occasionally met upon the frontier.

While surveying Indian lands in the wilds of Western Texas, during the summer of 1854, I encountered a deputy surveyor traveling on foot, with his compass and chain upon his back. I saluted him very politely, remarking that I presumed he was a surveyor, to which he replied, "I reckon, *stranger*, I ar that thar individoal."

I had taken the magnetic variations several times, always with nearly the same results (about 10° 20′); but, in order to verify my observations, I was curious to learn how they accorded with his own working, and accordingly inquired of him what he made the variation of the compass in that particular locality. He seemed struck with astonishment, took his compass from his back and laid it upon a log near by, then facing me, and pointing with his hand toward it, said,

"Straanger, do yer see that thar instru-*ment*?" to which I replied in the affirmative. He continued,

"I've owned her well-nigh goin on twenty year. I've put her through the perarries and through the timber, and now look yeer, straanger, you can just bet your life on't she never *var*-ried arry time, and if you'll just follow her sign you'll knock the centre out of the north star. She never lies, she don't."

He seemed to consider my interrogatory as a direct insinuation that his compass was an inperfect one, and hence his indignation. Thinking that I should not get any very important intelligence concerning the variation of the needle from this surveyor, I begged his pardon for questioning the accuracy of his instru-*ment*, bid him good-morning, and continued on my journey.

BLACK BEAVER.

In 1849, I met with a very interesting specimen of the Delaware tribe whose name was Black Beaver. He had for ten years been in the employ of the American Fur Company, and, during this time, had visited nearly every point of interest within the limits of our unsettled territory. He had set his traps and spread his blanket upon the head waters of the Missouri and Columbia; and his wanderings had led him south to the Colorado and Gila, and thence to the shores of the Pacific in Southern California. His life had been that of a veritable cosmopolite, filled with scenes of intense and startling interest, bold and reckless adventure. He was with me two seasons in the capacity of guide, and I always found him perfectly reliable, brave, and competent. His reputation as a resolute, determined, and fearless warrior, did not admit of question, yet I have never seen a man who wore his laurels with less vanity.

When I first made his acquaintance, I was puzzled to know what to think of him. He would often, in speaking of the Prairie Indians, say to me,

"Captain, if you have a fight, you mustn't count much on me, for I'ze a big coward. When the fight begins I 'spect you'll see me run under the cannon; Injun mighty 'fraid of big gun."

I expressed my surprise that he should, if what he told me was true, have gained such a reputation as a warrior; whereupon he informed me that many years previous, when he was a young man, and before he had ever been in battle, he, with about twenty white men and four Delawares, were at one of the Fur Company's trading-posts upon the Upper Missouri, engaged in trapping beaver. While there, the stockade fort was attacked by a numerous band of Blackfeet Indians, who fought bravely, and seemed determined to annihilate the little band that defended it.

After the investment had been completed, and there appeared no probability of the attacking party's abandoning their purpose, "One d—d fool Delaware" (as Black Beaver expressed it) proposed to his countrymen to make a sortie, and thereby endeavor to effect an impression upon the Blackfeet. This, Beaver said, was the last thing he would ever have thought of suggesting, and it startled him prodigiously, causing him to tremble so much that it was with difficulty he could stand.

He had, however, started from home with the fixed purpose of becoming a distinguished brave, and made a great effort to stifle his emotion. He assumed an air of determination, saying that was the very idea he was just about to propose; and, slapping his comrades upon the back, started toward the gate, telling them to follow. As soon as the gate was passed, he says, he took particular care to keep in the rear of the others, so that, in the event of a retreat, he would be able to reach the stockade first.

They had not proceeded far before a perfect shower of arrows came falling around them on all sides, but, fortunately, without doing them harm. Not fancying this hot reception, those in front proposed an immediate retreat, to which he most gladly acceded, and at once set off at his utmost speed, expecting to reach the fort first. But he soon discovered that his comrades were more fleet, and were rapidly passing and leaving him behind. Suddenly he stopped and called out to them, "Come back here, you cowards, you squaws; what for you run away and leave brave man to fight alone?" This taunting appeal to their courage turned them back, and, with their united efforts, they succeeded in beating off the enemy immediately around them, securing their entrance into the fort.

Beaver says when the gate was closed, the captain in charge of the establishment grasped him warmly by the hand, saying, "Black Beaver, you are a brave man; you have done this day what no other man in the fort would have the courage to do, and I thank you from the bottom of my heart."

In relating the circumstance to me he laughed most heartily, thinking it a very good joke, and said after that he was regarded as a brave warrior.

The truth is, my friend Beaver was one of those few heroes who never sounded his own trumpet; yet no one that knows him ever presumed to question his courage.

At another time, while Black Beaver remained upon the head waters of the Missouri, he was left in charge of a "*caché*," consisting of a quantity of goods buried to prevent their being stolen by the Indians. During the time he was engaged upon this duty, he amused himself by hunting in the vicinity, only visiting his charge once a day. As he was making one of these periodical visits, and had arrived upon the summit of a hill overlooking the locality, he suddenly discovered a large number of hostile Blackfeet occupying it, and he supposed they had appropriated all the goods. As soon as they espied him, they beckoned for him to come down and have a friendly chat with them.

Knowing that their purpose was to beguile him into their power, he replied that he did not feel in a talking humour just at that time, and started off in another direction, whereupon they hallooed after him, making use of the most insulting language and gestures, and asking him if he considered himself a man thus to run away from his friends, and intimating that, in their opinion, he was an old woman, who had better go home and take care of the children.

Beaver says this roused his indignation to such a pitch, that he stopped, turned round, and replied, "Maybe so; s'pose three or four of you Injuns come up here alone, I'll show you if I'ze old womans." They did not, however, accept the challenge, and Beaver rode off.

Although the Delawares generally seem quite happy in their social relations, yet they are not altogether exempt from some of those minor discords which occasionally creep in and mar the domestic harmony of their more civilized pale-faced brethren.

I remember, upon one occasion, I had bivouacked for the night with Black Beaver, and he had been endeavoring to while away the long hours of ths evening by relating to me some of the most thrilling incidents of his highly-adventurous and erratic life, when at length a hiatus in the conversation gave me an opportunity of asking him if he was a married man. He hesitated for some time; then looking up and giving his fore-finger a twirl, to imitate the throwing of the lasso, replied, "One time me catch 'um wife. I pay that woman, *his modder*, one hoss—one saddle—one bridle—two plug tobacco, and plenty goods. I take him home to my house—got plenty meat—plenty corn—plenty everything. One time me go take walk, maybe so three, maybe so two hours. When I come home, that woman he say, 'Black Beaver, what for you go way long time?' I say, 'I not go nowhere; I just take one littel walk.' Then that woman he* get heap mad, and say, 'No, Black Beaver, you not take no littel walk. I know what for you go way; *you go see nodder one woman.*' I say, 'Maybe not.' Then that woman he cry long time, and all e'time now he mad. You never see 'Merican woman that a-way?"

I sympathized most deeply with my friend in his distress, and told him, for his consolation, that, in my opinion, the women of his nation were not peculiar in this respect; that they were pretty much alike all over the world, and I was under the impression that there were well-authenticated instances, even among white women, where they had subjected themselves to the same causes of complaint so feelingly depicted by him. Whereupon he very earnestly asked, "What you do for cure him? Whip him?" I replied, "No; that, so far as my observation extended, I was under the impression that this was generally regarded by those who had suffered from its effects, as one of those chronic and vexatious complaints which would not be benefited by the treatment he suggested, even when administered in homœopathic doses, and I believed it was now admitted by all sensible men that it was better in all such cases to let nature take its course, trusting to a merciful Providence."

At this reply, his countenance assumed a dejected expression; but at length he brightened up again and triumphantly remarked, "I tell you, my friend, what I do; I ketch 'um nodder one wife when I go home."

Black Beaver had visited St. Louis and the small towns upon the Missouri frontier, and he prided himself not a little upon his acquaintance with the customs of the whites, and never seemed more happy than when an opportunity offered to display this knowledge in the presence of his Indian companions. It so happened, upon one occasion, that I had a Comanche guide who bivouacked at the same

* The N. A. Indian, like the African Negro, translates his vernacular into English. Few savage or barbarian languages have distinctions of gender; thus a woman is always "he."—Ed.

fire with Beaver. On visiting them one evening according to my usual practice, I found them engaged in a very earnest and apparently not very amicable conversation. On inquiring the cause of this, Beaver answered,

"I've been telling this Comanche what I seen 'mong the white folks."

I said, "Well, Beaver, what did you tell him?"

"I tell him 'bout the steam boats, and the rail-roads, and the heap o' houses I seen in St. Louis."

"Well, sir, what does he think of that?"

"He say I'ze d—d fool."

"What else did you tell him about?"

"I tell him the world is round; but he keep all e'time say, Hush, you fool! do you spose I'ze child? Have'nt I got eyes? Can't I see the prairie? You call him round? He say, too, maybe so I tell you something you not know before. One time my grandfather he make long journey that way (pointing to the west). When he get on big mountain, he seen heap water on t'other side, jest so flat he can be, and he seen the sun go right straight down on t'other side. I then tell him all these rivers he seen, all e'time the water he run; s'pose the world flat the water he stand still. Maybe so he not b'lieve me?"

I told him it certainly looked very much like it. I then asked him to explain to the Comanche the magnetic telegraph. He looked at me earnestly, and said,

"What you call that magnetic telegraph?"

I said, "You have heard of New York and New Orleans?"

"Oh yes," he replied.

"Very well; we have a wire connecting these two cities, which are about a thousand miles apart, and it would take a man thirty days to ride it upon a good horse. Now a man stands at one end of this wire in New York; and, by touching it a few times, he inquires of his friend in New Orleans what he had for breakfast. His friend in New Orleans touches the other end of the wire, and in ten minutes the answer comes back—ham and eggs. Tell him that, Beaver."

His countenance assumed a most comical expression; but he made no remark until I again requested him to repeat what I had said to the Comanche, when he observed,

"No, captain, I not tell him that, for I don't b'lieve that myself."

Upon my assuring him that such was the fact, and that I had seen it myself, he said,

"Injun not very smart; sometimes he's big fool, but he holler pretty loud; you hear him maybe half a mile; you say 'Merican man he talk thousand miles. I 'spect you try to fool me now, captain; *maybe so you lie.*"

The Indians living between the outer white settlements and the nomadic tribes of the Plains form intermediate social links in the chain of civilization.

The first of these occupy permanent habitations; but the others, although they cultivate the soil, are only resident while their crops are growing, going out into the prairies after harvest to spend the winter in hunting. Among the former may be mentioned the Cherokees, Creeks, Choctaws, and Chickasaws, and of the latter are the Delawares, Shawnees, Kickapoos, etc., who are perfectly familiar with the use of the rifle, and, in my judgment, would make as formidable partisan warriors as can be found in the universe.

THE WILD TRIBES OF THE WEST.

These are very different in their habits from the natives that formerly occupied the country bordering upon the Atlantic coast. The latter lived permanently in villages,* where they cultivated the soil, and never wandered very far from them. They did not use horses, but always made their war expeditions on foot, and never came into action unless they could screen themselves behind the cover of trees. They inflicted the most inhuman tortures upon their prisoners, but did not, that I am aware, violate the chastity of women.

The prairie tribes have no permanent abiding-places;

* The Eastern wigwam was a larger and more substantial tenement than the western lodge.—Ed.

they never plant a seed, but roam for hundreds of miles in every direction over the plains. They are perfect horsemen, and seldom go to war on foot. Their attacks are made in the open prairies, and when unhorsed they are powerless. They do not, like the eastern Indians, inflict upon their prisoners prolonged tortures, but invariably subject all females that have the misfortune to fall into their merciless clutches to an ordeal worse than death.

It is highly important to every man passing through a country frequented by Indians to know some of their habits, customs, and propensities; as this will facilitate his intercourse with friendly tribes, and enable him, when he wishes to avoid a conflict, to take precautions against coming in collision with those who are hostile.

Almost every tribe has its own way of constructing its lodges, encamping, making fires, its own style of dress, by some of which peculiarities the experienced frontiersman can generally distinguish them.

The Osages, for example, make their lodges in the shape of a wagon-top, of bent rods or willows covered with skins, blankets, or the bark of trees.

The Kickapoo lodges are made in an oval form, something like a rounded haystack, of poles set in the ground, bent over, and united at top; this is covered with cloths or bark.

The Witchetaws, Wacos, Towackanies, and Tonkowas erect their hunting-lodges of sticks put up in the form of the frustrum of a cone and covered with brush.

All these tribes leave the framework of their lodges standing when they move from camp to camp, and this, of course, indicates the particular tribe that erected them.

The Delawares and Shawnees * plant two upright forked poles, place a stick across them, and stretch a canvas covering over it, in the same manner as with the "tente d'abri."

The Sioux, Arapahoes, Cheyennes, Utes, Snakes, Black-

* Add Cherokees and Choctaws,—Ed.

feet, and Kioways make use of the Comanche lodge, covered with dressed buffalo hides.*

All the Prairie Indians I have met with are the most inveterate beggars. They will flock around strangers, and, in the most importunate manner, ask for everything they see, especially tobacco and sugar; and, if allowed, they will handle, examine, and occasionally pilfer such things as happen to take their fancy. The proper way to treat them is to give them at once such articles as are to be disposed of, and then, in a firm and decided manner, let them understand that they are to receive nothing else.

A party of Keechis once visited my camp with their principal chief, who said he had some important business to discuss, and demanded a council with the "capitan." After consent had been given, he assembled his principal men, and, going through the usual preliminary of taking a "big smoke," he arose, and with a great deal of ceremony commenced his pompous and flowery speech, which, like all others of a similar character, amounted to nothing, until he touched upon the real object of his visit. He said he had traveled a long distance over the prairies to see and have a talk with his white brothers; that his people were very hungry and naked. He then approached me with six small sticks, and, after shaking hands, laid one of the sticks in my hand, which he said represented sugar, another signified tobacco, and the other four, pork, flour, whisky, and blankets, all of which he assured me his people were in great need of, and must have. His talk was then concluded, and he sat down, apparently much gratified with the graceful and impressive manner with which he had executed his part of the performance,

It then devolved upon me to respond to the brilliant effort of the prairie orator, which I did in something like the following manner. After imitating his style for a

* The Sacs, Foxes, Winnebagos, or Puants and Menomenes build elliptical lodges, thirty to forty feet long by fourteen to fifteen feet wide, and large enough to shelter from twenty to sixty people. The covering is of plaited rush mats bound to the poles, and a small aperture in the lodge acts as chimney.—Ed.

short time, I closed my remarks, by telling him that we were poor infantry soldiers, who were always obliged to go on foot; that we had become very tired of walking, and would like very much to ride. Furthermore, I had observed that they had among them many fine horses and mules. I then took two small sticks, and imitating as nearly as possible the manner of the chief, placed one in his hand, which I told him was nothing more or less than a first-rate horse, and then the other, which signified a good large mule. I closed by saying that I was ready to exchange presents whenever it suited his convenience.

They looked at each other for some time without speaking, but finally got up and walked away, and I was not troubled with them again.*

INDIAN FIGHTING.

The military system, as taught and practised in our army up to the time of the Mexican war, was, without doubt, efficient and well-adapted to the art of war among civilized nations. This system was designed for the operations of armies acting in populated districts, furnishing ample resources, and against an enemy who was tangible, and made use of a similar system.

The vast expanse of desert territory that has been annexed to our domain within the last few years, is peopled by numerous tribes of marauding and erratic savages, who are mounted upon fleet and hardy horses, making war the business and pastime of their lives, and acknowledging none of the ameliorating conventionalities of civilized warfare. Their tactics are such as to render the old system almost wholly impotent.

To act against an enemy who is here to-day and there

* In the old times, crafty North American Indians have tried "dreaming dreams," against white men, and have lost by the proceeding. Thus, while the red-face saw in sleep his pale-faced brother giving him a fine cloth coat, the pale-face perceived his red-faced brother making over to him a valuable tract of country. The visions, of course, soon ceased.—Ed.

to-morrow; who at one time stampedes a herd of mules upon the head waters of the Arkansas, and when next heard from, is in the very heart of the populated districts of Mexico, laying waste haciendas, and carrying devastation, rapine, and murder in his step; who is every where without being any where; who assembles at the moment of combat, and vanishes whenever fortune turns against him; who leaves his women and children far distant from the theatre of hostilities, and has neither towns or magazines to defend, nor lines of retreat to cover; who derives his commissariat from the country he operates in, and is not encumbered with baggage-wagons or pack-trains; who comes into action only when it suits his purposes, and never without the advantage of numbers or position—with such an enemy the strategic science of civilized nations loses much of its importance, and finds but rarely, and only in peculiar localities, an opportunity to be put in practice.

Our little army, scattered has it has been over the vast area of our possessions, in small garrisons of one or two companies each, has seldom been in a situation to act successfully on the offensive against large numbers of these marauders, and has often been condemned to hold itself almost exclusively upon the defensive. The morale of the troops must thereby necessarily be seriously impaired, and the confidence of the savages correspondingly augmented. The system of small garrisons has a tendency to disorganize the troops in proportion as they are scattered, and renders them correspondingly inefficient.* The same results have been observed by the French army in Algeria, where, in 1845, their troops were, like ours, disseminated over a vast space, and broken up into small detachments stationed in numerous entrenched posts. Upon the sudden appearance of Abd el Kader in the plain of Mitidja, they were defeated with serious losses, and were from day to day obliged to abandon these useless stations, with all the

* I have treated of this important subject—the deficiency of centralization in the American and the Anglo-Indian armies—in the City of the Saints, chap. 1.—Ed.

supplies they contained. A French writer, in discussing this subject, says:

"We have now abandoned the fatal idea of defending Algeria by small entrenched posts. In studying the character of the war, the nature of the men who are to oppose us, and of the country in which we are to operate, we must be convinced of the danger of admitting any other system of fortification than that which is to receive our grand depots, our magazines, and to serve as places to recruit and rest our troops, when exhausted by long expeditionary movements.

"These fortifications should be established in the midst of the centres of action, so as to command the principal routes, and serve as pivots to expeditionary columns.

"We owe our success to a system of war which has its proofs in twice changing our relations with the Arabs. The system consists altogether in the great mobility we have given to our troops. Instead of disseminating our soldiers, with the vain hope of protecting our frontiers with a line of small posts, we have concentrated them, to have them at all times ready for emergencies; and, since then, the fortune of the Arabs has waned, and we have marched from victory to victory.

"This system which has thus far succeeded, ought to succeed always; and to conduct us, God willing, to the peaceful possession of the country."

In reading a treatise upon war as it is practised by the French in Algeria, by Colonel A. Laure, of the 2nd Algerine Tirailleurs, published in Paris in 1858, I was struck with the remarkable similarity between the habits of the Arabs and those of the wandering tribes that inhabit our Western prairies. Their manner of making war is almost precisely the same, and a successful system of strategic operations for one will, in my opinion, apply to the other.

As the Turks have been more successful than the French in their military operations against the Arab tribes, it may not be altogether uninteresting to inquire by what means the inferior soldiers have accomplished the best results.

The author above mentioned, in speaking upon this subject, says:

"In these latter days, the world is occupied with the organization of mounted infantry, according to the example of the Turks, where, in the most successful experiments that have been made, the mule carries the foot-soldier.

"The Turkish soldier mounts his mule, puts his provisions upon one side and his accoutrements upon the other, and, thus equipped, sets out upon long marches, traveling day and night, and only reposing occasionally in bivouac. Arrived near the place of operations (as near the break of day as possible), the Turks dismount in the most profound silence, and pass in succession the bridle of one mule through that of another, in such a manner that a single man is sufficient to hold forty or fifty of them by retaining the last bridle, which secures all the others; they then examine their arms, and are ready to commence their work. The chief gives his last orders, posts his guides, and they make the attack, surprise the enemy, generally asleep, and carry the position without resistance. The operation terminated, they hasten to beat a retreat, to prevent the neighbouring tribes from assembling, and thus avoid a combat.

"The Turks had only 3,000 mounted men and 10,000 infantry in Algeria, yet these 13,000 men sufficed to conquer the same obstacles which have arrested us for twenty-six years, notwithstanding the advantage we had of an army which was successively re-inforced until it amounted to a 100,000.

"Why not imitate the Turks, then; mount our infantry upon mules, and reduce the strength of our army?

"The response is very simple:

"The Turks are Turks—that is to say, Mussulmans—and indigenous to the country; the Turks speak the Arabic language; the Deys of Algeria had less country to guard than we, and they cared very little about retaining possession of it. They were satisfied to receive part of its revenues. They were not permanent; their dominion was held by a thread. The Arab dwells in tents; his magazines are in caves.

When he starts upon a war expedition, he folds his tent, drives far away his beasts of burden, which transport his effects, and only carries with him his horse and arms. Thus equipped, he goes every where ; nothing arrests him; and often, when we believe him twenty leagues distant, he is in ambush at precisely rifle-range from the flanks of his enemy.

"It may be thought the union of contingents might retard their movements; but this is not so. The Arabs, whether they number 10,000 or a 100,000, move with equal facility. They go where they wish, and as they wish, upon a campaign; the place of rendezvous merely is indicated, and they arrive there.

"What calculations can be made against such an organization as this?

"Strategy evidently loses its advantages against such enemies; a general can only make conjectures; he marches to find the Arabs, and finds them not; then, again, when he leasts expects it, he suddenly encounters them.

"When the Arab despairs of success in battle, he places his sole reliance upon the speed of his horse to escape destruction; and as he is always in a country where he can make his camp beside a little water ; he travels until he has placed a safe distance between himself and his enemy."

No people probably on the face of the earth are more ambitious of martial fame, or entertain a higher appreciation for the deeds of a daring and successful warrior, than the North American savages. The attainment of such reputation is the paramount and absorbing object of their lives. All their aspirations for distinction invariably take this channel of expression. A young man is never considered worthy to occupy a seat in council until he has encountered an enemy in battle; and he who can count the greatest number of scalps is the most highly honored by his tribe. This idea is inculcated from their earliest infancy. It is not surprising, therefore, that, with such weighty inducements before him, the young man who, as yet, has gained no renown as a brave or warrior, should be less discriminate in his attacks than older men who have already acquired a name. The young braves should, therefore be closely watched when encountered on the Plains.

The prairie tribes are seldom at peace with all their neighbors, and some of the young braves of a tribe are almost always absent upon a war excursion. These forays sometimes extend into the heart of the northern states of Mexico, where the Indians have carried on successful invasions for many years. They have devastated and depopulated a great portion of Sonora and Chihuahua. The objects of these forays are to steal horses and mules, and to take prisoners; and if it so happens that a war-party has been unsuccessful in the accomplishment of these ends, or has had the misfortune to lose some of its number in battle, they become reckless, and will often attack a small party with whom they are not at war, provided they hope to escape detection. The disgrace attendant upon a return to their friends without some trophies as an offset to the loss of their comrades is a powerful incentive to action, and they extend but little mercy to defenseless travelers who have the misfortune to encounter them at such a conjuncture.

While *en route* from New Mexico to Arkansas in 1849, I was encamped near the head of the Colorado River, and wishing to know the character of the country for a few miles in advance of our position, I desired an officer to go out and make the reconnoissance. I was lying sick in my bed at the time, or I should have performed the duty myself. I expected the officer would have taken an escort with him, but he omitted to do so, and started off alone. After proceeding a short distance, he discovered four mounted Indians coming at full speed directly towards him, when, instead of turning his own horse towards camp, and endeavoring to make his escape (he was well mounted), or of halting, and assuming a defensive attitude, he deliberately rode up to them; after which the tracks indicated that they proceeded about three miles together, when the Indians most brutally killed and scalped my most unfortunate but too credulous friend, who might probably have saved his life, had he not, in the kindness of his excellent heart, imagined that the savages would reciprocate his friendly advances. He was most woefully mistaken, and his life paid the forfeit of his generous and noble disposition.

I have never been able to get any positive information as to the persons who committed this murder; yet circumstances render it highly probable that they were a party of young Indians who were returning from an unsuccessful foray, and they were unable to resist the temptation of taking the scalp and horse of the lieutenant.

A small number of white men, in traveling upon the Plains, should not allow a party of strange Indians to approach them unless able to resist an attack under the most unfavorable circumstances.

It is a safe rule, when a man finds himself alone in the prairies, and sees a party of Indians approaching, not to allow them to come near him; and, if they persist in so doing, to signal them to keep away. If they do not obey, and he be mounted upon a fleet horse, he should make for the nearest timber. If the Indians follow and press him too closely, he should halt, turn round, and point his gun at the foremost, which will often have the effect of turning them back, but he should never draw trigger unless he finds that his life depends upon the shot; for, as soon as his shot is delivered, his sole dependence, unless he have time to reload, must be upon the speed of his horse.

The Indians of the Plains, notwithstanding the encomiums that have been heaped upon their brethren who formerly occupied the Eastern States for their gratitude, have not, so far as I have observed, the most distant conception of that sentiment. You may confer numberless benefits upon them for years, and the more that is done for them the more they will expect. They do not seem to comprehend the motive which dictates an act of benevolence or charity, and they invariably attribute it to fear or the expectation of reward. When they make a present, it is with a view of getting more than its equivalent in return.*

* Such is the morale of all savages. The battle of life, and the

I have never yet been able to discover that the Western wild tribes possessed any of those attributes which among civilized nations are regarded as virtues adorning the human character. They have yet to be taught the first rudiments of civilization, and they are at this time as far from any knowledge of Christianity, and as worthy subjects for missionary enterprise, as the most untutored natives of the South Sea Islands.*

The only way to make these merciless freebooters fear or respect the authority of our government is, when they misbehave, first of all to chastise them well by striking such a blow as will be felt for a long time, and thus show them that we are superior to them in war. They will then respect us much more than when their good-will is purchased with presents.

The opinion of a friend of mine, who has passed the last twenty-five years of his life among the Indians of the Rocky Mountains, corroborates the opinions I have advanced upon this head; and although I do not endorse all

---

selection of species, compels every man to do unto his neighbour what he would *not* have his neighbour do unto him. The word "gratitude" is not to be found in the dialects of the wild men. Even in Hindostan, it must be borrowed from Arabic or Persian. And when trying to obtain an African equivalent for "honest," the nearest approach to it is "one who does not steal."—Ed.

* Maugre some evidence to the contrary, I still believe that the North American Aborigen, like the Tasmanian and the Australian, is but a temporary denizen of the world who fails to succeed in the first struggle with nature. He is, like a wild animal, to be broken but not to be tamed; as the wolf can be taught to refrain from worrying, but cannot be made to act as a dog. In his wild state, the Indian falls before the white man. Settled and semi-civilized he dies of acute disease. He has virtually disappeared from the wide regions east of the Mississipi, and the same causes, still ceaselessly operating, point to his annihilation when the Prairie lands shall have become the grazing grounds of the Western World.

It is a false sentimentalism that cannot look facts in the face; an unsound reverence that models Providence after its own fashion. The best and wisest book of this, or, perhaps, of any age—I allude to the "Origin of Species,"—which opens up the grandest views of life, is based upon a practical justification of the ways of eternal wisdom to man.—Ed.

of his sentiments, yet many of them are deduced from long and matured experience and critical observation. He says :—

"They are the most onsartainest varmits in all creation, and I reckon tha'r not mor'n half human; for you never seed a human, arter you'd fed and treated him to the best fixins in your lodge, jist turn round and steal all your horses, or ary other thing he could lay his hands on. No, not adzackly. He would feel kinder grateful, and ask you to spread a blanket in his lodge ef you ever passed that a-way. But the Injun he don't care shucks for you, and is ready to do you a heap of mischief as soon as he quits your feed. No, Cap.," he continued, "it's not the right way to give um presents to buy peace; but ef I war governor of these yeer United States, I'll tell you what I'd do. I'd invite um all to a big feast, and make b'lieve I wanted to have a big talk; and as soon as I got um all together, I'd pitch in and sculp about half of um, and then t'other half would be mighty glad to make a peace that would stick. That's the way I'd make a treaty with the dog'ond, red-bellied varmints; and as sure as you're born, Cap., that's the only way."

I suggested to him the idea, that there would be a lack of good faith and honor in such a proceeding, and that it would be much more in accordance with my notions of fair dealing to meet them openly in the field, and there endeavour to punish them if they deserved it. To this he replied :—

"Tain't no use to talk about honour with them, Cap.; they hain't got no such thing in um; and they won't show fair fight, any way you can fix it. Don't they kill and sculp a white man when-ar they get the better on him? The mean varmints, they'll never behave themselves until you give um a clean out and out licking. They can't onderstand white folk's ways, and they won't learn um; and ef you treat um decently, they think you are afeard. You may depend on't, Cap., the only way to treat Injuns is to thrash them well at first, then the balance will sorter take to you and behave themselves."

The wealth of the Prairie Indians consists almost exclusively in their horses, of which they possess large numbers; and they are in the saddle from infancy to old age. Horsemanship is with them, as with the Arab of the Sahara, a necessary part of their education. The country they occupy is unsuited to cultivation, and their only avocations are war, rapine, and the chase. They have no fixed habitations, but move from place to place with the seasons and the game. All their worldly effects are transported in their migrations, and wherever their lodges are pitched there is their home. They are strangers to all cares, creating for themselves no artificial wants, and are perfectly happy and contented so long as the buffalo is found within the limits of their wanderings. Every man is a soldier, and they generally exhibit great confidence in their own military prowess.

MEETING INDIANS.

On approaching strangers, these people put their horses at full speed, and persons not familiar with their peculiarities and habits might interpret this as an act of hostility; but it is their custom with friends as well as enemies, and should not occasion groundless alarm.*

When a party is discovered approaching thus, and are near enough to distinguish signals, all that is necessary, in order to ascertain their disposition, is to raise the hand with the palm in front, and gradually push it forward and back several times. They all understand this to be a command to halt; and if they are not hostile, it will at once be obeyed.

After they have stopped, the right hand is raised again as before, and slowly moved to the right and left, which signifies "I do not know you. Who are you?" As all the wild tribes have their peculiar pantomimic signals by which they are known, they will then answer the inquiry

* A well known Moorish practice. The South African Kafirs, according to M. Delegorgue, have retained the custom at the *levées* of their Kings.—ED.

by giving their signal. If this should not be understood, they may be asked if they are friends, by raising both hands grasped in the manner of shaking hands, or by locking the two fore-fingers firmly while the hands are held up. If friendly, they will respond with the same signal; but, if enemies, they will probably disregard the command to halt, or give the signal of anger by closing the hand, placing it against the forehead, and turning it back and forth while in that position.

The pantomimic vocabulary is understood by all the Prairie Indians, and when oral communication is impracticable, it constitutes the court or general council language of the Plains. The signs are exceedingly graceful and significant; and, what was a fact of much astonishment to me, I discovered they were very nearly the same as those practised by the mutes in our deaf and dumb schools, and were comprehended by them with perfect facility.*

The Comanche is represented by making with the hand a waving motion in imitation of the crawling of a snake.

The Cheyenne, or "Cut-arm," by drawing the hand across the arm, to imitate cutting it with a knife.

The Arapahoes, or "Smellers," by seizing the nose with the thumb and fore-finger.

The Sioux, or "Cut-throats," by drawing the hand across the throat.

The Pawnees, or "Wolves," by placing a hand on each side of the forehead, with two fingers pointing to the front, to represent the narrow, sharp ears of the wolf.

The Crows, by imitating the flapping of the bird's wings with the palms of the hands.†

When Indians meet a party of strangers, and are disposed to be friendly, the chiefs, after the usual salutations

* See note at the end of this chapter.—Ed.

† The Kiowas, or Prairie-men, make the signs of the Prairie, and of water-drinking. The Yutas (Utahs), "they who live on mountains," have a complicated sign which denotes "living on mountains." The Blackfeet pass the right-hand, bent spoon-fashion, from the heel to the little toe of the right foot.—Ed.

have been exchanged, generally ride out and accompany the commander of the party some distance, holding a friendly talk, and, at the same time, indulging their curiosity by learning the news, etc. Phlegmatic and indifferent as they appear to be, they are very inquisitive and observing, and, at the same time, exceedingly circumspect and cautious about disclosing their own purposes.

They are always desirous of procuring, from whomsoever they meet, testimonials of their good behavior, which they preserve with great care, and exhibit upon all occasions to strangers as a guarantee of future good conduct.

On meeting with a chief of the Southern Comanches in 1849, after going through the usual ceremony of embracing, and assuring me that he was the best friend the Americans ever had among the Indians, he exhibited numerous certificates from the different white men he had met with, testifying to his friendly disposition. Among these was one that he desired me to read with special attention, as he said he was of the opinion that perhaps it might not be so complimentary in its character as some of the others. It was in these words:

> "The bearer of this says he is a Comanche chief, named Senaco; that he is the biggest Indian and best friend the whites ever had; in fact, that he is a first-rate fellow; but I believe he is a d—d rascal, *so look out for him.*"

I smiled on reading the paper, and, looking up, found the chief's eyes intently fixed upon mine with an expression of the most earnest inquiry. I told him the paper was not so good as it might be, whereupon he destroyed it.

Five years after this interview, I met Senaco again near the same place. He recognized me at once; and, much to my surprise, pronounced my name quite distinctly.

A circumstance which happened in my interview with this Indian, shows their character for diplomatic policy.

I was about locating and surveying a reservation of land upon which the government designed to establish the Comanches, and was desirous of ascertaining whether they were disposed voluntarily to come into the measure. In this connection, I stated to him that their Great Father, the President, being anxious to improve their condition, was willing to give them a permanent location, where they could cultivate the soil, and, if they wished it, he would send white men to teach them the rudiments of agriculture, supply them with farming utensils, and all other requisites for living comfortably in their new homes. I then desired him to consult with his people, and let me know what their views were upon the subject.

After talking a considerable time with his head men, he rose to reply, and said, "He was very happy to learn that the President remembered his poor red children in the Plains, and he was glad to see me again, and hear from me that their Great Father was their friend; that he was also very much gratified to meet his agent who was present, and he should remember with much satisfaction the agreeable interview we had had upon that occasion." After delivering himself of numerous other non-committal expressions of similar import, he closed his speech, and took his seat without making the slightest allusion to the subject in question.

On reminding him of this omission, and again demanding from him a distinct and categorical answer, he, after a brief consultation with his people, replied that his talk was made and concluded, and he did not comprehend why it was that I wanted to open the subject anew. But, as I continued to press him for an answer, he at length said, "You come into our country and select a small patch of ground, around which you run a line, and tell us the President will make us a present of this to live upon, when everybody knows that the whole of this entire country, from the Red River to the Colorado, is now, and always has been, ours from time immemorial. I suppose, however, if the President tells us to confine ourselves to these narrow limits, we shall be forced to do so, whether we desire it or not."

He was evidently averse to the proposed change in their mode of life, and has been at war ever since the establishment of the settlement.

The mode of life of the nomadic tribes, owing to their unsettled and warlike habits, is such as to render their condition one of constant danger and apprehension. The security of their numerous animals from the encroachments of their enemies, and habitual liability to attack, compels them to be at all times upon the alert. Even during profound peace they guard their herds both night and day, while scouts are often patrolling upon the surrounding heights to give notice of the approach of strangers, and enable them to secure their animals and take a defensive attitude.

When one of these people conceives himself injured, his thirst for revenge is insatiable. Grave and dignified in his outward bearing, and priding himself upon never exhibiting curiosity, joy, or anger, yet when once roused he evinces the implacable dispositions of his race; the affront is laid up and cherished in his breast, and nothing can efface it from his mind until ample reparation is made. The insult must be atoned for by presents, or be washed out with blood.

WAR EXPEDITIONS.

When a chief desires to organize a war-party, he provides himself with a long pole, attaches a red flag to the end of it, and trims the top with eagle feathers. He then mounts his horse in his war-costume, and rides around through the camp singing the war-song. Those who are disposed to join the expedition, mount their horses and fall into the procession; after parading about for a time, all dismount, and the war-dance is performed. This ceremony is continued from day to day, until a sufficient number of volunteers are found to accomplish the objects desired, when they set out for the theatre of their intended exploits.

As they proceed upon their expedition, it sometimes happens that the chief with whom it originated, and who invariably assumes the command, becomes discouraged at not finding an opportunity of displaying his warlike abilities, and abandons the enterprise; in which event, if others of the party desire to proceed farther, they select another leader, and push on, and thus so long as any one of the party holds out.

A war-party is sometimes absent for a great length of time, and for days, weeks, and months their friends at home anxiously await their return, until, suddenly, from afar, the shrill war-cry of an *avant courier* is heard proclaiming the approach of the victorious warriors. The camp is in an instant alive with excitement and commotion. Men, women, and children swarm out to meet the advancing party. Their white horses are painted and decked out in the most fantastic style, and led in advance of the triumphal procession; and, as they pass around through the village, the old women set up a most unearthly howl of exultation, after which the scalp-dance is performed with all the pomp and display their limited resources admit of, the warriors having their faces painted black.

When, on the other hand, the expedition terminates disastrously by the loss of some of the party in battle, the relatives of the deceased cut off their own hair, and the tails and manes of their horses, as symbols of mourning, and howl and cry for a long time.

In 1854, I saw the widow of a former chief of the Southern Comanches, whose husband had been dead about three years, yet she continued her mourning tribute to his memory, by crying daily for him and refusing all offers to marry again.

The prairie warrior is occasionally seen with the rifle in his hand, but his favorite arm is the bow, the use of which is taught him at an early age. By constant practice, he acquires a skill in archery that renders him no less formidable in war than successful in the chase. Their bows are usually made of the tough and elastic wood of the "*bois d'arc*," strengthened and re-inforced with sinews of the deer wrapped firmly around, and strung with a cord of the same material. They are from three to four feet long. The arrows, which are carried in a quiver upon the back, are about twenty inches long, of flexible wood, with a triangular iron point at one end, and at the other two feathers intersecting at right angles.*

At short distances (about fifty yards), the bow, in the hands of the Indian, is effective, and in close proximity with the buffalo throws the arrow entirely through his huge carcase. In using this weapon the warrior protects himself from the missiles of his enemy with a shield made of two thicknesses of undressed buffalo hide filled in with hair.

The Comanches, Sioux, and other prairie tribes make their attacks upon the open prairies. Trusting to their wonderful skill in equitation and horsemanship, they ride around their enemies with their bodies thrown upon the opposite side of the horse, and discharge their arrows in rapid succession while at full speed; they will not, however, often venture near an enemy who occupies a defensive position. If, therefore, a small party be in danger of an attack from a large force of Indians, they should seek the cover of timber or a park of wagons, or, in the absence of these, rocks or holes in the prairies which afford good cover.

Attempts to stampede animals are often made when parties first arrive in camp, and when every one's attention is pre-occupied in the arrangements therewith connected. In a country infested by hostile Indians, the ground in the vicinity of which it is proposed to encamp should be cautiously examined for tracks and other Indian *signs*, by making a circuit around the locality previous to unharnessing the animals.

After Indians have succeeded in stampeding a herd of horses or mules, and desire to drive them away, they are in the habit of pushing them forward as rapidly as possible for the first few days, in order to place a wide interval between themselves and any party that may be in pursuit.

In running off stolen animals, the Indians are generally divided into two parties, one for driving, and the other to act as a rear guard. Before they reach a place where they

* I have always seen *three* feathers, as in Europe, Asia, and Africa.—ED

propose making a halt, they leave a vidette upon some prominent point to watch for pursuers and give the main party timely warning, enabling them to rally their animals and push forward again.

TRACKING INDIANS.

When an Indian sentinel intends to watch for an enemy approaching from the rear, he selects the highest position available, and places himself near the summit, in such an attitude that his entire body shall be concealed from the observation of any one in the rear, his head only being exposed above the top of the eminence.* Here he awaits with great patience so long as he thinks there is any possibility of danger, and it will be difficult for an enemy to surprise him or to elude his keen and scrutinizing vigilance. Meanwhile his horse is secured under the screen of the hill, all ready when required. Hence it will be evident, that, in following Indian depredators, the utmost vigilance and caution must be exercised to conceal from them the movements of their pursuers. They are the best scouts in the world, proficient in all the artifices and stratagems available in border warfare, and, when hotly pursued by a superior force, after exhausting all other means of evasion, they scatter in different directions; and if, in a broken or mountainous country, they can do no better, abandon their horses and baggage, and take refuge in the rocks, gorges, or other hiding-places. This plan has several times been resorted to by Indians in Texas when surprised, and notwithstanding their pursuers were directly upon them, the majority made their escape, leaving behind all their animals and other property.

For overtaking a marauding party of Indians who have advanced eight or ten hours before the pursuing party are in readiness to take the trail, it is not best to push forward rapidly at first, as this will weary and break down horses. The Indians must be supposed to have at least fifty or sixty miles the start; it will, therefore, be useless to think

* The face is concealed by a tuft of grass or a bunch of wild sage held in the hand.—ED.

of overtaking them without providing for a long chase. Scouts should be continually kept out in front upon the trail to reconnoitre and give preconcerted signals to the main party when the Indians are espied.

In approaching all eminences or undulations in the prairies, the commander should be careful not to allow any considerable number of his men to pass upon the summits, until the country around has been carefully reconnoitred by the scouts, who will cautiously raise their eyes above the crests of the most elevated points, making a scrutinizing examination in all directions; and, while doing this, should an Indian be encountered who has been left behind as a sentinel, he must, if possible, be secured or shot, to prevent his giving the alarm to his comrades. These precautions cannot be too rigidly enforced when the trail becomes "warm;" and if there be a moon it will be better to lie by in the daytime and follow the trail at night, as the great object is to come upon the Indians when they are not anticipating an attack. Such surprises, if discreetly conducted, generally prove successful.

As soon as the Indians are discovered in their bivouac, the pursuing party should dismount, leave their horses under charge of a guard in some sequestered place, and, before advancing to the attack, the men should be instructed in signals for their different movements, such as all will easily comprehend and remember. As, for example, a pull upon the right arm may signify to face to the right, and a pull upon the left arm to face to the left; a pull upon the skirt of the coat, to halt; a gentle push on the back, to advance in ordinary time; a slap on the back, to advance in double quick time, etc., etc.

These signals, having been previously well understood and practised, may be given by the commander to the man next to him, and from him communicated in rapid succession throughout the command.

I will suppose the party formed in one rank, with the commander on the right. He gives the signal, and the men move off cautiously in the direction indicated. The importance of not losing sight of his comrades on his right and left, and of not allowing them to get out of his reach, so as to break the chain of communication, will be apparent to all, and great care should be taken that the men do not mistake their brothers in arms for the enemy. This may be prevented by having two *pass-words,* and when there is any doubt as to the identity of two men who meet during the night-operations, one of these words may be repeated by each. Above all, the men must be fully impressed with the importance of not firing a shot until the order is given by the commanding officer, and also that a rigorous personal accountability will be enforced in all cases of a violation of this rule.

If the commander gives the signal for commencing the attack by firing a pistol or gun, there will probably be no mistake, unless it happens through carelessness by the accidental discharge of fire-arms.

I can conceive of nothing more appalling, or that tends more to throw men off their guard and produce confusion, than a sudden and unexpected night-attack. Even the Indians, who pride themselves upon their coolness and self-possession, are far from being exempt from its effects; and it is not surprising that men who go to sleep with a sense of perfect security around them, and are suddenly aroused from a sound slumber by the terrific sounds of an onslaught from an enemy, should lose their presence of mind.

TELEGRAPHING BY SMOKES.

The transparency of the atmosphere upon the Plains is such that objects can be seen at great distances; a mountain, for example, presents a distinct and bold outline at fifty or sixty miles, and may occasionally be seen as far as a hundred miles.

The Indians, availing themselves of this fact, have been in the habit of practising a system of telegraphing by means of smokes during the day and fires by night; and, I dare say, there are but few travelers who have crossed the mountains to California that have not seen these signals made and responded to from peak to peak in rapid succession.

The Indians thus make known to their friends many items of information highly important to them. If enemies or strangers make their appearance in the country, the fact is telegraphed at once, giving them time to secure their animals and to prepare for attack, defence, or flight.*

War or hunting parties, after having been absent a long time from their erratic friends at home, and, not knowing where to find them, make use of the same preconcerted signals to indicate their presence.

Very dense smokes may be raised by kindling a large fire with dry wood, and piling upon it the green boughs of pine, balsam, or hemlock. This throws off a heavy cloud of black smoke which can be seen very far.

This simple method of telegraphing, so useful to the savages both in war and in peace, may, in my judgment, be used to advantage in the movements of troops cooperating in separate columns in the Indian country.

I shall not attempt at this time to present a matured system of signals, but will merely give a few suggestions tending to illustrate the advantages to be derived from the use of them.

For example, when two columns are marching through a country at such distances apart, that smokes may be seen from one to the other, their respective positions may be

* When Indians are pursued by a large force, and do not intend to make resistance, they generally scatter as much as possible, in order to perplex and throw off those who follow their trail; but they have an understanding where they are to rendezvous in advance. Sometimes, however, circumstances may arise during a rapid flight, making it necessary for them to alter these plans, and turn their course in another direction. When this happens, they are in the habit of leaving behind them some well-understood signals to indicate to their friends in the rear the change in their movements.

For instance, they will sometimes leave a stick or other object to attract attention ; and, under this, bury an arrow pointing in the new direction they intend to take. They will then continue on for a time in the course they have been pursuing, until they get upon hard ground, where it is difficult to see their tracks, then gradually turn their course in the new direction.—AUTHOR.

made known to each other at any time by two smokes raised simultaneously or at certain pre-concerted intervals.

Should the commander of one column desire to communicate with the other, he raises three smokes simultaneously, which, if seen by the other party, should be responded to in the same manner. They would then hold themselves in readiness for any other communications.

If an enemy is discovered in small numbers, a smoke raised twice at fifteen minutes' interval would indicate it; and, if in large forcc, three times with the same intervals might be the signal.

Should the commander of one party desire the other to join him, this might be telegraphed by four smokes at ten minutes' interval.

Should it become necessary to change the direction of the line of march, the commander may transmit the order by means of two simultaneous smokes raised a certain number of times to indicate the particular direction; for instance, twice for north, three times for south, four times for east, and five times for west; three smokes raised twice for north-east, three times for north-west, etc., etc.*

By multiplying the combinations of signals a great variety of messages might be transmitted in this manner; but, to avoid mistakes, the signals should be written down, and copies furnished the commander of each separate party, and they need not necessarily be made known to other persons.

During the day an intelligent man should be detailed to keep a vigilant look-out in all directions for smokes, and he should be furnished with a watch, pencil, and paper, to make a record of the signals, with their number, and the time of the intervals between them.

* This rude semaphore is known to most savages. The Western Africans, to quote no others, still telegraph to slavers in the offing by means of smokes.—Ed.

NOTE (Referred to at Page 143).

Referring to a previous page, I here present the reader with a few specimens of pantomimic expressions, borrowed from the City of the Saints, chap. ii. An illustrated description of the natural gestures used by Surdo-Mutes would be highly desirable, as a basis for the formation of an organized system of easy communication between men ignoring each other's tongues. I venture to recommend the subject to those who have studied signs as well as words. My calculation is, that with 100 vocables, and an intelligible pantomime, one may express any want or wish. It sounds like reducing the speaking man to the level of the dumb; but Nature herself gives the hint.

The following vocabulary, if I may so call it, consists of about a hundred word-signs, and the reader will be surprised to see how much can be explained by it.

Halt! — Raise the hand, with the palm in front, and push it backwards and forwards several times—a gesture well known in the East.

I don't know you! — Move the raised hand, with the palm in front, slowly to the right and left.

I am angry!—Close the fist, place it against the forehead, and turn it to and fro in that position.

Are you friendly?—Raise both hands, grasped, as if in the act of shaking hands, or lock the two forefingers together while the hands are raised.

These signs will be found useful upon the prairie in case of meeting a suspected band. The Indians, like the Bedouin and North-African Moslems, do honour to strangers and guests by putting their horses to speed, couching their lances, and other peculiarities, which would readily be dispensed with by gentlemen of peaceful pursuits and shaky nerves. If friendly, the band will halt when the hint is given and return the salute: if surly, they will disregard the command to stop, and probably will make the sign of anger. Then—ware scalp!

Come!—Beckon with the forefinger, as in Europe, not as is done in the East.

Come back!—Beckon in the European way, and draw the forefinger towards yourself.

Go!—Move both hands edgeways (the palms fronting the breast) towards the left with a rocking-horse motion.

Sit!—Make a motion towards the ground, as if to pound it with the ferient of the closed hand.

Lie down!—Point to the ground, and make a motion as if of lying down.

Sleep!—Ditto, closing the eyes.

Look! — Touch the right eye with the index and point it outwards.

Hear !—Tap the right ear with the index tip.

Colours are expressed by a comparison with some object in sight. Many things, as the blowing of wind, the cries of beasts and birds, and the roaring of the sea are imitated by sound.

See !—Strike out the two forefingers forward from the eyes.

Smell !—Touch the nose tip. A bad smell is expressed by the same sign, ejaculating at the same time "pooh!" and making the sign of bad.

Taste !—Touch the tongue tip.

Eat ! —Imitate the action of conveying food with the fingers to the mouth.

Drink ! —Scoop up with the hand imaginary water into the mouth.

Smoke !—With the crooked index describe a pipe in the air, beginning at the lips; then wave the open hand from the mouth to imitate curls of smoke.

Speak !—Extend the open hand from the chin.

Fight !—Make a motion with both fists to and fro, like a pugilist of the eighteenth century who preferred a high guard.

Kill !—Smite the sinister palm earthwards with the dexter fist sharply, in sign of "going down;" or strike out with the dexter fist towards the ground, meaning to "shut down;" or pass the dexter index under the left forefinger, meaning to "go under."

To show that fighting is actually taking place, make the gestures as above described; tap the lips with the palm like an Oriental woman when "keening," screaming the while O-a! O-a! to imitate the war-song.

Wash !—Rub the hand as with invisible soap in imperceptible water.

Think !—Pass the forefinger sharply across the breast from right to left.

Hide !—Place the hand inside the clothing of the left breast. This means also to put away or to keep secret. To express "I won't say," make the sign of "I" and "no" (which see), and hide the hand as above directed.

Love !—Fold the hands crosswise over the breast, as if embracing the object, assuming at the same time a look expressing the desire to carry out the operation. This gesture will be understood by the dullest squaw.

Tell truth !—Extend the forefinger from the mouth ("one word").

Tell lie !—Extend the two first fingers from the mouth ("double tongue," a significant gesture).

Steal !—Seize an imaginary object with the right hand from under the left fist. To express horse-stealing, they saw with the right hand down upon the extended finger of the left, thereby denoting rope-cutting.

Trade or Exchange!—Cross the forefingers of both hands before the breast—"diamond cut diamond."

This sign also denotes the Americans, and indeed any white men, who are generically called by the Indians west of the Rocky Mountains "Shwop," from our swap or swop, an Anglo-Romany word for barter or exchange.

The pronouns are expressed by pointing to the person designated. For "I," touch the nose-tip, or otherwise indicate self with the index. The second and third persons are similarly made known.

Every animal has its precise sign, and the choice of gesture is sometimes very ingenious. If the symbol be not known, the form may be drawn on the ground; and the strong perceptive faculties of the savage enable him easily to recognise even rough draughts. A cow or a sheep denotes white men, as if they were their totems. The Indian's high development of locality also enables him to map the features of a country readily and correctly upon the sand. Moreover, almost every grand feature has a highly significant name—the Flint-water River, for instance, and nothing is easier than to combine the signs.

The *bear* is expressed by passing the hand before the face to mean ugliness, as the same time grinning and extending the fingers like claws.

The *buffalo* is known by raising the forefingers crooked inwards, in the semblance of horns on both sides of the head.

The *elk* is signified by simultaneously raising both hands, with the fingers extended on both sides of the head, to imitate palmated horns.

For the *deer*, extend the thumbs and the two forefingers of each hand on each side of the head.

For the *antelope*, extend the thumbs and forefingers along the sides of the head to simulate ears and horns.

Mountain sheep are denoted by placing the hands on a level with the ears, the palms facing backwards, and the fingers slightly reversed, to imitate the ammonite-shaped horns.

For the *beaver*, describe a parenthesis, *e.g.* ( ), with the thumb and index of both hands, and then with the dexter index imitate the wagging of the tail.

The *dog* is shown by drawing horizontally across the breast, from right to left the two forefingers slightly opened. This is a highly appropriate and a traditional gesture. Before the introduction of horses, the dog was taught to carry the tent-poles, and the motion expressed the lodge-trail.

To denote the *mule* or *ass*, the long ears are imitated by the indices on both sides and above the head.

For the *crow*, and indeed any bird, the hands are flapped near the shoulders. If specification be required, the cry is imitated, or some peculiarity is introduced. The following will show the ingenuity with which the Indian can convey his meaning under difficulties. A Yuta wishing to explain that the torpedo or gymnotus eel is found in Cottonwood Kanyon Lake, took to it thus :—He made the body by extending his sinister index to the fore, touched it with the dexter index at two points on both sides to show legs, and finally sharply withdrew his right forefinger, to convey the idea of an electric shock.

Some of the symbols of relationship are highly appropriate, and not ungraceful or unpicturesque. Man is denoted by a sign somewhat too expressive for description ; woman, by passing the hand down both sides of the head, as if smoothing or stroking the long hair. A son or daughter is expressed by making with the hand a movement denoting issue from the loins ; if the child be small, a bit of the index held between the antagonised thumb and medius is shown. The same sign of issue expresses both parents, with additional explanations. To say, for instance, "*my mother*," you would first pantomime "*I*," or, which is the same thing, "*my*," then "*woman*," and, finally, the symbol of parentage. "*My grandmother*" would be conveyed in the same way, adding to the end clasped hands, closed eyes, and like an old woman's bent back. The sign for brother and sister is perhaps the prettiest: the two first fingertips are put into the mouth, denoting that they fed from the same breast. For the wife (squaw is now becoming a word of reproach amongst the Indians) the dexter forefinger is passed between the extended thumb and index of the left.

Of course, there is a sign for every weapon. The *knife* (scalp or other) is shown by cutting the sinister palm with the dexter ferient downwards and towards oneself; if the cuts be made upward with the palm downwards, meat is understood. The *tomahawk*, hatchet, or axe, is denoted by chopping the left hand with the right; the *sword*, by the motion of drawing it; the *bow*, by the movement of bending it ; and a *spear* or *lance* by an imitation of darting it. For the *gun*, the dexter thumb and fingers are flashed or scattered, *i.e.*, thrown outwards and upwards to denote fire. The same movement, made lower down, expresses a *pistol*. The *arrow* is expressed by nocking it upon an imaginary bow, and by "snapping" with the index and medius. The *shield* is shown by pointing with the index over the left shoulder, where it is slung ready to be brought over the breast when required.

The following are the most useful words:—

Yes.—Wave the hands straight forwards from the face.

No.—Wave the hand from right to left, as if motioning away. This sign also means, "I'll have nothing to do with you." Done slowly and insinuatingly, it informs a woman that she is *charmante*, "not to be touched" being the idea.

Good.—Wave the hand from the mouth, extending the thumb from the index, and closing the other three fingers. This sign means also, "I know." "I don't know" is expressed by waving the right hand, with the palm outwards, before the right breast; or by moving about the two forefingers before the breast, meaning "two hearts."

Bad.—Scatter the dexter fingers outwards, as if spirting away water from them.

Now (*at once*).—Clap both palms together sharply and repeatedly; or make the sign of "to-day."

Day.—Make a circle with the thumb and forefinger of both, in sign of the sun. The hour is pointed out by showing the luminary's place in the heavens. The moon is expressed by a crescent with the thumb and forefinger: This also denotes a month. For a year give the sign of rain or snow.

Many Indians ignore the quadripartite division of the seasons, which seems to be an invention of European latitudes; the Persians, for instance, know it, but the Hindus do not. They have, however distinct terms for the month, all of which are pretty and descriptive, appropriate and poetical; *e.g.*, the moon of light nights, the moon of leaves, the moon of strawberries, for April, May, and June. The Ojibwe have a queer quarternal division, called Of Sap, Of Abundance, Of Fading, and Of Freezing. The Dakota reckon five moons to winter, and five to summer, leaving one to spring, and one to autumn; the year is lunar, and as the change of season is denoted by the appearance of sore eyes and of racoons, any irregularity throws the people out.

Night.—Make a closing movement, as if of the darkness, by bringing together both hands with the dorsa upwards and the fingers to the fore. The motion is from right to left; and, at the end, the two indices are alongside and close to each other. This movement must be accompanied by bending forward with bowed head, otherwise it may be misunderstood for the freezing over of a lake or river.

To-day.—Touch the nose with the index tip, and motion with the fist towards the ground.

Yesterday.—Make, with the left hand, the circle which the sun describes from sunrise to sunset, or invert the direction from sunset to sunrise with the right hand.

To-morrow.—Describe the motion of the sun from east to west. Any number of days may be counted upon the fingers. The latter, I need hardly say, are the only numerals in the pantomimic vocabulary.

Among the Dakotas, when they have gone over the fingers and thumbs of both hands, one is temporarily turned down for one ten: at the end of another ten a second finger is turned down, and so on, as amongst children who are learning to count. "Opawinge," one hundred, is derived from "pawinga," to go round in circles, as the fingers have all been gone over again for their respective tens; "keptopawinge" is from "ake," and "opawinge,"—"hundred again," being about to recommence the circle of their fingers already completed in hundreds. For numerals above a thousand there is no method of computing. There is a sign and word for one half of a thing, but none to denote any smaller aliquot part.

Peace.—Intertwine the fingers of both hands.

Friendship.—Clasp the left with the right hand.

Glad (pleased).—Wave the open hand outwards from the breast, to express "good heart."

A Cup.—Imitate its form with both hands, and make the sign of drinking from it. In this way any utensil can be intelligibly described—of course provided that the interlocutor has seen it.

Paint.—Daub both the cheeks downwards with the index.

Looking-glass.—Place both palms before the face, and admire your countenance in them.

Bead.—Point to a bead, or make the sign of a necklace.

Wire.—Show it, or where it ought to be, in the ear-lobe.

Whiskey.—Make the sign of "bad" and "drink" for "bad water."

Blanket or Clothes.—Put them on in pantomime.

A Lodge.—Place the fingers of both hands ridge-fashion before the breast.

Fire.—Blow it and warm the hands before it. To express the boiling of a kettle, the sign of fire is made low down, and an imaginary pot is eaten from.

It is cold.—Wrap up, shudder, and look disagreeable.

Rain.—Scatter the fingers downwards. The same sign denotes snow.

Wind.—Stretch the fingers of both hands outward, puffing violently the while.

A Storm.—Make the rain sign; then, if thunder and lightning are to be expressed, move, as if in anger, the body to and fro, to show the wrath of the elements.

A Stone.—If light, act as if picking it up: if heavy, as if dropping it.

A Hill.—Close the finger-tips over the head; if a mountain is to be expressed, raise them high. To denote an ascent on rising ground, pass the right palm over the left hand, half doubling up the latter, so that it looks like a ridge.

A Plain.—Wave both the palms outward and low down.

A River.—Make the sign of drinking, and then wave both the palms outwards. A rivulet, creek, or stream is shown by the drinking sign, and by holding the index tip between the thumb and medius; an arroyo (dry water-course), by covering up the tip with the thumb and middle finger.

A Lake.—Make the sign of drinking, and form a basin with both hands. If a large body of water is in question, wave both palms outwards, as in denoting a plain. The prairie savages have never seen the sea, so it would be vain to attempt explanation.

A Book.—Place the right palm on the left palm, and then open both before the face.

A Letter.—Write with the thumb and dexter index on the sinister palm.

A Waggon.—Roll hand over hand, imitating a wheel.

A Waggon-road.—Make the waggon sign, and then wave the hand along the ground.

Grass.—Point to the ground with the index, and then turn the fingers upwards to denote growth. If the grass be long, raise the hand high ; and if yellow, point out that colour.

The pantomime, as may be seen, is capable of expressing detailed narratives. For instance, supposing an Indian would tell the following tale :—"Early this morning, I mounted my horse, rode off at a gallop, traversed a kanyon or ravine, then over a mountain to a plain where there was no water, sighted bison, followed them, killed three of them, skinned them, packed the flesh upon my pony, remounted and returned home"—he would symbolise it thus :—

Touches nose—"*I.*"

Opens out the palms of his hand—"*this morning.*"

Points to east—"*early.*"

Places two dexter forefingers astraddle over sinister index—"*mounted my horse.*"

Moves both hands upwards and rocking-horse fashion towards the left—"*galloped.*"

Passes the dexter hand right through thumb and forefinger of the sinister, which are widely extended—"*traversed a kanyon.*"

Closes the finger-tips high over the head, and waves both palms outwards—"*over a mountain to a plain.*"

Scoops up with the hand imaginary water into the mouth, and then waves the hand from the face to denote "no"—"*where there was no water.*"

Touches eyes—"*sighted.*"

Raises the forefingers crooked inwards on both sides of the head—"*bison.*"

Smites the sinister palm downwards with the dexter fist—"*killed.*"

Shows three fingers—"*three of them.*"

Scrapes the left palm with the edge of the right hand—"*skinned them.*"

Places the dexter on the sinister palm, and then the dexter palm on the sinister dorsum—"*packed the flesh upon my pony.*"

Straddles the two forefingers on the index of the left—"*remounted ;*" and finally,

Beckons towards self—"*returned home.*"

To conclude, I can hardly flatter myself that these descriptions have been made quite intelligible to the reader. They may, however, serve to prepare his mind for a *vivâ voce* lesson upon the prairies, should fate have such thing in store for him.—Ed.

CHAPTER VII.

Hunting.—Its Benefits to the Soldier.—Buffalo.—Deer.—Antelope. —Bear.—Big-horn, or Mountain Sheep.—Their Habits, and Hints upon the best Methods of hunting them.

HUNTING.

I KNOW of no better school of practice for perfecting men in target-firing, and the use of fire-arms generally, than that in which the frontier hunter receives his education. One of the first and most important lessons that he is taught, impresses him with the conviction that, unless his gun is in good order, and steadily directed upon the game, he must go without his supper; and if ambition does not stimulate his efforts, his appetite will, and ultimately lead to success and confidence in his own powers.

The man who is afraid to place the butt of his piece firmly against his shoulder, or who turns away his head at the instant of pulling trigger (as soldiers often do before they have been drilled at target-practice), will not be likely to bag much game, or to contribute materially towards the result of a battle. The successful hunter, as a general rule, is a good shot, will always charge his gun properly, and may be relied upon in action. I would, therefore, when in garrison or at permanent camps, encourage officers and soldiers in field-sports. If permitted, men very readily cultivate a fondness for these innocent and healthy exercises, and occupy their leisure time in their pursuits; whereas, if confined to the narrow limits of a frontier camp or garrison, having no amusements within their reach, they are prone to indulge in practices which are highly detrimental to their physical and moral condition.

By making short excursions about the country, they acquire a knowledge of it, become inured to fatigue, learn the art of bivouacking, trailing, etc., etc., all of which will be found serviceable in border warfare; and, even if they should perchance now and then miss some of the minor routine duties of the garrison, the benefits they would derive from hunting would, in my opinion, more than counterbalance its effects. Under the old regime, it was thought that drills, dress-parades, and guard-mountings, comprehended the sum total of the soldier's education, but the experience of the last ten years has taught us that these are only the rudiments, and that to combat successfully with Indians, we must receive instruction from them, study their tactics, and, where they suit our purposes, copy from them.

The union of discipline with the individuality, self-reliance, and rapidity of locomotion of the savage is what we should aim at. This will be the tendency of the course indicated; and it is conceived by the writer that an army composed of well-disciplined hunters will be the most efficient of all others against the only enemy we have to encounter within the limits of our vast possessions.

I find some pertinent remarks upon this subject in a very sensible essay by "a late captain of infantry" (U.S.). He says:—

"It is conceived that scattered bands of mounted hunters, with the speed of a horse and the watchfulness of a wolf or antelope, whose faculties are sharpened by their necessities; who, when they get short of provisions, separate and look for something to eat, and find it in the water, in the ground, or on the surface; whose bill of fare ranges from grass-seed, nuts, roots, grasshoppers, lizards, and rattle-snakes, up to the antelope, deer, elk, bear, and buffalo, and who have a continent to roam over, will be neither surprised, caught, conquered, overawed, or reduced to famine by a rumbling, bugle-blowing, drum-beating town passing through their country on wheels at the speed of a loaded wagon.*

"If the Indians are in the path and do not wish to be seen, they cross a ridge, and the town moves on, ignorant whether there are fifty Indians within a mile, or no Indian within fifty miles. If the Indians wish to see, they return to the crest of the ridge, crawl up to the edge, pull up a bunch of grass by the roots, and look through or under it at the procession."

Although I would always encourage men in hunting when permanently located; yet, unless you are good woodsmen, it is not safe to permit them to go out alone in marching through the Indian country, as, aside from the danger of encountering Indians, they would be liable to become bewildered and lost, and this might detain the entire party in searching for them. The better plan upon a march is for three or four to go out together, accompanied by a good woodsman, who will be able with certainty to lead them back to camp.

The little group could ascertain if Indians are about, and would be strong enough to act on the defensive against small parties of them; and, while they are amusing themselves, they may perform an important part as scouts and flankers.

An expedition may have been perfectly organised, and everything provided that the wisest forethought could suggest, yet circumstances beyond the control of the most experienced traveler may sometimes arise to defeat the best concerted plans. It is not, for example, an impossible contingency that the traveler may, by unforeseen delays,

* The late "Captain of Infantry (U.S.)" is Captain Patterson. Sir Francis Head ("Gallop over the Pampas,") falls into the same error of praising savage at the expense of civilized warfare. Without entering into the subject further than is necessary, I may remark, that the Sindh Camel Corps would more than match in marching any equestrian Indians, from the Comanche to the Pampero. The reader will find the matter discussed at greater length in the City of the Saints, chap. i.—Ed.

consume his provisions, lose them in crossing streams, or have them stolen by hostile Indians, and be reduced to the necessity of depending upon game for subsistence. Under these circumstances, a few observations upon the habits of the different animals that frequent the Plains and on the best methods of hunting them may not be altogether devoid of interest or utility in this connection.

THE BUFFALO.

The largest and most useful animal that roams over the prairies is the buffalo. It provides food, clothing, and shelter to thousands of natives whose means of livelihood depend almost exclusively upon this "gigantic monarch of the prairies."

Not many years since they thronged in countless multitudes over all that vast area lying between Mexico and the British possessions; but now their range is confined within very narrow limits, and a few more years will probably witness the extinction of the species.

The traveler, in passing from Texas or Arkansas through southern New Mexico to California, does not, at the present day, encounter the buffalo; but upon all the routes north of latitude 36° the animal is still found between the 99th and 102nd meridians of longitude.

Although generally regarded as migratory in their habits, yet the buffalo often *winter* in the snows of a high northern latitude. Early in the spring of 1858, I found them in the Rocky Mountains, at the head of the Arkansas and South Platte Rivers; and there was every indication that this was a permanent abiding place for them.

There are two methods generally practised in hunting the buffalo, viz.: running them on horseback, and stalking, or still-hunting. The first method requires a sure-footed and tolerably fleet horse that is not easily frightened. The buffalo cow, which makes much better beef than the bull, when pursued by the hunter runs rapidly, and, unless the horse be fleet, it requires a long and exhausting chase to overtake her.

When the buffalo are discovered, and the hunter intends

to give chase, he should first dismount, arrange his saddle-blanket and saddle, buckle the girth tight, and make everything about his horse furniture snug and secure. He should then put his arms in good firing order, and, taking the lee side of the herd, so that they may not get "*the wind*" of him, he should approach in a walk as close as possible, taking advantage of any cover that may offer. His horse then, being cool and fresh, will be able to dash into the herd, and probably carry his rider very near the animal he has selected before he becomes alarmed.

If the hunter be right-handed, and uses a pistol, he should approach upon the left side, and when nearly opposite and close upon the buffalo, deliver his shot, taking aim a little below the centre of the body, and about eight inches behind the shoulder. This will strike the vitals, and generally render another shot unnecessary.

When a rifle or shot-gun is used, the hunter rides up on the right side, keeping his horse well in hand, so as to be able to turn off if the beast charges upon him ; this, however, never happens except with a buffalo that is wounded, when it is advisable to keep out of his reach.

The buffalo has immense powers of endurance, and will run for many miles without any apparent effort or diminution in speed. The first buffalo I ever saw I followed about ten miles, and when I left him he seemed to run faster than when the chase commenced.

As a long buffalo-chase is very severe labor upon a horse, I would recommend to all travelers, unless they have a good deal of surplus horse-flesh, never to expend it in running buffalo.

Still-hunting, which requires no consumption of horse-flesh, and is equally successful with the other method, is recommended. In stalking on horse-back, the most broken and hilly localities should be selected, as these will furnish cover to the hunter, who passes from the crest of one hill to another, examining the country carefully in all directions. When the game is discovered, if it happen to be on the lee side, the hunter should endeavor, by making a wide détour, to get upon the opposite side, as he will find it impossible to approach within rifle range with the wind.

When the animal is upon a hill, or in any other position where he cannot be approached without danger of disturbing him, the hunter should wait until hc moves off to more favorable ground; and this will not generally require much time, as they wander about a great deal when not grazing; he then pickets his horse,and approaches cautiously, seeking to screen himself as much as possible by the undulations in the surface, or behind such other objects as may present themselves; but if the surface should offer no cover, he must crawl upon his hands and knees when near the game, and in this way he can generally get within rifle range.

Should there be several animals together, and his first shot take effect, the hunter can often get several other shots before they become frightened. A Delaware Indian and myself once killed five buffaloes out of a small herd, before the remainder were so much disturbed as to move away; although we were within the short distance of twenty yards, yet the reports of our rifles did not frighten them in the least, and they continued grazing during all the time we were loading and firing.

The sense of smelling is exceedingly acute with the buffalo, and they will take the wind from the hunter at as great a distance as a mile.

When the animal is wounded, and stops, it is better not to go near him until he lies down, as he will often run a great distance if disturbed; but if left to himself, will, in many cases, die in a short time.

The tongues, humps, and marrow-bones are regarded as the choice parts of the animal. The tongue is taken out by ripping open the skin between the prongs of the lower jaw-bone and pulling it out through the orifice. The hump may be taken off by skinning down on each side of the shoulders and cutting away the meat, after which the hump-ribs can be unjointed where they unite with the spine. The marrow, when roasted in the bones, is delicious.

THE DEER.

Of all game quadrupeds indigenous to this continent, the common red deer is probably more widely dispersed from north to south and from east to west over our vast possessions than any other. They are found in all latitudes, from Hudson's Bay to Mexico, and they clamber over the most elevated peaks of the western sierras with the same ease that they range the eastern forests or the ever-green glades of Florida. In summer they crop the grass upon summits of the Rocky Mountains, and in winter, when the snow falls deep, they descend into sheltered valleys, where they fall an easy prey to the Indians.

Besides the common red deer of the Eastern States, two other varieties are found in the Rocky Mountains, viz., the "black-tailed deer," which takes its name from the fact of its having a small tuft of black hair upon the end of its tail, and the *lony-tailed* species. The former of these is considerably larger than the eastern deer, and is much darker, being of a very deep-yellowish iron-gray, with a yellowish red upon the belly. It frequents the mountains, and is never seen far away from them. Its habits are similar to those of the red deer, and it is hunted in the same way. The only difference I have been able to discern between the long-tailed variety and the common deer is in the length of the tail and body. I have seen this animal only in the neighbourhood of the Rocky Mountains; but it may resort to other localities.

Although the deer are still abundant in many of our forest districts in the east, and do not appear to decrease very rapidly, yet there has, within a few years, been a very evident diminution in the numbers of those frequenting our Western prairies. In passing through Southern Texas in 1846, thousands of deer were met with daily; and, astonishing as it may appear, it was no uncommon spectacle to see from one to two hundred in a single herd; the prairies seemed literally alive with them; but in 1855 it was seldom that a herd of ten was seen in the same localities. It seemed to me that the vast herds first met with could not have been killed off by the hunters in that sparsely-populated section; and I was puzzled to know what had become of them. It is possible they may have moved off into Mexico. They certainly are not in our territory at the present time.

Twenty years' experience in deer-hunting has taught me several facts relative to the habits of the animal which, when well understood, will be found of much service to the inexperienced hunter, and greatly contribute to his success. The best target-shots are not necessarily the most skilful deer-stalkers. One of the great secrets of this art is in knowing how to approach the game without giving alarm; and this cannot easily be done unless the hunter sees it before he is himself discovered. There are so many objects in the woods resembling the deer in colour that none but a practised eye can often detect the difference.

When the deer is reposing, he generally turns head from the wind, in which position he can see an enemy approaching from that direction; and his nose will apprise him of the presence of danger from the opposite side. The best method of hunting deer, therefore, is *across the wind.*

While the deer are feeding, early in the morning and a short time before dark in the evening,* are the best times to stalk them, as they are then busily occupied and less on the alert. When a deer is espied with his head down, cropping the grass, the hunter advances cautiously, keeping his eyes constantly directed upon him, and screening himself behind intervening objects, or, in the absence of other cover, crawls along upon his hands and knees in the grass, until the deer hears his steps and raises his head. when he must instantly stop and remain in an attitude fixed and motionless as a statue, for the animal's vision is his keenest sense. When alarmed he will detect the

* In most countries wild animals become very shy about evening time, when instinct warns them to seek safe places for the night's rest.—ED.

slightest movement of a small object, and, unless the hunter stands or lies perfectly still, his presence will be detected. If the hunter does not move, the deer will, after a short time, recover from his alarm, and resume his grazing, when he may be again approached. The deer always exhibits his alarm by a sudden jerking of the tail just before he raises his head.

I once saw a Delaware Indian walk directly up within rifle range of a deer that was feeding upon the open prairie and shoot him down; he was, however, a long time in approaching, and made frequent halts whenever the animal flirted his tail and raised his head. Although he often turned toward the hunter, yet he did not appear to notice him, probably taking him for a stump or a tree.

When the deer are lying down in the smooth prairie, unless the grass is tall, it is difficult to get near them, as they are generally looking around, and become alarmed at the least noise.

The Indians are in the habit of using a small instrument which imitates the bleat of the young fawn, with which they lure the doe within range of their rifles. The young fawn gives out no scent upon its track until it is sufficiently grown to make good running, and instinct teaches the mother that this wise provision of nature to preserve the helpless little quadruped from the ravages of wolves, panthers, and other carnivorous beasts, will be defeated if she remains with it, as her tracks cannot be concealed. She, therefore, hides her fawn in the grass, where it is almost impossible to see it, even when very near it, goes off to some neighbouring thicket within call, and makes her bed alone. The Indian pot-hunter, who is but little scrupulous as to the means he employs in accomplishing his ends, sounds the bleat along near the places where he thinks the game is lying, and the unsuspicious doe, who imagines that her offspring is in distress, rushes with headlong impetuosity toward the sound, and often goes within a few yards of the hunter to receive her death-wound.

This is cruel sport, and can only be justified when meat

is scarce, which is very frequently the case in the Indian's larder.

It does not always comport with a man's feelings of security, especially if he happens to be a little nervous, to sound the deer-bleat in a wild region of country. I once undertook to experiment with the instrument myself, and made my first essay in attempting to call up an antelope which I discovered in the distance. I succeeded admirably in luring the wary victim within shooting range, had raised upon my knee, and was just in the act of pulling trigger, when a rustling in the grass on my left drew my attention in that direction, where, much to my surprise, I beheld a huge panther within about twenty yards, bounding with gigantic strides directly toward me. I turned my rifle, and in an instant, much to my relief and gratification, its contents were lodged in the heart of the beast.

Many men, when they suddenly encounter a deer, are seized with nervous excitement, called, in sporting parlance, the "*buck fever,*" which causes them to fire at random. Notwithstanding I have had much experience in hunting, I must confess that I am never entirely free from some of the symptoms of this malady, when firing at large game; and I believe that in four out of five cases where I have missed the game, my balls have passed too high. I have endeavoured to obviate this by sighting my rifle low; and it has been attended with more successful results. The same remarks apply to most other men I have met with. They fire too high when excited.*

THE ANTELOPE.

This animal frequents the most elevated bleak and naked prairies in all latitudes from Mexico to Oregon, and constitutes an important item of subsistence with many of the Prairie Indians. It is the most wary, timid, and fleet animal that inhabits the Plains. It is about the size of a small deer, with a heavy coating of coarse, wiry hair, and

* High firing, with some recruits, is a kind of disease. I have seen men elevate their pieces to an angle of 45°.

its flesh is more tender and juicy than that of the deer. It seldom enters a timbered country, but seems to delight in cropping the grass from the elevated swells of the prairies. When disturbed by the traveler, it will circle around him with the speed of the wind, but does not stop until it reaches some prominent position, whence it can survey the country on all sides, and nothing seems to escape its keen vision. They will sometimes stand for a long time and look at a man, provided he does not move or go out of sight; but if he goes behind a hill, with the intention of passing around and getting nearer to them, he will never find them again in the same place. I have often tried the experiment, and invariably found, that, so soon as I went where the antelope could not see me, he moved off. Their sense of hearing, as well as vision, is very acute, which renders it difficult to stalk them. By taking advantage of the cover afforded in broken ground, the hunter may, by moving slowly and cautiously over the crests of the irregularities in the surface, sometimes approach within rifle-range.

The antelope possesses a greater degree of curiosity than any other animal I know of, and will often approach very near a strange object.* The experienced hunter, taking advantage of this peculiarity, lies down and secretes himself in the grass, after which he raises his handkerchief, hand, or foot, so as to attract the attention of the animal, and thus often succeeds in beguiling him within shooting distance.

In some valleys near the Rocky Mountains, where the pasturage is good during the winter season, they collect in immense herds. The Indians are in the habit of surrounding them in such localities and running them with their horses until they tire them out, when they slay large numbers.

The antelope makes a track much shorter than the deer,

* Curiosity is a *faiblesse* with many species of wild animals. A red flag hoisted high will cause a hippopotamus to raise his head out of water, for a full minute.—Ed.

very broad and round at the heel, and quite sharp at the toe; a little experience renders it easy to distinguish them.

THE BEAR.

Besides the common black bear of the Eastern States, several others are found in the mountains of California, Oregon, Utah, and New Mexico, viz., the grizzly, brown, and cinnamon varieties; all have nearly the same habits, and are hunted in the same manner.

From all I had heard of the grizzly bear, I was induced to believe him one of the most formidable and savage animals in the universe, and that the man who would deliberately encounter and kill one of these beasts had performed a signal feat of courage which entitled him to a lofty position among the votaries of Nimrod. So firmly had I become impressed with this conviction, that I should have been very reluctant to fire upon one had I met him when alone and on foot. The grizzly bear is assuredly the monarch of the American forests, and, so far as physical strength is concerned, he is perhaps without a rival in the world; but, after some experience in hunting, my opinions regarding his courage and his willingness to attack men have very materially changed.

In passing over the elevated table-lands lying between the two forks of the Platte River in 1858, I encountered a full-grown female grizzly bear with two cubs, very quietly reposing upon the open prairie, several miles distant from any timber. This being the first opportunity that had ever occurred to me for an encounter with the ursine monster, and being imbued with the most exalted notions of the beast's proclivities for offensive warfare, especially when in the presence of her offspring, it may very justly be imagined that I was rather more excited than usual. I, however, determined to make the assault. I felt the utmost confidence in my horse, as she was afraid of nothing; and, after arranging everything about my saddle and arms in good order, I advanced to within about eighty yards before I was discovered by the bear, when she raised upon her haunches and gave me a scrutinizing examination. I seized this opportune moment to fire, but missed my aim, and she started off, followed by her cubs at their utmost speed. After reloading my rifle, I pursued, and, on coming again within range, delivered another shot, which struck the large bear in the fleshy part of the thigh, whereupon she set up a most distressing howl and accelerated her pace, leaving her cubs behind. After loading again I gave the spurs to my horse and resumed the chase, soon passing the cubs, who were making the most plaintive cries of distress. They were heard by the dam; but she gave no other heed to them than occasionally to halt for an instant, turn around, sit up on her posteriors, and give a hasty look back; but, as soon as she saw me following her, she invariably turned again and redoubled her speed. I pursued about four miles and fired four balls into her before I succeeded in bringing her to the ground; and, from the time I first saw her until her death-wound, notwithstanding I was very often close upon her heels, she never came to bay or made the slightest demonstration of resistance. Her sole purpose seemed to be to make her escape, leaving her cubs in the most cowardly manner.

Upon three other different occasions I met the mountain bears, and once the cinnamon species, which is called the most formidable of all; and, in none of these instances, did they exhibit the slightest indication of anger or resistance, but invariably ran from me. Such is my experience with this formidable monarch of the mountains. It is possible that if a man came suddenly upon the beast in a thicket, where it could have no previous warning, he might be attacked; but, it is my opinion, that if the bear gets *the wind* or sight of a man at any considerable distance, it will endeavor to get away as soon as possible. I am so fully impressed with this idea that I shall hereafter hunt bear with a feeling of as much security as I would have in hunting the buffalo.*

* It is not the experience of Europe and Asia. The bear hunter

The grizzly, like the black bear, hybernates in winter, and makes his appearance in the spring with his claws grown out long and very soft and tender; he is then poor, and unfit for food.

I have heard a very curious fact stated by several old mountaineers regarding the mountain bears, which, of course, I cannot vouch for; but it is given by them with great apparent sincerity and candor. They assert that no instance has ever been known of a female bear having been killed in a state of pregnancy. This singular fact in the history of the animal seems most inexplicable to me, unless she remain concealed in her brumal slumber until after she has been delivered of her cubs.

I was told by an old Delaware Indian that when the bear has been traveling against the wind and wishes to lie down, he always turns in an opposite direction, and goes some distance away from his first track before making his bed. If an enemy then comes upon his trail, his keen sense of smell will apprise him of the danger. The same Indian mentioned, that when a bear had been pursued and sought shelter in a cave, he had often endeavoured to eject him with smoke, but that the bear would advance to the mouth of the cave, where the fire was burning, and put it out with his paws, then retreat into the cave again.* This would indicate that Bruin is endowed with some glimpses of reason beyond the ordinary instincts of the brute creation in general, and, indeed, is capable of discerning the connection between cause and effect. Notwithstanding the extraordinary intelligence which this quadruped exhibits upon some occasions, upon others he shows himself to be one of the most stupid brutes imaginable. For example, when he has taken possession of a

---

of the Pyrenees seldom passes through life unscathed; and there are probably more hair-breadth escapes from the bear of the Himalayas than from the tiger of the plains.—ED.

* All bear countries have some superstition about the beast. Persians will gravely assure you, that to compass the traveller's destruction, "Ephraim" will bind round his head a turban of grass, and mount an ass like a Mullah.—ED.

cavern, and the courageous hunter enters with a torch and rifle, it is said he will, instead of forcibly ejecting the intruder, raise himself upon his haunches and cover his eyes with his paws, so as to exclude the light, apparently thinking that in this situation he cannot be seen. The hunter can then approach as close as he pleases, and shoot him down.

THE BIG-HORN.

The big-horn or mountain sheep, which has a body like the deer, with the head of a sheep, surmounted by an enormous pair of short, heavy horns, is found throughout the Rocky Mountains, and resorts to the most inaccessible peaks, and to the wildest and least frequented glens. It clambers over almost perpendicular cliffs with the greatest ease and celerity, and skips from rock to rock, cropping the tender herbage that grows upon them.

It has been supposed by some, that this animal leaps down from crag to crag, lighting upon its horns, as an evidence of which, it has been advanced that the front part of the horns is often much battered. This, I believe, to be erroneous, as it is very common to see horns that have no bruises upon them.

The old mountaineers say they have often seen the bucks engaged in desperate encounters with their huge horns, which, in striking together, made loud reports. This will account for the marks sometimes seen upon them.

The flesh of the big-horn, when fat, is more tender, juicy, and delicious, than that of any other animal I know of, but it is a *bonne bouche* which will not grace the tables of our city epicures until a railroad to the Rocky Mountains affords the means of transporting it to a market a thousand miles distant from its haunts.

In its habits, the mountain sheep greatly resembles the chamois of Switzerland, and it is hunted in the same manner. The hunter traverses the most inaccessible and broken localities, moving along with great caution, as the least unusual noise causes them to flit away like a phantom, and they will be seen no more. The animal is gregarious, but it is seldom that more than eight or ten are found in a flock. When not grazing, they seek the sheltered sides of the mountains, and repose among the rocks.

ITINERARIES.

LIST OF ITINERARIES:

SHOWING THE DISTANCES BETWEEN CAMPING-PLACES, THE CHARACTER OF THE BOARDS, AND THE FACILITIES FOR OBTAINING WOOD, WATER, AND GRASS ON THE PRINCIPAL ROUTES BETWEEN THE MISSISSIPI RIVER AND THE PACIFIC OCEAN.

I.—*From Fort Smith, Arkansas, to Santa Fé and Albuquerque, New Mexico.* By Captain R. B. Marcy, U. S. A.

Miles.

From Fort Smith to—

15. Strickland's Farm.—The road crosses the Poteau River at Fort Smith, where there is a ferry; it then follows the Poteau bottom for ten miles. This part of the road is very muddy after heavy rains. At 14 miles, it passes the Choctaw Agency, where there are several stores. There is the greatest abundance of wood, water, and grass at all camps for the first 200 miles. Where any of these are wanting it will be specially mentioned. The road passes through the Choctaw settlements for about 150 miles, and corn and supplies can be purchased from these Indians at reasonable rates.

11. Camp Creek.—Road crosses a prairie of three miles in length, then enters a heavy forest. The camp is on a small branch, with grass plenty in a small prairie about 400 yards to the left of the road.

12. Coon Creek.—Road passes through the timber, and is muddy in a rainy season.

12. Sans Bois Creek.—Prairie near; some Choctaw houses at the crossing.

14. Bend of Sans Bois Creek.—Indian farm.

15. South Fork of Canadian, or "Gain's Creek."—Road traverses a very rough and hilly region. There is a ford and a ferry upon the creek. Indian farm on the west bank.

12. First ford of Coal Creek.—Road crosses over a rolling prairie, and at four miles the Fort Washita road turns to the left.

Second ford of Coal Creek.—Indian Farm.

4. Little Cedar Mountain.—Very rough, mountainous road.

6. Stony Point.—Very rough, mountainous road.

5. Shawnee Village.—Several Indian houses.

14. Shawnee Town.—Road passes several small prairies. Indian settlement; store on opposite bank of Canadian River, near the camp.

21. Delaware Mountain.—Road passes over a very beautiful country, with small streams of good water frequent, and good camps. It crosses small prairies and groves of timber.

5. Boggy River.—Road passes a country similar to that mentioned above.

3. Clear Creek.—Road turns to the right near a prominent round mound. Beautiful country, diversified with prairies and timbered lands.

7. Branch of Topofki Creek.—Beautiful country and fine roads.

9½. Cane Creek.—Excellent camp.

Miles.

5. Small Branch.—Road passes about two miles from the old "Camp Arbuckle," built by Captain Marcy in 1853, since occupied by Black Beaver and several Delaware families.

11½. Mustang Creek.—Road runs on the dividing ridge between the waters of the Washita and Canadian, on a high prairie.

17½. Choteau's Creek.—Road passes on the high prairie opposite Choteau's old trading-house, and leaves the outer limits of the Indian settlements. Excellent road, and good camps at short distances.

11¾. Choteau's Creek.—Road runs up the creek; is smooth and good.

12¾. Head of Choteau's Creek.—Road runs up the creek, and is good.

17¼. Branch of Washita River.—Road runs over an elevated prairie country, and passes a small branch at six miles from last camp.

5¾. Branch of "Spring Creek."—Good camp.

16. Head of "Spring Creek."—Road traverses a high prairie country, is smooth and firm.

13. Red Mounds.—Road runs over a high rolling prairie country, and is excellent.

5. Branch of Washita River.—Good road.

15¾. Branch of Canadian.—Road continues on the ridge dividing the Washita and Canadian Rivers; is smooth and firm.

17¾. Branch of Washita River.—Road continues on the "divide."

18. Branch of Canadian.—Road continues on the divide from one to four miles from the Canadian.

19. On Canadian River.—Good Road.

16. Little Washita River.—Good road; timber becoming scarce.

13. Branch of Canadian.—Good road.

17½. Antelope Buttes.—Road runs along the Canadian bottom and in places is sandy.

14. Rush Lake.—Small pond on the prairie. No wood within half a mile; some buffalo chips; poor water.

16. Branch of Washita River.—Good road on the divide.

10¼. Dry River.—Road descends a very long hill, and crosses the dry river near the Canadian. Water can be found by digging about a foot in the sand of the creek. Good grass on the west bank.

17. Branch of Canadian.—Road winds up a very long and abrupt hill, but is smooth and firm.

22½. Timbered Creek.—Road passes over a very elevated prairie country, and descends by a long hill into the beautiful valley of Timbered Creek.

11½. Spring Branch.—Good camp.

14. Spring Branch.—Good camp.

17¾. Branch of Canadian.—Road passes a small branch 3½ miles from the last camp.

18⅜. Branch of Canadian.—Road passes a small branch of the Canadian at 8 miles from the last camp.
17⅞. Spring Branch.—Good road.
9½. Branch of Canadian.—Good road and camp.
18½. Branch of the Canadian.—Good road and camp.
10¼. Pools of Water.—Good camp.
10. Large Pond.—Good camp.
25. Pools of Water.—No wood; water brackish. The road passes over a very elevated and dry country, without wood or water.
18½. Head of Branch.—At 13½ miles the road crosses a branch of the Canadian.
19¾. Laguna Colorado.—Road here falls into an old Mexican cart-road. Good springs on the left up the creek, with wood and grass abundant.
7. Pools of Water.—Road runs through cedars.
10⅜. Pajarito Creek.—Grass begins to be rather short in places, but is abundant on the creek.
13½ Gallenas Creek.—Good camp.
15. 2d Gallenas Creek.—Good road.
16½. Pécos River at Anton Chico.—This is the first settlement after leaving Camp Arbuckle. Corn and vegetables can be purchased here. Grass is generally short here.
15. Pécos River opposite Questa.—Road runs through the cedar, and is firm and good. Camp is in sight of the town of Questa, upon a very elevated bluff.
21¾. Laguna Colorado.—Road passes through a wooded country for a portion of the distance, but leaves it before reaching camp, where there is no wood, but water generally sufficient for trains. In very dry seasons, it has been known to fail. The road forks here, the right leading to Santa Fé *via* Galistio (45½ miles), and the left to Albuquerque.
22½. San Antonio.—Good road.
18¾. Albuquerque.—Good road.

Total distance from Fort Smith to Albuquerque, 814¾ miles.
Total distance from Fort Smith to Santa Fé, 819 miles.

II.—*From Fort Leavenworth to Santa Fé by the way of the upper ferry of the Kansas River and the Cimarron.*

[In this table, the distances, taken by an odometer, are given in miles and hundredths of a mile. The *measured* distances between the crossing of the Arkansas and Santa Fé are from Major Kendrick's published table. Wood, water, and grass are found at all points where the absence of them is not stated.]

From Fort Leavenworth to—
2·88. Salt Creek.
9·59. Stranger's Creek.

Miles.
13·54. Stranger's Creek.
9·60. Grasshopper Creek.
6·50. "
2·86. "
2·60. "
4·54. Soldier's Creek.
2·45. Upper Ferry, Kansas River.
7·41. Pottawatomie Settlement.
5·75. Pottawatomie Creek.
3·89. White Wakarussi Creek.
7·78. " "
6·27. " "
0·73. Road from Independence—No place to encamp.
5·72. White Wakarussi Creek.
2·51. " "
2·82. 142-mile Creek.
7·80. Bluff Creek.
5·77. Rock Creek.
5·08. Big John Spring.
2·29. Council Grove.
7·97. Elm Creek.—Water generally.
8·06. Diamond Spring.
1·42. Diamond Creek.
15·46. Lost Spring.—No wood.
9·25. Mud Creek.—Water uncertain; no wood.
7·76. Cottonwood Creek.
6·16. Water Holes.—Water generally; no wood.
12·44. Big Turkey Creek.—No water.
7·83. Little Turkey Creek.—Water uncertain; no wood.
18·19. Little Arkansas River.
10·60. Owl Creek.—Water generally in holes above and below crossing.
6·39. Little Cow Creek.—Water only occasionally.
2·93. Big Cow Creek.—Water holes, 10 miles (estimated). Water uncertain; no wood.
18·24. Bend of the Arkansas.
6·66. Walnut Creek.
16·35. Pawnee Rock.—Teams sometimes camp near here and drive stock to the Arkansas to water. No wood.
5·28. Ash Creek.—Water above and below crossing, uncertain.
6·65. Pawnee Fork.—Best grass some distance above crossing.

From Pawnee Fork to the lower crossing of the Arkansas, a distance of 98½ miles, convenient camping-places can be found along the Arkansas; the most prominent localities are therefore only mentioned. A supply of fuel should be laid in at Pawnee Fork to last till you pass Fort Mann, though it may be obtained, but inconveniently, from the

Miles.

opposite side of the Arkansas. Dry Route branches off at 3½ miles (estimated). This route joins the main one again 10 miles this side of Fort Mann. It is said to be a good one, but deficient in water, and without wood.

11·43. Coon Creek.

46·58. Jackson's Island.

5·01. Dry Route comes in.

10·05. Fort Mann.

23·34. Lower Crossing of the Arkansas.—The Bent's Fort Route branches off at this point. For the distances upon this route, see next table. A supply of wood should be got from this vicinity, to last till you reach Cedar Creek.

15·68. Water-hole.—Water uncertain ; no wood.

30·02. Two Water-holes.—Water uncertain ; no wood.

14·14. Lower Cimarron Springs.—No wood.

20·00. Pools of Water.—Water uncertain ; no wood.

19·02. Middle Springs of the Cimarron.—No wood.

12·93. Little Crossing of the Cimarron.—No wood.

14·10. Upper Cimarron Springs.—No wood. Pools of water, 7 miles (estimated). No wood.

19·05. Cold Spring.—A tree here and there in the vicinity. Pools of water, 11 miles (estimated). Water uncertain ; no wood.

16·13. Cedar Creek.—M'Nees' Creek, 10 miles (estimated). Water indifferent and uncertain; scant pasture; no wood. Arroyo del la Seña, 2½ miles (estimated). No water.

21·99. Cottonwood Creek.—No water. Arroyo del Burro, 5 miles (estimated).

15·17. Rabbit-ear Creek.—10 miles (estimated), springs. Round Mound, 8 miles (estimated). No water; no wood; no camping-place. Rock Creek, 10 miles (estimated). Grazing scant; no wood.

26·40. Whetstone Creek.—Spring; no wood. Arroyo Don Carlos, 10½ miles (estimated). Water, etc., to the left of the road.

14·13. Point of Rocks.—Water and grass *up the cañon*, just after crossing the *point*; scattering shrub cedars on the neighboring heights.

16·62. Sandy Arroyo.—Water uncertain; no wood. Crossing of Canadian River, 4¾ miles (estimated). Grazing above the crossing; willows.

10·05. Rio Ocaté.—Wood ⅓ of a mile to right of road; grass in the cañon. Pond of water, 13½ miles (estimated). No wood.

19·05. Wagon Mound.—Santa Clara Springs. Wood brought from the Rio Ocaté. Rio del Perro (Rock Creek), 17½ miles (estimated).

21·62. Cañon del Lobo.—Rio Moro, 3½ miles (estimated) Rio Sapillo, 1 mile (estimated). The Bent's Fort Route comes in here.

Miles.
18·00. Las Vegas.—Forage purchasable.
13·05. Tacolote.—Forage purchasable. Ojo Vernal, 5 miles (estimated). No grass to speak of.
14·00. San Miguel.—Forage purchasable; no grass.
21·18. Ruins of Pecos.—Grazing very scant. Cottonwood Creek, 4½ miles (estimated). Water uncertain; no grass.
13·41. Stone Corral.—No grass.
10·80. Santa Fé.—Forage purchasable; no grazing.

III.—*Camping-places upon a road discovered and marked out from Fort Smith, Arkansas, to Doña Aña and El Paso, New Mexico, in* 1849. By Captain R. B. Marcy, U.S.A.

Miles.
Fort Smith to—
65. South Fork of the Canadian.—The road from Fort Smith to the South Fork of the Canadian follows the same track as the road to Albuquerque and Santa Fé, and by reference to the tables of distances for that road the intermediate camps will be found.
15. Prior's Store.—Grass, wood, and water near.
17½. Little Boggy.—Good camp. Wherever there are not the requisites of wood, water, and grass for encamping, it will be specially noted; when they are not mentioned they will always be found.
13. Little Boggy.—Good camp.
15½. Boggy Depôt.—Store and blacksmith's shop.
12⅗. Blue River.—The road passes over a flat section, which is muddy after rains.
8½. Fort Washita.—Good camp half a mile before reaching the fort. The road forks at the Indian village on the Boggy, the left being the most direct. There are settlers along the road, who will give all necessary information to strangers. Corn plenty.
22. Preston Texas, on Red River.—The road from Fort Washita runs through the Indian settlements, passing many places where good camps may be found, and crosses the Red River at Preston. There is a ferry here; also stores and a blacksmith's shop.
20. M'Carty's.—Road runs through a heavy-timbered country, crossing several streams where there are good camps.
14⅗. Elm Fork of the Trinity, at Gainesville.—Road passes over a section diversified by prairies and groves of timber.

Miles.

12. Elm Fork of Trinity.—Good Camp.

11. Elm Fork of Trinity.—Excellent camps. Road passes over a beautiful country rapidly settling up with farmers, who cultivate and sell grain at low rates.

9. Turkey Creek.—Tributary of Red River. Road emerges from the upper "Cross Timbers" two miles from camp.

26¾. Buffalo Springs.—Springs of good water, but of limited amount, in a ravine.

12. On a Ravine.—Pools of good water and a small running stream, not reliable.

13½. On a Ravine.—Pools of water.

17¼. On a Ravine.—Pools of water.

17¼. Running branch of Cottonwood Spring.—Branch about two feet wide, good water; wood about half a mile distant.

14. Fort Belknap.—Good road through post-oak timber. County seat and town at Fort Belknap. Good camp on the west side of the Brazos, whioh is always fordable except in very high water.

14. Small Branch.—Water in holes.

18. Water-holes.—Pools of water. Road passes over prairie and timbered lands, is very smooth and level.

7½. Steam's Farm, on Clear Fork of the Brazos River.—Good road; excellent camp, with abundance of wood, water, and grass. Indian reservation here.

13. Elm Creek, or Qua-qua-ho-no.—Good road over rolling prairie and mesquite lands.

17. Ravine.—Pools of standing water. Good road.

18. Ravine --Pools of standing water. Good road.

27. Small Creek.—Tributary of the Brazos. Good road.

6. Pools of water.—Good camp.

8½. Small Branch.—Good water.

20½. Tributary of the Colorado.—Brackish water.

3¼. Rio Colorado.—Brackish water. Road very excellent.

12 1/10. Spring on the Road.—Good water.

22 9/10. Big spring to the left of the road, affording a great amount of water, which runs off in a small stream.

23. Laguna Colorado.—Water somewhat sulphurous; fuel, mesquite roots; grass abundant.

35. Mustang Pond.—This pond is north of the road about two miles, and was found in 1849, but emigrants and others have not been able to find it since. For this reason, I would advise travelers to fill their water-kegs at the Laguna Colorado, as in a very dry season, they might not be able to get any water until they reached the Sand Hills. The road is excellent over the "Llano Estacado," or Staked Plain.

34½. Sand Hills.—Water in holes. The water is good here, and can always be relied on as permanent. The road through the

Miles.

Sand Hills is very heavy; and I would advise travelers with loaded wagons to make half loads.

$31\frac{1}{2}$. Laguno near the Pecos River.—Road passes through the hills, and descends the high prairie to the valley of the Pecos. Laguna on the left.

$15\frac{5}{8}$. Crossing of Pecos.—Water deep and not fordable; river forty-two yards wide. A road leads up the eastern bank of the Pecos to a ford with rock bottom. Good camps can be had at almost any point on the Pecos. The water is brackish, but can be used without harm.

$54\frac{1}{2}$. Pecos River.—Point of the river where the road turns off toward Delaware Creek.

$9\frac{1}{8}$. Delaware Creek.—Good road after leaving the Pecos River. The road on the Pecos is good in the bottom in very dry weather, but after heavy rains it is submerged, and very muddy. Travelers should then turn off to the bluffs. The water in Delaware Creek is brackish.

$11\frac{7}{8}$. Ojo de San Martin.—Fine spring of fresh water, also mineral spring. Good road up Delaware Creek.

$15\frac{3}{10}$ Independence Spring.—Large spring of excellent water. Look out for Indians.

$5\frac{1}{10}$. Ojo del Camins.—Good spring in the pine timber at the base of the mountain.

$4\frac{1}{2}$. Peak of the Guadalupe.—Spring at the foot of the mountain. Road descends the mountain, and is very steep.

$23\frac{7}{8}$. Ojo del Cuerbo.—Road descends through a very rough and sinuous ravine, and crosses a long prairie to camp at a pond of standing water. No wood.

26. Cornudas (Wells).—Well in the rocks; plenty of water for small parties. Road good.

$8\frac{3}{4}$. Sierra del Alamo.—Road good; water limited in quantity. There is a small spring upon the side of the mountain. No wood except a few mesquite roots.

$22\frac{1}{4}$. Waco Tanks.—Good water in a large reservoir in the rocks. The road here branches, the left leading to El Paso and the right to Doña Aña.

28. El Paso, on the Rio del Norte.—Road good, with some sand; no water upon it.

The distance from the "Waco Tanks" to Doña Aña is sixty-three miles, but forty miles of the road is over heavy sand, and no water until reaching the mountain, twenty-five miles from Doña Aña. I would recommend travelers to take the El Paso road in preference.

Total distance from Fort Smith to El Paso, 860 miles.

IV.—*From St. Joseph, Missouri, to Great Salt Lake City.*

EMIGRANTS' ITINERARY,

Showing the distances between camping-places, the several mail-stations where mules are changed, the hours of travel, the character of the roads, and the facilities for obtaining water, wood, and grass on the route along the southern bank of the Platte River, from St. Joseph Mo. *via* Great Salt Lake City, to Carron Valley. From a Diary kept by Richard F. Burton between the 7th August and the 19th October, 1860.

No. of Mail.		Miles	Start.	Arrival.	Date.
1.	Leave St. Joseph, Missouri, in N. lat. 39° 40′, and W. long. 94° 50′. Cross Missouri River by steam ferry. Five miles of bottom land, bend in river and settlements. Over rolling prairie 2000 feet above sea-level. After 6 miles, Troy, capital of Doniphan Co. Kansas T. about a dozen shanties. Dine and change mules at Cold Spring—good water and grass. Road from Fort Leavenworth (N. lat. 39° 21′ 14″, and W. long. 94° 44′) falls in at Cold Spring, distant 15 miles. From St. Joseph to Cold Spring there are two routes, one lying north of the other, the former 20, the latter 24 miles in length.	20—24	A.M. 9.30	P.M. 3	Aug. 7
2.	After 10 miles, Valley Home, a white-washed shanty. At Small Branch on Wolf River, 12 miles from Cold Spring, is a fiumara on north of road, with water, wood, and grass. Here the road from Fort Atchinson falls in. Kennekuk station, 44 miles from St. Joseph. Sup and change mules.	22—23	P.M. 4	P.M. 8	Aug. 7
3.	Two miles beyond Kennekuk is the first of the three Grasshopper Creeks, flowing after rain to the Kansas River. Road rough and stony, water, wood, and grass. Four miles beyond the First Grasshopper is Whitehead, a young settlement on Big Grasshopper, water in pools, wood, and grass. Five and a half miles beyond is Walnut Creek, in Kikapoo Co. pass over Corduroy bridge, roadside dotted with shanties. Thence to Locknan's, or Big Muddy Station.	25	P.M. 9	A.M. 1	Aug. 7, 8

No. of Mail.		Miles	Start.	Arrival.	Date.
4.	Seventeen miles beyond Walnut Creek, the Third Grasshopper, also falling into the Kansas River. Good camping-ground. Ten miles beyond lies Richland, deserted site. Thence to Seneca, capital of Nemehaw Co. A few shanties on N. bank of Big Nemehaw Creek, a tributary of the Missouri River, which affords water, wood, and grass.	18	A.M. 3	A.M. 6	Aug. 8
5.	Cross Wildcat Creek and other nullahs. Seven miles beyond Seneca lies Ashpoint, a few wooden huts, thence to "Uncle John's Grocery," where liquor and stores are procurable. Eleven miles from Big Nemehaw, water, wood, and grass are found at certain seasons near the head of a ravine. Thence to Vermilion Creek, which heads to the N.E. and enters the Big Blue 20 miles above its mouth. The ford is miry after rain, and the banks are thickly wooded. Water is found in wells 40—43 ft. deep. Guittard's Station.	20	A.M 8	NOON. 12	Aug. 8
6.	Fourteen miles from Guittard's, Marysville, capital of Washington Co. affords supplies and a blacksmith. Then ford the Big Blue, tributary to Kansas River, clear and swift stream. Twelve miles W. of Marysville is frontier line between Kansas and Nebraska. Thence to Cottonwood Creek, fields in hollow near the stream.	25	P.M. 1	P.M. 6	Aug. 8
7.	Store at the crossing very dirty and disorderly. good water in spriug 400 yards N. of the road, wood and grass abundant. Seventeen and a half miles from the Big Blue is Walnut Creek, where emigrants encamp. Thence to West Turkey or Rock Creek in Nebraska T. a branch of the Big Blue: its approximate altitude is 1485 feet.	26	P.M. 6	P.M. 11	Aug. 8
8.	After nineteen miles of rough road and mosquitos, cross Little Sandy, five miles E. of Big Sandy, water and trees plentiful. There Big Sandy deep and heavy bed. Big Sandy Station.	23	P.M. 12	A.M. 4	Aug. 9
9.	Cross hills forming divide of Little Blue River ascending valley sixty miles long. Little Blue fine stream of clear water falling into Kansas River, everywhere good supplies and good camping-ground. Along left bank to Kiowa.	19	A.M. 6	A.M. 10	Aug. 9
10.	Rough roads of spurs and gullies runs up				

No. of Mail.		Miles	Start.	Arrival.	Date.
	valley 2 miles wide. Well wooded chiefly with cotton wood and grass abundant. Ranch at Liberty Farm on the Little Blue.	25	A.M. 11	P.M. 3	Aug. 9
11.	Cross divide between Little Blue and Platte River, rough road, mosquitos troublesome. Approximate altitude of dividing ridge 2025 feet. Station at Thirty-two Mile-Creek, a small wooded and winding stream flowing into the Little Blue.	24	P.M. 4	P.M. 9	Aug. 9
12.	After twenty-seven miles strike valley of the Platte, along southern bank of river, over level ground, good for camping, fodder abundant. After seven miles Fort Kearny in N. lat. 40° 38′ 45″, and W long. 98° 58′ 11″: approximate altitude 2350 feet above the sea level. Grocery, cloths, provisions, and supplies of all kinds are to be procured from the sutler's store. Beyond Kearny a rough and bad road leads to "Seventeen-Mile-Station."	34	P.M. 10.30	A.M. 8	Aug. 10
13.	Along south bank of Platte. Buffalo chips used for fuel. Sign of Buffalo appears. Plum Creek Station on a stream where there is a bad crossing in wet weather.	21	A.M. 9.30	P.M. 1.15	Aug. 10
14.	Beyond Plum Creek, Willow Island Ranch, where supplies are procurable. Road along Platte, wood scarce, grass plentiful, buffalo abounds; after twenty miles "Cold Water Ranch." Halt and change at Midway Station.	25	P.M. 2.30	P.M. 8	Aug. 10
15.	Along Valley of Platte, road muddy after rain, fuel scarce, grass abundant, camp traces everywhere. Ranch at Cottonwood Station, at this season the western limit of buffalo.	27	P.M. 9	A.M. 1.45	Aug. 11
16.	Up Valley of Platte. No wood, buffalo chips for fuel. Good camping-ground, grass on small branch of Platte. To Junction House Ranch and thence to station at Frémont Springs.	30	A.M. 6.15	A.M. 11	Aug. 11
17.	Road passes O'Fallon's Bluffs. "Half-way House" a store and ranch, distant 120 miles from Fort Kearny, 400 from St. Joseph, forty from the lower crossing, and sixty-eight from the upper crossing of the South Fork (Platte River). The station is called Alkali Lake.	25	NOON. 12	P.M. 5	Aug. 11
18.	Road along river, no timber, grass, buffalo chips, and mosquitos. Station at Diamond Springs near Lower Crossing.	25	P.M. 6	P.M. 10 15	Aug. 11

No. of Mail.		Miles	Start.	Arrival.	Date.
19.	Road along river. Last four miles very heavy sand, avoided by Lower Crossing. Poor accommodation at Upper Ford or Crossing on the eastern bank, where the mail passes the stream *en route* to Gt. S. L. City, and the road branches to Denver City and Pike's Peak.	25	P.M. 11	A.M. 3·15	Aug. 12
20.	Ford Platte 600 yards wide, 2·50 ft. deep, bed gravelly and solid, easy ford in dry season. Cross divide between North and South Forks along bank of Lodge Pole Creek. Land arid, wild sage for fuel. Lodge Pole Station.	35	AM. 6.30	P.M. 12·45	Aug. 11
21.	Up Lodge Pole Creek over spur of table-land, then striking over the prairie finishes the high divide between the Forks. Approximate altitude 3600 feet. On the right is Ash-Hollow, where there is plenty of wood and a small spring. Station is mud springs, a poor ranch.	25	P.M. 3	P.M. 5·45	Aug. 12
22.	Route lies over rolling divide between the Forks, crossing Omoha, Lawrence, and other creeks where water and grass are procurable. Cedar is still found in hill-gullies. About half a mile north of Chimney Rock is a ranch where the cattle are changed.	25	A. M. 8	P. M. 12·30	Aug. 13
23.	Road along south bank of North Fork of Platte River. Wild sage only fuel in valley; small spring on top of first hill. Rugged labyrinth of paths abreast cf Scott's Bluffs, which lie 5 miles S. of river in N. lat. 41° 48′ 26″, and W. long, 103° 45′ 02″. Water found in first ravine of Scott's Bluffs 200 yards below the road, cedars on heights. To Station.	24	P. M. 1·30	P. M. 5·30	Aug. 13
24.	Road along river, crosses Little Kiowa Creek, a tributary to Horse Creek, which flows into the Platte. Ford Horse Creek, a clear shallow stream with a sandy bottom. No wood below the hills.	16	P. M 6·3	P. M. 8 30	Aug. 13
25.	Route over sandy and heavy river bottom and rolling ground, leaving the Platte on the right: cottonwood and willows on the banks. Ranch at Laramie City kept by M. Badeau, a Canadian, who sells spirits, Indian goods, and outfit.	26	A. M. 6	P. M. 10·20	Aug. 14
26.	After 9 miles of rough road cross Laramie Fork and enter Fort Laramie, N. lat. 420° 12′ 38″, and W. long, 104° 31′ 26″. Alt. 4519 feet. Military post with post-office,				

).of ail.		Miles	Start.	Arrival,	Date.
	sutler's stores, and other conveniences. Thence to Ward's Station on the Central Star, small ranch and store.	18	P. M. 12·	P. M. 4	Aug. 14
7.	Rough and bad road. After 14 miles, cross Bitter Cottonwood Creek, water rarely flows after rain 10 feet wide and 6 inches deep, grass and fuel abundant. Pass Indian shop and store. At Bitter Creek branch of Cottonwood the road to Salt Lake City forks. Emigrants follow Upper or South road over spurs of Black Hills, some way south of river to avoid kanyons and to find grass. The station is called Horseshoe Creek. Residence of road agent, Mr. Slade, one of the worst places on the line.	25	P. M. 5	P. M. 9·30	Aug. 14
8.	Road forks, one line follows Platte, the other turns to the left, over "cut off;" highly undulating ridges crooked and deeply dented with dry beds of rivers; land desolate and desert. No wood nor water till end of stage. La Bonté River and Station, unfinished ranch in Valley, water and grass.	25	A. M. 10·45	A. M. 2·45	Aug. 15
9.	Road runs 6 miles (wheels often locked), on rugged red land, crosses several dry beds of creeks, and springs with water after melting of snow and frosts in dry season, thence into Valley of Platte. After 17 miles, it crosses the La Prêle (Rush River), a stream 16 feet wide, where water and wood abound. At Box-Elder Creek Station good ranch and comfortable camping-ground.	25	P. M. 4	P. M. 9	Aug. 15
0.	Along the Platte River now shrunk to 100 yards. After 10 miles, M. Bisonnette, at Deer Creek, a post offiee, blacksmith's shop, and store near Indian Agency. Thence a waste of wild sage to Little muddy, a creek with water. No accommodation nor provisions at station.	20	A. M 8·3	NOON. 12	Aug. 16
1.	After 8 miles cross vile bridge over Snow Creek. Thence up river valley along S. bank of Platte to lower ferry. To Lower Bridge, old station of troops. To Upper Bridge, where ferry has now been done away with.	18	P. M. 1·15.	P. M 4·15	Aug. 16
).	Road ascends hill 7 miles long, land rough, barren, and sandy in dry season. After 10 miles, red spring near the Red Buttes, old trading-place and post office. Road then				

No. of Mail.		Miles	Start.	Arrival.	Date.
	leaves Platte River and strikes over high, rolling, and barren prairie. After 18 miles "Devil's Backbone." Station at Willow Springs, wood, water, and grass, good place for encampment, but no accommodation nor provisions. On this stage mineral and alkaline waters dangerous to cattle abound.	28	A. M. 6·30	P. M. 12·50	Aug. 1
33.	After 3 miles, Green Creek, not to be depended upon, and Prospect Hill, a good look out. Then, at intervals of 3 miles, Harper's, Woodworth's, and Greasewood Creeks, followed by heavy sand. At 17 miles "Saleratus Lake" on west of road. Four miles beyond is "Independence Rock," Ford Sweetwater, leaving "Devil's Gate" on right. Pass blacksmith's shop. Sage only fuel. Plante or Muddy Station, family of Canadians, no conveniences.	33	P.M. 2·30	P.M. 9·15	Aug. 17
34.	Along winding banks of Sweetwater. After 4 miles, "Alkali Lake," S. of road. Land dry and stony, stunted cedars in hills. After 12 miles, "Devil's Post-Office," singular bluff on left of road, and opposite ranch kept by Canadian. Mail Station "Three Crossings," at Ford No. 3, excellent water, wood, grass, game, and wild currants.	25	A.M. 7	A.M. 11	Aug. 18
35.	Up kanyon of Sweetwater. Ford river 5 times, making total of 8. After 16 miles, "Ice Springs," in swampy valley, and one quarter of a mile beyond "Warm Springs." Then rough descent and waterless stretch. Descend by "Lander's cut-off" into fertile bottom. "Rocky Ridge Station," at Muskrat Creek good cold spring, grass, and sage fuel.	35	A.M. 5·45	P.M. 12·45	Aug. 1
36.	Up bed of creek, and ascending long hills leave Sweetwater. After 4 miles, 3 alkaline ponds S. of road. Rough path. After 7 miles, "Strawberry Creek," 6ft. wide, good camping ground, willows and poplars. One mile beyond is Quaking Asp Creek, often dry. Three miles beyond lies M'Achran's branch, 33 × 2. Then "Willow Creek," 10 × 2, good camping-ground. At Ford No. 9, Canadian ranch and store. Long table-land leads to "South Pass," dividing trip between Atlantic and Pacific, and thence 2 miles to station at "Pacific Springs," water, tolerable grass, sage fuel, and mosquitos.	35	A.M. 7·45	P M. 3	Aug. 2

No. of Mail		Miles	Start.	Arrival.	Date.
37.	Cross Miry Creek. Road down Pacific Creek, water scarce for 20 miles. After 11 miles, "Dry Sandy Creek," water scarce and too brackish to drink, grass little, sage and greasewood plentiful. After 16 miles, "Sublett's cut-off," or the "Dry Drive," turns N. westward to Soda Springs and Fort Hall: the left fork leads to Fort Bridger and Gt. St. L. City. Four miles beyond junction is "Little Sandy Creek," 20—25 × 2, grass, timber, and good camping-ground. Eight miles beyond is "Big Sandy Creek," clear, swift, and with good crossing 110 × 2. Southern route best, along old road, no water for 49 miles. Big Sandy Creek Station.	33	A.M. 8	P.M. 12·50	Aug. 21
38.	Desolate road cuts off bend of river, no grass nor water. After 12 miles "Simpson's Hollow." Fall into Valley of Green River half a mile wide, water 110 yards broad. After 20½ miles, Upper Ford, Lower Ford 7 miles below Upper. Good camping-ground on bottom; at station in Green River grocery, stores, and ferry-boat when there is high water.	32	P.M. 1·45	P.M. 6·30	Aug. 21
39.	Diagonal ford over Green River, good camping-ground in bottom. Follow valley for 4 miles, grass, and fuel. Michel Martin's store and grocery. Road leaves river and crosses waterless, divide to Black's Fork 100 × 2, grass and fuel. Wretched station at Ham's Fork.	24	A.M. 8	NOON. 12	Aug. 22
	Ford Ham's Fork. After 12 miles road forks at the 2nd striking of Ham's Fork, both branches leading to Fort Bridger. Mail takes left-hand path. Then Black's fork 20 × 2, clear and pretty valley, with grass and fuel, cottonwood, and yellow currants. Cross stream 3 times. After 12 miles, "Church Butte." Ford Smith's Fork 30ft. wide, and shallow, tributary of Black's Fork. Station at Millersville on Smith's Fork, large store, and good accommodation.	20	P.M. 2	P.M. 5·15	Aug 22.
41.	Road runs up valley of Black's Fork. After 12 miles, Fort Bridger in N. lat. 41° 18′ 12″, and W. long. 110° 32′ 23″, on Black's Fork of Green River. Commands Indian trade, fuel, corn, little grass. Post-office, sutler's store, grocery, and other conveniences. Thence rough and rolling ground to Muddy Creek				

No. of Mail.		Miles.	Start.	Arrival.	Date.
	Hill, steep and stony descent. Over fertile bottom to Big Muddy and Little Muddy Creek, which empties into Black's Fork below Fort Bridger. At Creek Station is a Canadian, provisions, excellent milk, no stores.	25	A.M. 8.30	P.M. 12·15	Aug. 23
42.	Rough country. Road winds along ridge to Quaking Asp Hill 7,900 (8,400?) feet above sea-level. Steep descent, rough and broken ground. After eighteen miles, Sulphur Creek Valley, stagnant stream, flowing after rain, ford bad and muddy. Station in fertile valley of Bear River, which turns northward and flows into E. side of Lake, wood, grass, and water. Poor accommodations at Bear River Station.	20	NOON. 12	P.M. 5·30	Aug. 23
43.	Road runs by Needle Rocks, falls into Valley of Egan's Creek. "Cache Cave" on right hand. Three Miles below Cave is Red Fork in Echo Kanyon, unfinished station at entrance. Rough road, steep ascents and descents along Red Creek Station, on Weber River, which falls into Salt Lake south of Bear River.	36	A.M. 8·15	P.M. 2·30	Aug. 24
44.	Road runs down Valley of Weber. Ford river. After 5½ miles is a salt spring where the road leaves the river, to avoid a deep kanyon, and turns left into a valley with rough paths, trying to wheels; then crosses mountain, and ascending long hill descends to Bauchemin's Creek, tributary to Weber River. Creek eighteen feet wide, swift, pebbly bed, good ford, grass and fuel abundant. Station called Carson's House; accommodations of the worst.	22	P.M. 4·30	P.M. 7·45	Aug. 24
45.	Ford Bauchemin's Creek thirteen times in eight miles. After two miles along a small watercourse ascend Big Mountain, whence first view of Great Salt Lake City, twelve miles distant. After fourteen miles Big Kanyon Creek. Six miles further, road leaves Big Kanyon Creek, and after steep ascent and descent makes Emigration Creek. Cross Little Mountain, two miles beyond Big Mountain, road rough and dangerous. Five Miles from Emigration Kanyon to Great Salt Lake City. Road through "Big Field" six miles square.	29	A.M. 7	P.M. 7·15	Aug. 28

GREAT SALT LAKE CITY N. lat. 40° 46′ 08″
W. long. 112° 06′ 08″ (g.)
Altitude 4300 feet.

The variation of compass at Temple Block in 1849 was 15° 47′ 23″, and in 1860 it was 15° 64′, a slow progress towards the east. (In the Wind River Mountains, as laid down by Col. Frémont in 1842 was E. 18°.) In Fillmore Valley it is now 18° 15′, and three years ago was about 17° east, the rapid progression to the east is accompanied with extreme irregularity, which the people attribute to the metallic constituents of the soil.

Total of days between St. Jo. and Great Salt Lake City .	19
Total Stages	45
Distance in statute miles	1136
From Fort Leavenworth to Great Salt Lake City . .	1168

V.—*From Salt Lake City to Sacramento and Benicia, California.*

Miles.

From Salt Lake City to—

18. Hait's Ranch.—Good road, and grass abundant until Bear River is crossed.

17½. Ford on Weber River.—Good road, and grass abundant.

15. Point of Mountain.—Spring water warm but pure.

12¾. Box Elder Creek.—Excellent water; grass and fuel abundant in the cañons.

23. Ferry on Bear River.—Four miles above the usual crossing. Excellent grass.

¾. West Bank.—Grass not good on the west bank.

6. Small Spring.—Cross Bear River below the mouth of the Mallade.

17½. Blue Springs.—Water and grass scarce, and of poor quality.

21¼. Deep Creek.—Heavy sage, but good grass on the right of the road, near sink.

20½. Cedar Springs.—Good grass on the hills, with fine water and wood; rolling country.

10. Rock Creek.—Plenty of grass to the left of the road; good camping-place.

14½. Raft River.—Good camp.

22½. Goose Creek Mountains.—Grass, wood, and water abundant; rough and mountainous country. Road from Fort Bridger comes in here *via* Soda Springs.

17¾. On Goose Creek.—Rough, broken country, with a good road, which runs along the creek for several miles.

28½. Head of 1000 Spring Valley.—Road runs over a rolling, barren

Miles.

section, with but little water except on the river far to the right.

25¾. 1000 Spring Valley.—Meadow grass; good fuel scarce. Camps can be found at short intervals along the road.

14. Head of Humboldt River.—Fine camping-places, and road generally good, running over a rolling country.

23. Slough of the Humboldt.—Extensive bottoms of good grass.

20. Humboldt River.—Along the entire course of the Humboldt good grass is found in the bottoms. The road, which follows the bottom, is hard and smooth, but cannot be traveled in seasons of very high water, as the bottom overflows. It is then necessary to take the road on the bluffs, where the grass is scarce. The river, when not above a fording stage, can be forded at almost any point, and good camps can be found at short intervals. There are spots along the river bottom where alkaline ponds are frequent. These are poisonous to cattle, and should be avoided by travelers. It is well along this river not to allow animals to drink any water except from the river where it is running.

20. Humboldt River.—The foregoing remarks apply for every camp on the Humboldt River.

22. Humboldt River.—Good camps along the Humboldt Valley.

23. Humboldt River.

13½. "

16½ "

25. "

13¾. "

24. "

24½. "

20¼. "

18¾. "

13½. "

18¼. Lawson's Meadows.—The road here forks, the left going by the Carson Valley and Sacramento route, and the right *via* Goose, Cleer, and Rhett lakes, Applegat's Pass of the Cascade Mountains, into Rogue River Valley, Fort Law, Oregon Territory, Yreka, Fort Jones, Fort Reading, and Sacramento River.

33½. On Humboldt River.—Grass and water poor all the distance to the Sink of the Humboldt.

19½. Sink of Humboldt River.—The water at the Sink is strongly impregnated with alkali; the road generally is good. Travelers should not allow their stock to drink too freely of this water.

26. Head Sink of Humboldt.—Road good.

45. Carson River.—Road crosses the desert, where there is no water for stock, but there is a well where travelers can purchase water for drinking. This part of the road should be traveled in the cool of the day and at night. Grass good, also the water.

Miles.

2. Carson River.—Good bunch-grass near the road.
30. Carson River.—26 miles of desert; poor grass.
14. Eagle Ranch.—Good grass and water.
13. Reese's Ranch.—Good grass and water.
12. Williams' Ranch.—Very good water and grass.
15. Hope Valley.—Road rough and rocky.
3. Near Sierra.—Good camp, with water and grass.
7. First Summit.—Road rough and rocky; good water; grass scarce.
2. Second Summit.—Road mountainous and very steep; snow nearly all the year.
10. Lakes.—Good camp.
12. Leek Springs.—Good grass near the road.
10. Trader's Creek.—Grass and fuel scarce.
12. Sly Park.—Grass and fuel near the road.

Forty Mile House.—Water plenty; grass scarce.
Sacramento Valley.—Water plenty; purchase forage.
Sacramento City.—Water plenty; purchase forage.

Total distance from Salt Lake City to Benicia, 973 miles.

At the Big Meadows, 23 miles from the Sink of the Humboldt, travelers should make a halt of a day or two to rest and recruit their animals, and to cut grass for crossing the desert, as this is the last good camping-place until reaching Carson River. The ground near this place is boggy, and animals should be watered with buckets. The camping-ground here is on the right bank of the river, and about half a mile to the left of the main road. The water is in a slough, near its head, where will be found some springs which run off a short distance, but soon sink.

The road across the desert is very sandy, especially toward the western extremity. Twenty miles from the Sink of the Humboldt there are four wells. About half a mile east of the mail station, the road leading to the wells turns to the right, where water can be purchased for from one to two shillings for each man and beast.

At 9½ miles beyond the mail station, on the desert, a road turns off from the main trace toward a very high sandy ridge, and directly upon the top of this ridge is the crater of an extinct volcano, at the bottom of which is a salt lake. Upon the extreme north end of this lake will be found a large spring of fresh water, sufficient for 1000 animals. From thence to "Ragtown," on Carson River, is three miles.

I would advise travelers, when their animals become exhausted before reaching this water, to take them out of harness and drive them to this place to recruit. There is some grass around the lake.

This desert has always been the most difficult part of the journey to California, and more animals have probably been lost here than at any other place. The parts of wagons that are continually met with here shows this most incontestably.

VI.—*From Great Salt Lake City to Los Angelos and San Francisco, California.*

Miles.

Salt Lake City to—

23⅝. Willow Creek.—Good Grass.
14. American Creek.—Good Grass.
11½. Provo City.—Town.
7¼. Hobble Creek.—Good camp.
6. Spanish Fork.—Good camp.
5. Peteetneet.—Good camp.
25. Salt Creek.—Several small streams between. Good camp.
18⅝. Toola Creek.—Ford. No wood; grass good.
6¼. Sevier River—Road is sandy, passing over a high ridge. Good camp.
25½. Cedar Creek.—Road rather mountainous and sandy. Good grass and wood.
17½. Creek.—This is the fourth stream south of Sevier River. Road crosses two streams. Good camp.
3⅝. Willow Flats.—The water sinks a little east of the road.
25. Spring.—Good grass and water.
22¼. Sage Creek.—Grass poor; wood and water.
5⅛. Beaver Creek.—Good wood, water, and grass.
27¼. North Cañon Creek.—In Little Salt Lake Valley. Good grass; no wood. The road is rough and steep for six miles.
5⅜. Creek.—Good wood, water, and grass.
6¾. Creek.—Good wood, water, and grass.
12⅞. Cottonwood Creek.—Good grass and water.
9. Cedar Springs.—Good camp.
23. Pynte Creek.—Good grass one mile up the cañon.
9. Road Springs.—Road is rough; good camp.
16. Santa Clara.—Road descending and rough; poor grass. From this point to Cahoon Pass look out for Indians.
17⅛. Camp Springs.—Two miles before reaching the springs the road leaves the Santa Clara. Good grass.
22⅞. Rio Virgin.—Road crosses over the summit of a mountain. Good road; grass poor.
39⅝. Rio Virgin.—Road runs down the Rio Virgin, crossing it ten times. Grass good down the river.
19⅝. Muddy Creek.—Road for half a mile is very steep and sandy. Good camp.

Miles.

$52\frac{5}{8}$. Las Vagas.—Water is sometimes found $2\frac{1}{2}$ miles west of the road in holes 23 miles from the Muddy, and some grass about a mile from the road. Good camp.

5. On Vagas.—Road runs up the river. Good grass.

17. Cottonwood Spring.—Poor grass.

$29\frac{3}{4}$. Cottonwood Grove.—No grass. Water and grass can be found four miles west by following the old Spanish trail to a ravine, and thence to the left in the ravine one mile.

$21\frac{3}{4}$. Resting Springs.—Good grass and water. Animals should be rested here before entering the desert.

7. Spring.—The spring is on the left of the road, and flows into Saleratus Creek. Animals must not be allowed to drink the Saleratus water.

$14\frac{1}{8}$. Salt Springs.—Poor grass and no fresh water.

$38\frac{3}{4}$. Bitter Springs.—Good road; poor grass.

$30\frac{3}{4}$. Mohave River.—Good road and good grass.

$51\frac{1}{2}$. On the Mohave.—Last ford. Good grass all the way up the Mohave.

17. Cahoon Pass.—At the summit.

10. Camp.—Road bad down the cañon.

$11\frac{1}{2}$. Coco Mongo Ranch.

10 Del Chino Ranch.—Williams

$19\frac{3}{8}$. San Gabriel River.

6. San Gabriel Mission.

$8\frac{1}{4}$. Puebla de los Angelos.

$65\frac{3}{4}$. Santa Clara River.—*On the Coast Route.* Good camps to San José.

$7\frac{1}{2}$. Buena Ventura Mission and River.—Road here strikes the Pacific shore.

26. Santa Barbara.—Town.

$45\frac{3}{4}$. San Yenness River.—At the Mission.

$78\frac{7}{8}$. Santa Margareta.—Old Mission.

$28\frac{3}{8}$. San Miguel.—Old Mission.

$24\frac{3}{4}$. San Antonio River.

$26\frac{3}{4}$. Rio del Monterey.

$15\frac{5}{8}$. Solida Mission.—At the ford of Rio del Monterey.

$37\frac{1}{2}$. San Juan Mission.

33. San José Pueblo.

75. San Francisco.

VII.—*From Great Salt Lake City to San Francisco.*

No. of Mail.		Miles	Start.	Arrival.	Date.
1. and 2.	Road through south of City, due south along right bank of Jordan. Crosses many creeks, viz., Kanyon Creek, 4¼ miles, Mill Creek, 2½ First or Great Cottonwood Creek, 2. Second ditto, 4. Fork of road, 1¼. Dry Creek, 3½. Willow Creek, 2¾. After 22—23 miles, hot and cold springs, and halfway house, the brewery under Point of the Mountain. Road across Ash Hollow or Jordan Kanyon, 2 miles. Fords river, knee deep, ascends a rough divide between Utah Valley and Cedar Valley 10 miles from camp, and finally reaches Cedar Creek and Camp Floyd.	44	10·30	9·30	Sept. 20
3.	Leaves Camp Floyd, 7 miles to divide of Cedar Valley. Crosses divide into Rush Valley, after total of 18·2 miles reaches Meadow Creek, good grass and water. Rush Valley Mail Station 1 mile beyond, food and accommodation.	20	10·30	9·30	Sept. 27
4.	Crosses remains of Rush Valley 7 miles. Up rough divide called Genl. Johnston's Pass. Spring often dry, 200 yards on right of road. At Point Look-Out leaves Simpson's Road, which runs south. Cross Skull Valley, bad road. To bench on eastern flank of desert. Station called Egan's Springs, Simpson's Springs, or Lost Springs, grass plentiful, water good.	27	A. M. 9·30	4·30	Sept. 28
5.	New station, road forks to S.-E. and leads after 5 miles to grass and water. After 8 miles River Bottom, 1 mile broad. Long line over desert to Express Station, called Dugway, no grass, and no water.	20	12	P. M. 5·30	Sept. 29
6.	Steep road 2½ miles to summit of Dugway Pass. Descend by rough incline, 8 miles beyond road forks to Devil's Hole, 90 miles from Camp Floyd on Simpson's route, and 6 miles S. of Fish Springs. Eight miles beyond Fork is Mountain Point, road winds S. and W. and then N. to avoid swamp, and crosses three sloughs. Beyond last is Fish Spring Station on bench, poor place,				

No. of Mail.		Miles	Start.	Arrival.	Date.
	water plentiful but bad. Cattle here drink for first time after Lost Springs, distant 48 miles.	28	P. M. 6·30	A. M. 3·30	Sept. 29
7.	Road passes many pools, Halfway forks S. to Pleasant Valley (Simpson's line). Road again rounds swamp, crossing S. end of Salt Plain. After 21 miles, "Willow Creek," water rather brackish. Station "Willow Springs" on bench below hills at W. end of Desert, grass and hay plentiful.	22	A. M. 10	3·30	Sept. 30
8.	Road ascending bench turns N. to find Pass. After 6 miles Mountain Springs, good water, grass, and fuel. Six miles beyond is Deep Creek Kanyon, dangerous ravine 9 miles long. Then descends into fertile and well watered valley, and after 7 miles enters Deep Creek Mail Station. Indian farm.	28	A. M. 8	P. M. 4	Oct. 1
9.	Along W. Creek. After 8 miles, "Eight Miles Springs," water, grass, and sage fuel. Kanyon after 2½ miles, 500 yards long and easy. Then 19 miles through Antelope Valley to station of same name, burnt in June 1860 by Indians. Simpson's route from Pleasant Valley, distant 12·5 miles, falls into E. end of Antelope Valley, from Camp Floyd 151 miles.	30	A. M. 8	P. M. 4	Oct. 3, 4
10.	Road over valley for 2 miles to mouth of Shell Creek Kanyon, 6 miles long. Rough road, fuel plentiful. Descends into Spring Valley, and then passes over other divides into Shell Creek, where there is a mail station; water, grass, and fuel abundant.	18	A. M. 6	P. M. 11	Oct. 5
11.	Descends rough road. Crosses Steptoe Valley and bridged creek. Road heavy, sand or mud. After 16 miles Egan's Kanyon, dangerous for Indians. Station at W. mouth, burned by Indians in Oct. 1860.	18	P. M. 2	P. M. 6	Oct. 5
12.	Pass divide, fall into Butte Valley, and cross its N. end. Bottom very cold. Mail Station half way up hill, very small spring, grass on N. side of hill. Butte Station.	18	P. M. 8	A. M. 3	Oct. 6
13.	Ascend long divide. 2 steep hills and falls. Cross N. end of Long Valley, all barren. Ascend divide and descend into Ruby Valley, road excellent, water, grass, and bottom, fuel distant. Good Mail Station.	22	A. M. 8	P. M. 1·45	Oct. 7
14.	Long divide, fuel plenty, no grass or water. After 10 miles road branches, right hand to Gravelly Ford of Humboldt River. Cross				

No. of Mails		Miles	Start.	Arrival	Date.
	dry bottom. Cross Smith's Fork of Humboldt River in Huntingdon Valley, little stream, bunch-grass and sage fuel on W. end. Ascend Chokop's Pass, Dugway and hard hill, descend into Moonshine Valley. Station at Diamond Springs; warm water but good.	23	A. M. 8	P. M. 1·45	Oct. 8, 9
15.	Cross Moonshine Valley. After 7 miles, sulphurous spring and grass. Twelve miles beyond, ascend divide, no water, fuel and bunch-grass plentiful. Then long divide. After 9 miles, station on Robert's Creek at E. end of Sheawit, or Roberts' Springs Valley.	28	A. M. 8	P. M. 1·45	Oct. 10
16.	Down Valley to west, good road, sage small, no fuel. After 12 miles, willows and water-holes, 3 miles beyond are alkaline wells. Station on bench, water below in dry creek, grass must be brought from 15 miles.	35	A. M. 6·30	P. M. 12·30	Oct. 11
17.	Cross long rough divide to Smoky Valley. At northern end creek called "Wanahonop," or "Netwood," *i. e.* trap. Thence long rough kanyon to Simpson's Park, grass plentiful, water in wells 10 feet deep. Simpson's Park in Shoshone country, and, according to Simpson's Itinerary, 348 miles from Camp Floyd.	25	A. M. 8·15	P. M. 2·25	Oct. 12
18.	Cross Simpson's Park. Ascend Simpson's Pass, a long kanyon, with sweet, "Sage Springs," on summit, bunch-grass plentiful. Descend to fork of road, right-hand to lower, left-hand to upper, ford of Reese's River. Water perennial and good, food poor.	15	A. M. 10	P. M. 2	Oct. 13
19.	Through remainder of Reese's River Valley. After long divide Valley of Smith's Creek, saleratus, no water nor grass. At last, station near kanyon, and hidden from view. Land belongs to Pa Yutas.	28	A. M. 7·20	P. M. 2·45	Oct. 14
20.	Ascend rough kanyon, and descend to barren and saleratus plain. Towards south of valley over bench-land, rough with rock and pitch-hole. "Cold Springs Station" half built, near stream, fuel scarce.	25	A.M. 8·15	P.M. 4·15	Oct. 15
21.	At west gate two miles from station, good grass. After eight miles, water. Two miles beyond is middle gate, water in fiumara, and grass near. Beyond gate two basins,				

[N]o.of [M]ail.		Miles	Start.	Arrival.	Date.
	long divides, winding road, to "Sand Springs Valley," bad water, little grass.	35	A.M. 9·50	P.M. 2·30	Oct. 16
22.	Cross valley, ten miles to summit, over slough inundations, and bad road. Summit shifting sand. Descend five miles to Carson Lake, water tolerable, tule abundant. Round S. side of lake to sink of Carson River Station, no provisions, pasture good, fuel scarce.	25	A.M. 11	P.M. 9	Oct. 17
23.	Cross long plain. Ascend very steep divide, and sight Sierra fifty miles distant. Descend to Carson River. Fort Churchill newly built. Sutler's stores, &c.	25	A.M. 9·30	P.M. 7·15	Oct. 18
[2]4.	Carson City. Carson City lies on the eastern foot of the Sierra Nevada, distant 552 statute miles, according to Captain Simpson, from Camp Floyd. The present itinerary reduces it to 544, and, adding 44 miles, to a total of 588 from Gt. S. L. City.	35	A.M. 11	P.M. 10·30	Oct. 19

III.—Capt. J. H. Simpson's Wagon Road from Camp Floyd to Genoa, Carson Valley, U. T. Explored by direction of General A. G. Johnston, commanding the Department of Utah between the 2nd May, and 12th June, 1859.

Places.	Intermediate Distances. Miles.	Camp to Camp. Miles	Total from Camp Floyd. Miles.	No. of Camp.	Wood.	Water.	Grass.
[Ca]mp Floyd, wood and grass in vicinity						W	
[M]eadow Creek	18·2	18·2	18·2	1			
[Cr]oss Meadow Creek (Rush Valley), mail station ¼ mile	1						
[Sp]ring ⅛ mile to right of Gen. Johnston's Pass, just after passing summit. This spring furnishes but little water, even in the spring, and in the summer would be most probably dry	8·9	9·9	28·1	2	W	W	G

Places.	Intermediate Distances. Miles.	Camp to Camp. Miles.	Total from Camp Floyd. Miles.	No. of Camp.	Wood.	Water.	Grass.
Simpson's Springs, Mail Station	16·2	16·2	44·3	3	W	W	G
Summit, Short-cut Pass	21·6						
1·6 miles below summit	1·6	23·2	67·5	4	Wil-low Sage		ver litt grs.
Tolerable grass skirting low range of rocks on right of road	7·8						G
A little grass, sage in valley	4·8				S		G
Devil's Hole, water slightly brackish	6·7					W	
Fish Springs, mail station	5·4	24·7	92·2	5	Ctw	W	G
Warm Springs	3·4				G W	W	G
Grass in considerable quantity of good character	26·4	29·7	12·19	6			G
Alkaline spring to right of road, water not drinkable	1						
Sulphur springs, water abundant and palatable	1·5	2·5	125·	7	W.S	W	G
Spring, Pleasant Valley, mail station	13·4	13·4	138·4	8	W	W	G
East side Antelope Valley		12·5	150·9	9	W	W	G
Spring Valley, good grass on west bench and slopes		19·	169·9	10	G W	W	G
Cross Marsh, road takes up a fine stream, grass all along	3·5						
Leave Creek	3·5				W	W	G
Spring, copious, grass fine	2·8				W	W	G
East side, Steptoe Valley, mail station	1·3	11·1	181·0	11	W	W	G
Steptoe Creek; dry in summer	6·5						
Mouth Egan Cañon	6·8	13·3	194·3	12	W	W	G
Spring, source of Egan Creek	1·8				W	W	G
West side of Butte Valley. Mail station. A very small spring, barely sufficient for cooking purposes, near top of hill; grass on N. side of same hill	16·2	18·1	212·4	13	W	W	G
Spring 1 mile west side of summit of range	12·	12·	224·4	14	W	W	G
Ruby Valley, mail station	9·2	9·2	233·6	15	G W	W	G
Smith's Fork, Humboldt R. Huntingdon's Creek	14·4						
Small mountain stream	3·3	17·6	251·2	16	G W	W	G
Spring left of road	1·2				G W	W	G
Near west foot of Cho-kupe Pass	5·8	7·1	258·3	17	G W	W	G
Spring in Pah-hun-nupe Valley	7·8						
Do. west side of Pah-hun-nupe Valley	5·6	13·3	271·6	18	S,W G W	W	G
She-a-wi-te (Willow) Creek	14·9	14·9	286·5	19	S.W	W	G

Places.	Intermediate Distances. Miles.	Camp to Camp. Miles.	Total from Camp Floyd. Miles.	No. of Camp.	Wood.	Water.	Grass.
Bed of Nash R. water in pools, probably not constant . . .	11·6						
Small spring, grass on mountain side, 2 miles off	5·9	17·5	304·	20	S.W	W	G
Wons-in-dam-me, or Antelope Creek .	7·	7·	311·	21	W	W	G
Creek	4·3				S.W	W	G
Creek west side of Valley . . .	9·5	13·7	324·7	22	S.W	W	G
Wan-a-ho-mo-pe (Netwood trap) Creek	13·6						
Do. do. do. . . .	4·6	18·2	342·9	23	S.W	W	G
Simpson's Park, according to topographers, Lt. Putnam and guide, Col. Reese	4·9	4·9	347·8	24	S.W	W	G
Small spring in Simpson's Pass (same authority)	3·						
Ford of Reese's River	8·2					W	G
Reese's River	2·6	13·8	361·6	25		W	G
Leave Reese's River	3·4					W	G
Small spring to left of road just before reaching summit of Pass . .	10·						
Lt. J. L. Kirby Smith's Creek . .	7·8	21·2	382·8	26	G W	W	G
Englemanns " . .	1·6					W	
Lt. Putnam's " . .	8·6	10·2	393·	27	S.W	W	G
Do. South Fork . . .	2·7				W	W	G
Rock Creek	3·				W	W	G
Do.	3·1	8·7	401·7	28	W	W	G
Do. Sinks	1·7						
Spring-water kegs should be filled for 2 days. Camp from this in alkaline flat	5·4					W	
Gibraltar Gate	0·6					W	
Creek joins Gibraltar Creek . .	4·2						
Middle Gate Spring	3·2	14·7	416·4	29	S.W	W	G
West Gate	3·5						
Dry wells, alkaline valley, very poor camp, water and grass alkaline, and little of either. Rabbit bush fuel	21·0	24·5	440·9	30	Rab. bush	W	G
Creek connecting the two lakes of Carson. Road can be shortened some eight or ten miles by striking across head of Alkaline Valley after getting about nine miles from camp 30, and then proceeding directly to shore of Carson Lake. It is not necessary to go so far north as the connecting creek referred to . .		16·6	457·5	31	Dry rush	W	R, G

Places.	Intermediate Distances. Miles.	Camp to Camp. Miles.	Total from Camp Floyd. Miles.	No. of Camp.	Wood.	Water.	Grass.
Leave Carson Lake	9·7					W	R. G
Walker's River	21·5	31·2	488·7	32	W	W	G
Do. do.		10·	498·7	33	W	W	G
Do. North bend		6·3	505·	34	W	W	G
Small spring, not sufficient for large command, grass half mile south	14·1				S. W	W	G
Carson River	1·9						
Do. do.	3·0	19·0	524·	35	W	W	G
Pleasant Grove, cross Carson River and get into Old Emigrant Road. Mail Station	9·0	9·0	533·	36	W	W	G
China town. Gold diggings . .	7·4					W	
Carson city. E. foot of Sierra Nevada	11·6	19·0	552·	37		W	G
Genoa do. do. do. .	12·9	12·9	564·9	38	W	W	G

To Brevet-Major F. J. Porter,
Assist.-Adj.-Genl.
Dept. Utah, Camp Floyd.

(Signed) J. H. Simpson,
Capt. Top Engineers.

IX.—*From Fort Bridger to the "City of Rocks."*
From Captain Handcock's Journal.

Miles.

Fort Bridger to—

9. Little Muddy Creek.—Water brackish in pools along the creek; tall bunch grass; sage for fuel. Road runs over a barren section, is rough, and passes one steep hill.

12⅓. Big Muddy Creek.—The road, with the exception of two or three bad gullies, is good for ten miles; it then follows the Big Muddy Bottom, which is flat and boggy. The camp is three miles above the crossing. Some grass; sage for fuel.

14⅓. Small Branch of the Muddy Creek.—Cross the River in three miles at a bad ford. A mile above camp the grass is good. Road generally good.

19½. On Small Creek.—Road continues up the Muddy 9½ miles to its head. It then ascends to the divide between Bear and

Miles.

Green Rivers, probably 800 feet in $1\frac{3}{5}$ miles. The descent on the other side is about the same. The road passes many fine springs. At one and two miles back it passes points of hills, where it is very rough. Good grass and sage at camp.

$8\frac{9}{10}$. Bear River.—Bad Creek to cross near the camp; thence to Bear River Valley the road is good. It then follows down the River, crossing Willow Creek. Good camp, with a large fine spring.

17. Bear River.—Good road along the river; plenty of wood, water, and grass at all points.

Foot of Grant's Mountain.—Road runs along Bear River; at $2\frac{1}{2}$ miles strikes Smith's Fork, a rapid trout stream. The road crosses the lower ford. A few miles farther on is a bad slough, which can be avoided by taking a round on the hills. Cross Thomas's Fork on a bridge, also a slough near it; toll \$2·00 for each team and wagon. The road then leaves Bear River Valley, and turns over a very steep hill. Good grass, wood, and water.

12. Bear River.—Road ascends Grant's Mountain 1,200 feet in $1\frac{1}{2}$ miles (double teams), then descends again into Bear River Valley at $4\frac{4}{5}$ miles. Good wood, water, and grass.

$17\frac{2}{5}$. Indian Creek.—Road crosses eight fine spring branches; camp is on a beautiful trout stream. Good wood, water, and grass.

11. Spring near Bear River.—Road is hilly, crossing two spring branches. Good wood, water, and grass. The camp is on the left, and near the road.

11. Bear River.—At $6\frac{7}{10}$ miles the road strikes a large group of springs, called "Soda Springs," and here crosses Pine Creek, on the left bank of which is a saleratus lake. Soon after, it strikes the main springs, and, after crossing another creek, the "Steamboat spring, may be seen in the bed of the river.

15. "Port Neuf," or Rock Creek.—At $2\frac{3}{10}$ miles the road leaves Bear River near where it runs through a cañon with high bluffs on each side. At this point, the California and Fort Hall roads separate. The California road (called Hudspeth's Cut-off) then crosses a valley between the Bear River and Port Neuf River Mountains, 9 miles. No water from camp to camp. Good camp.

15. Marsh Creek.—About two miles above the main road, the creek can be forded; a road leads to it from the descent into the valley. Road good; water and grass plènty; no wood.

$16\frac{1}{5}$. Paunack Creek.—First part of the road is hilly; the remainder good. Good camp.

$7\frac{1}{5}$. Mallade River.—At $7\frac{1}{5}$ miles the road crosses the Mallade

Miles.

River. Good camp 140 miles from Salt Lake City. Good Road.

$22\frac{3}{10}$. Small Creek.—The road ascends a ridge through a cañon, and descends to a valley on the other side. From the Camp to the summit of the ridge is $6\frac{1}{5}$ miles; the descent is $3\frac{7}{10}$ miles. It then crosses a valley 8 miles wide, and strikes a cañon which leads to the top of a hill over a rough road. Plenty of wood, water, and grass at camp, but no water between this and the last camp.

$9\frac{3}{5}$. Small Creek.—Road after five miles strikes a cañon with a long but gentle ascent. Two miles from the entrance of this cañon is a spring branch. There is wood and some grass and water at this place.

$11\frac{1}{5}$. Spring Branch.—The road passes through a cañon, and at 5 miles strikes the head of a spring branch, which it follows down $2\frac{1}{2}$ miles to the junction with a larger branch which is bridged. At nine-tenths of a mile, another fork enters. Grass very fine here. Road follows down this across the main branch, and the camp is 2 miles below. Good camp.

$18\frac{1}{2}$. Decassure Creek, or Raft River.—Road continues down the creek $2\frac{3}{10}$ miles, and crosses, then ascends by a steep hill to an elevated sage plain, leaving the creek at $11\frac{4}{5}$ miles, and passes a slough with water. Good camp.

$17\frac{9}{10}$. Spring Branch.—The road crosses the creek near the last camp, and follows up a valley, crossing in five miles several spring branches. At $2\frac{9}{10}$ miles it crosses the creek again, and follows up the valley 2 miles further, then crosses a high sage plain $8\frac{9}{10}$ miles long, when it strikes a spring 150 yards to the left of the road, where there is an excellent camp in a beautiful valley.

10. Junction of Salt Lake City Road.—Road passes several small branches in 3 miles, then commences ascending through a cañon, which, in $2\frac{1}{5}$ miles, leads to the entrance to the "City of Rocks," and passes through these for three miles. It then crosses a ridge, leaving the City of Rocks, and, at ten miles from last camp intersects the road from Salt Lake City. At $1\frac{2}{5}$ miles beyond this, a road leads off to the right to a spring branch 3 miles, where there is a good camp, near the foot of Goose Creek Mountain. From this point Californian travelers can refer to the itinerary of the route from Salt Lake City to Sacramento.

X.—*From Soda Springs to the City of Rocks, known as Hudspeth's Cut-off.*

Miles.

Soda Springs to—

20. Bear River.—The road runs down Bear River, crossing some small streams. Good camp.
10. Portner Creek.—Camp at the head of the creek. Good wood, water, and grass.
12. Fork of Portner Creek.—Good camp.
15. Pauack Creek.—Road crosses a summit. Good road and camp.
12. Snake Spring.—Good camp.
12. Utha Spring.—Good camp.
15. Decassure Creek.—Road crosses a small stream; rather bad crossing. Good camp.
18. City of Rocks.—Junction of Salt lake road. Good camp.

XI.—*Sublet's Cut-off, from the junction of the Salt Lake and Fort Hall Roads.*

Miles.

Junction to—

7. Big Sandy.
44. Green River.—From the Big Sandy to Green River (upper road) there is an abundance of grass in places along the road, but no water.
6. Small Creek.—The road runs up the creek. Good grass.
4. On the Creek.—Good grass and water.
12. Small Spring.—The spring is on the left of the road. Good grass.
9. Ham's Fork.—Good wood, water, and grass.
6. Spring.—On the summit of a mountain. Good grass.
6. Muddy Creek.—Wood, water, and grass.
10. Spring.—In Bear River Valley. Good wood, water, and grass.
6. Smith's Fork.—In Bear River Valley. Good wood, water, and grass.
10. Tomaus' Fork.—Road runs down Bear River. Good wood, water, and grass.
7. Spring Creek.—Wood, water, and grass.
7. Smith's Ford.—Road crosses over a spur of the mountain; long and gradual ascent; descent rather abrupt. Good wood, water, and grass.
8. Telleck's Fork.—Road runs down Bear River. Good camp.
4. Small Creek.—Good camp.
4. Small Creek.—Good camp.

Miles.
7. Small Creek.—Good camp.
12. Soda Springs.—Left side of the road, among some cedars, is a good camp.

Here take the left-hand road to California, called *Hudspeth's Cut-off.*

XII.—*From Lawson's Meadows, on the Humboldt River, to Fort Reading,* via *Rouge River Valley, Fort Lane, Oregon Territory, Yreka, and Fort Jones.*

Miles.
Lawson's Meadows to—

18½. Mountain Spring.—Road leaves the Humboldt, and takes a north-westerly course 12 miles to a spring of good water. Good bunch-grass to the left of the road, and a small spring at the camp. The road is plain on leaving the river; but, after a few days, it becomes faint. Road from this point passes over a desert country for about 60 miles, without good water or much grass.

38½. Black Rock Spring.—Road level and hard, with little vegetation. In 14 miles pass springs, but the water is not good. In 16 miles, the road passes a slough which is difficult to cross; water not good, but can be given to cattle in small quantities. In five miles from this, the road passes Black Rock, mentioned by Colonel Frémont in his trip from Columbia River in 1843-4. Three miles further, pass boiling springs, very hot, but good cooled. Grass pretty good.

20¼. Mountain Rill.—Water good; bunch-grass in the vicinity. In 8 miles' travel the road passes a beautiful creek of pure water, with good grass.

5¾. Lake (Marshy).

10½. High Rock Cañon.—This cañon is 25 miles long, with wild and curious scenery. Road crosses the creek frequently, and the mud is bad. In the autumn the road is good.

14¾. High Rock Cañon.
Small Creek.—Beautiful country, with the greatest abundance of water and grass; also fuel.

25¼. Pine Grove Creek.—Road passes over an interesting country, well supplied with wood, water, and grass, and passes around the south end of a salt lake.

18½. West Slope of Sierra.—Road passes over the mountain, which is steep but not rocky, then descends to a small creek of good water which runs into Goose Lake. Good grass and fuel.

Miles.

Look out for the Indians, as they are warlike and treacherous here.

7¾. East shore of Goose Lake.—Excellent camp.

16¼. West shore of Goose Lake.—This is a beautiful sheet of fresh water; great quantities of water-fowl resort to this lake.

16¼. Slough Springs.—The road passes over a very rocky divide, covered with loose volcanic debris, very hard for animals, and wearing to their feet. They should be well shod before attempting the passage.

18½. Marshy Lake.—Road difficult for wagons.

15. Clear Lake.—Beautiful lake of pure water, with good grass around its shore.

25¼. East shore of Rhett's Lake.—Road tolerable over a rolling, rocky country, between lakes. The road crosses Lost River over a natural bridge, on a solid smooth ledge of rock.

19. West shore of Rhett's Lake.—Plenty of wood, water, and grass along this road.

21. Klamath River.—Road leaves Rhett's Lake, and enters the forest and mountains; tolerably good. Good camp.

15¼. Cascade Mountains.—The road passes over high mountains, through lofty pine trees. Camp is at Summit Meadows. Good water and grass; also fuel.

14¼. Western slope of Cascade Mountains.—Rough roads.

19¼. Rogue River Valley.—Road descends into the settlements in six miles, where there is a lovely fertile valley, well settled with farmers.

23¾. Fort Lane.—Near "Table Rock," on Rogue River, eight miles from Jacksonville. Dragoon post.

22¾. Rogue River Valley.—Good camp.

18. Siskiyou Mountains.—Road crosses the Siskiyou Mountains, and is difficult for wagons.

18. Yreka.—Flourishing mining city.

18. Fort Jones.—Infantry post, in Scott's Valley.

20. Scott's Mountain,—Good camp at the foot of the mountain. Road passes over the mountains; but is impassable for wagons.

90. Shasta City.—Good grass, wood, and water.

180. Sacramento City.

XIII.—*From Soda Springs to Fort Wallah Wallah and Oregon City, Oregon,* via *Fort Hall.*

Miles.

Soda Springs to—

25. Portner Creek.—Good camp. Take the right-hand road.

Miles.

10. Ross's Creek.—Good camp.
10. Fort Hall Valley.—Good camp. Road runs down the creek.
8. Snake River.—Good camp. Road crosses the river bottom.
5. Fort Hall.
15. Small Branch.—Camp is three miles below the crossing of Port Neuf River, which is fordable. Good wood, water, and grass.
10. American Falls.—Good camp.
13. Raft River.—Road rough and rocky. Sage for fuel; grass scarce.
17. Bend of Swamp Creek.—Grass scarce.
20. On Snake River.—Road crosses Swamp and Goose Creeks. Wood on the hills; grass short.
25. Rock Creek.—Road crosses one small creek, and is very rough and rocky for several miles, when it enters a sandy region, where the grass is scarce; sage plenty, and willows on the creek.
24. Snake River.—Road crosses several small branches. There is but little grass, except in narrow patches along the river bottom.
26. Fishing Falls.—Road very crooked and rough, crossing two small streams.
29. Snake River.—Road crosses several small creeks, but leaves the main river to the north, and runs upon an elevated plateau. Good grass at camp.
16. Snake River (ford).—Road tortuous; ford good in low water.
19. Small Branch—Road crosses Snake River, and follows up a small branch, leaving the river to the left; good grass. Road ascends to a high plateau, which it keeps during the whole distance.
26. River "Aux Rochers."—Road passes Hot Springs, and is rough. Wood, water, and grass plenty.
22. Small Creek.—Road crosses two small branches, and is very rocky, but, at camp, grass, wood, and water are abundant.
23. Rio Boisè.—Road crosses one small creek, and follows along the Boisè River. Good wood, water, and grass.
26. Fort Boisè.—Road follows the south bank of Boisè River to the fort.
2. Fort Boisè.—Road crosses Boisè River. Good ford at ordinary stages. Grass good in the river bottom.
20. River "Aux Matthews."—Good road; grass abundant, but coarse; wood and water plenty.
27. Snake River.—Road passes over a rough country. Grass scarce, and of a poor quality.
20. Burnt River.—Road leaves Snake River, and takes across Burnt River, following up the north side of this to the camp. It is mountainous and rough, but the grass is good, and there is wood along the river.

Miles.

22. Burnt River.—Road continues up the river, and is still rough and mountainous. Grass and wood plenty.
26. Small branch.—Road passes over a divide to "Powder River." It is still rough, but getting better. The grass is good.
13. Powder River.—Good road ; grass plenty.
21. Creek.—Road passes a divide, crossing several small streams, and is smooth, with plenty of grass and fuel.
20. Creek.—Road crosses one small branch, and is rather rough. The grass and fuel are good and abundant.
21. Creek.—Road follows down the creek for ten miles, then turns up a small branch, and is good. There is plenty of grass and fuel.
12. Branch.—Road crosses a divide and strikes another branch.
5. Small branch of the Umatilah River.—Good road, with plenty of wood and grass.
16. Branch of Wallah Wallah River.—Wood, water, and grass.
18. Wallah Wallah River.—Wood, water, and grass.
18. Wallah Wallah River.—Wood. water, and grass.
Columbia River at Fort Wallah.—Wood water, and grass.
10. Butler Creek.—Good camp.
18. Well's Spring.—Good camp.
12. Willow Creek.—Good camp.
13. Cedar Spring.—Good camp.
6. John Day's River.—Good camp.
5. Forks of Road.—No camping. Left-hand road for wagons, and right-hand for pack-trains. This itinerary takes the left.
10. Ouley's Camp.—Good camp.
19. Soot's River.—Good camp.
6. Fall River.—Good camp.
10. Utah's River.—Good camp.
18. Soot's River.—Good camp.
6. Soot's River.—Good camp. Road follows up the river, crossing it several times.
16. Sand River Fork.—Good grass a mile and a half to the left of the road.
8. Good Camp.
15. Royal Hill Camp.—Good camp.
17. Sandy River.—But little grass.
45. Down the River.—Good camps all the distance.
25. Oregon City.—Good camps all the distance.
75. Salem.—Good camps all the distance.

XIV.—*Route for pack trains from John Day's River to Oregon City.*

Miles.

John Day's River to—

17. Columbia River.—From John Day's River to the forks of the road, and thence by the right-hand fork to the Columbia. Good camp.

2½. Soot's River Ferry.—Good camp.

15. Dalles.—Good camp.

25. Dog River.—Good camp.

15. Cascade Mountains.—One bad place.

9. Ouley's Rock.—Good camp.

20. Image Plain Ferry.—Good camp.

15. Portland.—Good camp.

12. Oregon City.—Good camp.

XV.—*From Indianola and Powder-horn to San Antonio, Texas.*

Miles.

Powder-horn to—

4. Indianola, Texas.—Steamers run from New Orleans five times a week to Powder-horn.

14. Chocolate Creek.—Good grass and water; fuel scarce. Road passes over a low flat country, which in wet weather is heavy and muddy.

12. Grove.—Grove of oak; good water and grass. The road passes over a hog-wallow prairie, which is very muddy, and almost impassable for loaded teams after rains. The grass is abundant everywhere in this section.

12½. Victoria.—The road is good, passing along near the east bank of the Guadalupe River. The country is thickly settled with farmers, who sell grain at reasonable rates. Grass abundant, also fuel.

34. Yorktown.—Road crosses the Guadalupe River on a bridge; toll one dollar for a six-mule team. It then crosses a low bottom for three miles; from thence the road is good, over a rolling country, with plenty of wood, water, and grass.

33. Cibello River.—Good road; wood, water, and grass plenty.

35. San Antonio.—Good road, with plenty of wood, water, and grass along the road. The Cibello is fordable at ordinary stages. The traveler can procure anything he may need at Victoria and at San Antonio.

XVI.—*Wagon-road from San Antonio, Texas, to El Paso, N.M., and Fort Yuma, Cal.*

[Distances in miles and hundredths of a mile.]

Miles.

San Antonio to—

6·41. Leona.
18·12. Castroville.
11·00. Hondo.
14·28. Rio Seco.
12·50. Sabinal.
13·46. Rio Frio.
15·12. Neuces.
10·27. Turkey Creek.
15·33. Elm Creek.—All good camps, with abundance of wood, water, and grass. Country mostly settled, and the road very good, except in wet weather, from San Antonio to Elm Creek.
7·00. Fort Clarke.—Good grass, wood, and water. Road level and good.
7·00. Piedra Pinta.—Good grass, wood, and water.
8·86. Maverick's Creek.—Good grass, wood, and water.
12·61. San Felipé.—Good grass, wood and water.
10·22. Devil's River.—First crossing. Good wood, water, and grass.
18·27. California Springs. Grass and water poor.
18·39. Devil's River.—Second crossing. Grass poor.
19·50. Devil's River.—Good camp. The only water between Devil's River and Live Oak Creek is at Howard's Springs. The road is very rough in places.
44·00. Howard's Springs.—Grass scarce; water plenty in winter; wood plenty.
30·44. Live Oak Creek.—Good water and grass. The road passes within 1½ miles of Fort Lancaster.
7·29. Crossing of Pecos River.—Bad water and bad camp. The water of the Pecos can be used.
5·47. Las Moras.—Good water, grass, and wood. The road is rough on the Pecos.
32·85. Camp on the Pecos River.—Wood and grass scarce.
16·26. Escondido Creek.—At the crossing. Water good; little grass or wood.
8·76. Escondido Spring.—Grass and water good; little grass.
19·40. Comanche Creek.—Grass and water good; little grass.
8·88. Leon Springs.—Grass and water good; no wood.
33·86. Barela Spring.—Grass and water good; wood plenty.
28·00. Fort Davis.—Good camp. From Fort Davis to Eagle Springs there is an ascent, and one of the very best of roads.
18·42. Barrel Springs.—Water good; grass and wood fair.

Miles.

13·58. Dead Man's Hole.—Good wood and water; grass scarce.
32·83. Van Horne's Wells.—No grass or wood; but they will be found two miles back.
19·74. Eagle Springs.—Grass and wood poor; water about half a mile from camp in a narrow cañon.
32·03. Mouth of Cañon "de los Camenos."—The road is rather rough. From here to Fort Bliss, opposite El Paso, the road runs near the river, and camps may be made anywhere. The wood, water, and grass are good at all points.
61·13. San Eluzario.—Mexican town.
9·25. Socorro.—Mexican town.
15·00. Fort Bliss, at El Paso.—United States military post and Mexican town.

Total distance from San Antonio to El Paso, 654·27 miles.

Miles.

El Paso to—

22. Cottonwood.—From El Paso to Messilla Valley, in the Gadsden Purchase, the road runs up the east bank of the Rio Grande to Fort Fillmore (N.M.), where it crosses the river into the Messilla Valley.
22. Fort Fillmore.
6. La Messilla.
65. Cook's Spring.—From Messilla Valley to Tucson the road is remarkably good, with good grass and water. The streams on this section are the Mimbres and San Pedro, both fordable, and crossed with little trouble. The Apache Indians are generally met with in this country. There is a flour-mill two miles below El Paso, where flour can be purchased at very reasonable prices.
18. Rio Mimbres.
17. Ojo la Vaca.
10. Ojo de Ynez.
34. Peloncilla.
18. San Domingo.
23. Apache Springs.
9. Cabesas Springs.
26. Dragon Springs.
18. Quercos Cañon.—Bunch-grass will be found sufficient for traveling purposes along this section of the road between El Paso and Tucson.
6. San Pedro Crossing.
20. Cienega.
13. Cienega Creek.
20. Mission of San Xavier.
8. Tucson.—Total distance from El Paso to Tucson, 305 miles.

Miles.
5. Pico Chico Mountain.
35. First Camp on Gila River.
29. Maricopa Wells.—The Maricopa Wells are at the western extremity of a fertile valley occupied by Pincos Indians, who cultivate corn and other grain.
40. Tezotal.—Across Jornada. There is but little grass here; but, in the season, the mesquite leaves are a good substitute.
10. Ten Mile Camp.
15. Oatman's Flat.—First crossing of the Gila River.
25. Second crossing of the Gila.—The traveler can generally find sufficient grass in the hills along the valley of the Gila.
32. Peterman's Station.
20. Antelope Peak.
24. Little Corral.
16. Fort Yuma.

The distance from El Paso to Fort Yuma is 644 miles.

XVII.—*From Fort Yuma to San Diego, California.*

[Distances in miles and huudredths of a mile.]

Miles.
Fort Yuma to—
10·00. Los Algodones.—Along the Colorado.
10·00. Cook's Wells.—Here commences the great desert; water nowhere good or reliable, until ariving at Carizo Creek. The points named are where deep wells have been dug. "New River," though usually set down, is a dry arroyo. The surface of the desert for seven miles on the eastern side is drifting sand and heavy for wagons. Then comes a section in the centre of the desert that is hard and level. On the west side there is about three miles of a mud flat.
21·90. Alamo Rancho.
16·40. Little Laguna.
4·50. New River.
5·80. Big Laguna.
26·40. Carizo Creek.—Water good; cane and brush for fuel, and they afford some forage for the animals; no grass.
16·60. Vallecito.—Grass poor; wood and water sufficient.
17·80. San Felipe.—Grass poor; wood scarce; water good.
15·80. Warner's Ranch.—The road passes through a beautiful oak grove, where there is an abundance of grass and water. This is the summit of the mountain. At the Ranch the grass is poor, and no wood. The water is good. The oak grove terminates six miles from Warner's.

Miles.
10·30. Santa Isabel.—Good grass, wood, and water. This was an old Spanish mission, but is now occupied by some Americans and Indians.
11·40. Laguna.—Two miles from last camp, is a good camping-place. The road passes over some steep hills, not high. This is the best camp on the road.
12·00. San Pasquel.—For the first nine miles, the road is level and good to the top of the mountain, where there is a good camping-place, with wood, water, and grass; thence the road descends a very steep hill. The camp is on the east side of the brook, near Soto's house.
18·80. Parrasquitas.—The road passes a good camp three miles from San Pasqual. Wood, water, and grass at Parrasquitas.
8·00. Fisher's House.—The road passes over several hills; and, at four miles, is a good camping-place. Wood, water, and grass at camp.
San Diego, California.—When animals are to be kept a considerable time at San Diego, they should be taken four or five miles up the river, as the grass is poor near the town.
Total distance from Fort Yuma to San Diego, 217 miles.

XVIII.—*From El Paso, New Mexico, to Fort Yuma, California,* viâ *Santa Cruz.*

[Distances in miles and hundredths of a mile.]

Miles.
From El Paso to—
26·10. Samalayuca.—Spring, with grass and wood.
38·00. Salado.—Bad water, with little grass and wood.
24·75. Santa Maria.—Good grass, wood, and water.
27·50. Mines of San Pedro.—Bad water; little grass or water.
19·20. Correlitos.—Good water, grass, and wood.
20·00. Janos.—Good water, grass, and wood.
12·00. Pelatudo.—Good water, grass, and wood.
30·00. San Francisco.—Water half-a-mile south of the road.
18·00. San Louis.—Good water, grass, and wood.
35·00. San Bernardino.—Good water, grass, and wood.
30·00. Ash Creek.—Grass, wood and water.
37·00. Head of San Pedro.—Grass and water.
24·00. Santa Cruz.—Good grass, wood, and water.
31·00. Cocospe.—Much grass; ten or twelve miles without water. Leave Santa Cruz River at old Rancho San Lazaro. No water till reaching the head of San Ignacio, except at nine miles; a spring, one mile west of the road.

Miles.

26·00. Hemores.—From Cocospe to Santa Anna, follow down the San Ignacio; and in many places there is wood and grass. Grass is much better at three miles from the river. At the foot of the hills there is abundance of grama-grass.

5·00. Terrenati.

4·00. San Ignacio.

5·20. Madina.

5·20. San Lorenzo.

2·60. Santa Marta.

5·20. Santa Anna.

26·00. Alamita.—Plenty of grass. Leave the river ten or twelve miles from Santa Anna, and no water thence to Alamita, which is a small rancho.

31·20. Altar.—No water; grass abundant.

13·00. Laguna.—Small water-hole; grass scanty and poor.

52·00. Sonia.—Sometimes water is found 25 miles from the Laguna, south of the road. There is a well at Sonia in the town, and sometimes water in a hole 300 yards south of the town, 100 yards west of the road.

10·40. El Paso.—Well at El Paso supplying 100 animals; water muddy and brackish; grass poor.

52·00. Sonorita.—No water on the road; at Sonorita are several brackish springs. Grass poor; bad campaigning place; saltpeter at the springs.

Quita Oaquita.—No water on the road. Saline spring at camp, better than at Sonorita, but the grass is not so good.

10·40. Agua Salado.—Water uncertain; grass poor.

23·40. Los Pleyes.—Water only in the rainy season, one mile west of the road, hidden by bushes, and difficult to find; grass pretty good.

28·60. Cabeza Prieta.—Natural tenajas in a ravine two miles from the road; follow a wagon-track up this ravine between a black and a red mountain. The water is good and abundant; grass tolerable.

31·00. Poso.—No water on the road until reaching Poso. Here it is abundant on the east side of the road; grass good one mile west.

13·00. Rio Gila.—But little good grass.

26·00. Fort Yuma, at the crossing of the Colorado River.—But little good grass for several miles.

Total Distance from El Paso to Fort Yuma, 756 miles

XIX.—*From Westport, Missouri, to the gold diggings at Pike's Peak and "Cherry Creek," N.T.,* via *the Arkansas River.*

Miles.

Westport to—

4¾. Indian Creek.—The road runs over a beautiful country. Indian Creek is a small wooded stream, with abundance of grass and water.

8¾. Cedar Creek.—The road passes over a fine country, and there is a good camping-place at Cedar Creek.

8½. Bull Creek.—The road is smooth and level, with less wood than before. Camping good.

9½. Willow Springs.—At nine miles, the road passes "Black Jack Creek," where there is a good camping-place. The road has but little wood upon it at firs; but it increases towards the end of the march. The road is level for some distance, but becomes more rolling, and the country is covered with the finest grass. Good camp at one mile from the main road.

20¼. 110-Mile Creek.—The road traverses the same character of country as yesterday, but with less woodland, is very smooth, and at nine and twelve miles passes "Rock Creeks," which have no running water in a dry season. Good camp.

22½. Prairie Chicken Creek.—At eight miles the road crosses Dwissler Creek, which is a fine little stream; four miles further First Dragoon Creek, and at one mile further the Second Dragoon Creek, both fine streams, well wooded, and good camping places. Good camp.

20. "Big Rock Creek."—At one mile the road crosses a small wooded branch. Three miles beyond, it crosses "Elm Creek," where a good camping-place may be found. At seven miles, it crosses 142-Mile Creek, and at thirteen miles it crosses Bluff Creek, where there is a good camping-place. Good camp.

20. "Council Grove," on "Elm Creek."—Road passes "Big John Spring" at thirteen miles, and is smooth and good. A fine camp is found three-fourths of a mile beyond the "Grove,' on Elm Creek, with abundance of wood, water, and grass.

16. Diamond Spring.—At eight miles the road crosses Elm Creek, and passes over a section similar to that east of Council Grove. It is fine in dry weather, but muddy after heavy rains. Good camp at Diamond Spring.

16. Lost Spring.—One mile from camp, the road passes a wooded creek. From thence there is no more wood or permanent water until arriving at camp. Take wood here for cooking, as there is not a tree or a bush in sight from Lost Spring. The country becomes more level, with grass everywhere. The road is muddy in wet weather.

Miles.

15¾. Cottonwood Creek.—Road continues over a prairie country, sensibly rising and improving. Wood, water, and grass at camp.

22. Turkey Creek.—The road is good, and at eighteen miles passes Little Turkey Creek. No wood, and the water poor at camp; grass good.

23. Little Arkansas River.—The road runs over a level prairie, and at 3½ miles passes "Big Turkey Creek," with the Arkansas River Valley in sight all day. After rains, there are frequent pools of water along the road. Good camp.

20. "Big Cow" Creek.—The road passes for ten miles over a level prairie to Charez Creek, which is a bushy gully; thence six miles to Little Cow Creek, which is a brushy stream, with here and there a tree. Good camp here to the left of the road, near a clump of trees. "Prairie-dog towns" commence to be seen. Road very level. Buffalo-grass here.

20. Big Bend of the Arkansas.—The road, at twelve miles, strikes the sand-hills of the Arkansas River. They are soon passed, however, and the level river bottom is reached. The river has a rapid current flowing over a quicksand bed. The road is generally good from the last camp. Wood, water, and grass at camp.

7. Walnut Creek. The road is good. Cool springs at this camp; good grass and wood.

21. Head of Coon Creek.—At five miles, the road forks, one following the river, the other a "short-cut" "dry route" to Fort Atkinson, where they unite on the river. The country rises for ten miles on the dry route, then descends to the river, and is covered with the short buffalo-grass. No wood at camp.

18. Arkansas River.—The road passes over an undulating and uninteresting prairie, with but little vegetation. The water in dry weather is in pools.

19. Arkansas River, at Fort Atkinson.—The road runs over a similar country to that of yesterday, with no wood near; plenty of buffalo-chips for cooking, and good grass.

18¾. Arkansas River.—At 4½ miles the road ascends a bluff covered with thick buffalo grass. On the river is heavy bottom grass. At seventeen miles pass a ford. Grass good at camp.

19¼. Arkansas River.—The road is sandy for fourteen miles, but not deep, except in places; thence to camp it is good. Good camp.

22. Arkansas River.—Country prairie, covered with short buffalo-grass; good camp.

22. Arkansas River.—The road is fine, crossing several dry beds of creeks, along which are seen a few scattering trees. Good camp on a dry creek near the river.

24. Arkansas River.—The road runs over a barren plain at the

Miles.

foot of the main plateau, and crosses two dry creeks near the camp, on which are cottonwood-trees. Plenty of wood at camp.

21. Arkansas River.—The road follows the base of the hills at from one to three miles from the river; good camp.

20. Arkansas River.—At seven miles, the road strikes the "Big Timbers," where there is a large body of cottonwood; thence for three miles the road is heavy sand; good camps along here.

13. Arkansas River.—At one mile, the road passes some old houses formerly used as a trading-post. Here terminates the "Big Timbers." Coarse grass at the camp.

15. Arkansas River.—At three miles, the road passes the mouth of Purgatoire Creek. Camp is below Bent's Fort. Good grass here.

24. Arkansas River.—Pass Bent's Fort. The grass is excellent in the vicinity of the fort, but after this it is not so good. The road runs over a high and considerably broken country; good camp.

11. Arkansas River.—Opposite the mouth of the Apishpa Creek; good camp. The Huerfano Mountains and Spanish Peaks are in sight from the camp. The "Cherokee Trail" comes in from Arkansas, near Bent's Fort, and leads to the gold diggings at Cherry Creek.

9. Arkansas River.—Opposite the mouth of the Huerfano Creek. Good camp, and a ford opposite Charles Audebee's House.

12. Arkansas River.—At this point the Cherokee trail bears to the right and leaves the river. The left-hand, or river road, runs up to the old pueblo at the mouth of the Fontaine qui Bouille Creek. The right-hand road leads to the gold diggings.

15$\frac{3}{4}$. Fontaine qui Bouille.—The road strikes in a north-west course over the rolling country, and comes upon the creek at a most beautiful camp, where there is a great abundance of good wood, water, and grass. The wood, water, and grass are good at all points on the Fontaine qui Bouille, and travelers can camp anywhere upon this stream.

17$\frac{1}{2}$. Fontaine qui Bouille.—Here the road forks, one running up the river, and the other striking directly across to the divide of the Arkansas and Platte. I prefer the left-hand road, as it has more water and better grass upon it.

6$\frac{1}{2}$. Forks of the "Fontaine qui Bouille." The road to Cherry Creek here leaves the "Fontaine qui Bouille" and bears to the right. There is a large Indian trail which crosses the main creek, and takes a north-west course toward "Pike's Peak." By going up this trail about two miles, a mineral spring will be found, which gives the spring its name of "The Fountain that Boils." This spring, or rather these springs,

Miles.

as there are two, both of which boil up out of solid rock, are among the greatest natural curiosities that I have ever seen. The water is strongly impregnated with salts, but is delightful to the taste, and somewhat similar to the Congress-water. It will well compensate anyone for the trouble of visiting it.

17½ Black Squirrel Creek.—This creek is near the crest of the high divide between the Arkansas and Platte Rivers. It is a small running branch, but always affords good water. There is pine timber here, and the grass is good on the prairies to the east. This is a locality which is very subject to severe storms, and it was here that I encountered the most severe snow-storm that I have ever known, on the 1st day of May, 1858. I would advise travelers to hasten past this spot as rapidly as possible during the winter and spring months, as a storm might prove very serious here.

14. Near the head of Cherry Creek.—The road crosses one small branch at four miles from Black Squirrel Creek; it then takes up to an elevated plateau, which in a rainy season is very muddy. The camp is at the first timber that is found, near the road, to the left. There is plenty of wood, water, and grass here. There is also a good camping-place at the small branch that is mentioned.

10. On Cherry Creek.—There is good grass, wood and water throughout the valley of Cherry Creek. The mountains are from five to ten miles distant, on the left or west of the road, and when I passed there was a great abundance of elk, deer, antelope, bear, and turkeys throughout this section.

7. On Cherry Creek.—Good camp.

11. On Cherry Creek.—Good camp.

17. Mouth of Cherry Creek, at the South Platte.—Good camp, and a town built up since I passed, called Denver City.

Total distance from Westport to the gold diggings, 685¼ miles.

XX.—*From St. Paul's, Min., to Fort Wallah Wallah, Oregon.*

Miles.

St. Paul's to—

17¼. Small Brook.—The wood, water, and grass are abundant as far as the "Bois des Sioux" River.

20¼, Cow Creek.—This stream is crossed on a bridge.

23¼. Small Lake.—North of the road. The road passes over a rolling prairie, and crosses Elk River on a bridge.

Miles.

17. Near Sauk Rapids.--The road crosses Elk River twice on bridges; Mississippi River near.

18. Russel's.—Ferry across the Mississippi River, then follow the Red River trail. Camp is on a cold spring brook.

6. Cold Spring Brook.—Cross Sauk River, 300 feet wide, 4½ feet deep.

19½. Lake Henry.—Road good.

18¾. Lightning Lake.—Cross Cow River in a ferry-boat; water 4½ feet deep.

17½. Lake.—One mile from Red River trail. Pass White Bean Lake.

9½. Pike Lake.—Pass the South Branch of the Chippeway River. Road runs over rolling prairie, and crosses a small branch.

19¼. Small Lake.—Cross Chippeway River in a boat. Road passes numerous lakes, and the best grass.

9¾. Small Lake.—Road passes rolling prairies, and crosses Rabbit River.

27. "Bois des Sioux" River.—Cross Bois des Sioux Prairie; rolling ground.

11. Wild Rice River.—Cross "Bois des Sioux" River, 70 feet wide, and 4 to 7 feet deep, muddy bottom and banks. Wood, water, and grass at all camps between this and Maple River.

4½. Small Creek.—Cross Wild Rice River on a bridge.

26½. Sheyene River.—Smooth prairie road.

16½. Maple River.—Cross Sheyene River on a bridge, and several small branches.

20. Small Creek.—Smooth road; no wood.

20. Pond.—Wet and marshy; numerous ponds in sight; no wood.

15. Pond.—No wood; approaching Sheyene River.

13½. Sheyene River.—Prairie more rolling; camp in the river bottom. Wood, water, and grass abundant.

7. Slough.—Cross Sheyene River, 50 feet wide, 3½ feet deep. No wood.

10. Lake.—Rolling prairie, with many marshes. Wood, water, and grass.

10½. Pond.—Low, wet prairie; no wood; plenty of grass and water.

18¼. Marsh.—Smooth prairie, generally dry.

20. "Rivière à Jaques."—Smooth prairie, with marshes. Road crosses the river several times. Wood, water, and grass.

21½. Pond.—Hilly and marshy prairie, with small ponds, and no wood.

12. Small Branch.—Marshy prairie, filled with ponds, with a thin, short grass, and no wood.

19¾. Lake.—On a high knoll. Road crosses the South Fork of Sheyene River; good crossing; thence rolling prairie, passing "Balto de Morale," also a narrow lake 4½ miles long.

16½. Pond.—Marshy prairie, ponds, and knolls; cross a small branch at 7¾ miles. No wood.

17¾. Pond.—Rolling prairie. Cross Wintering River, a deep muddy

Miles.

stream 100 feet wide, also marshy prairies and ponds. No wood.

16. Small branch.—Tributary of Mouse River. Road skirts the valley of Mouse River, crossing the ravines near their heads.

15¼. Pond.—Undulating prairie with occasional marshes; the road then turns up the high ridge called "Grand Coteau." No wood.

20¼. Lake.—Hilly road approaching Grand Coteau. No wood.

20. Lake.—Rolling prairie; smooth, good road; no wood.

15½. Pond.—Road passes Grand Coteau at 11 miles, and runs between two lakes. No wood, but plenty of "bois de vache" for fuel.

19¼. Branch of White Earth River.—Country rolling and hilly. Road passes wood at eight miles from camp.

23¼. Pond.—For two miles the road passes over a low, flat country, after which the country is hilly. No wood.

23½. Pond.—Rolling and hilly country, with rocky knobs. At 18 miles cross branch of Muddy Creek 15 feet wide. Wood in ravines near this stream. No wood at camp.

20. Pond.—Rolling country. At 11 miles there is water in a ravine. To the left there is more water, but the country is rough. No wood.

16¼. Fort Union.—Road descends a hill to the fort; before this it passes over high, firm prairie. Good grass near in the hills.

6½. Pond.—No wood; good grass.

6. Little Muddy River.—Good camp.

15½. Creek.—Two good camps between this and the last. Wood, water, and grass.

10. Big Muddy River.—Drift-wood for fuel.

11. Marsh near Missouri.—Good camp.

18. Poplar River.—Good camp. One or two good camps between this and the last camp.

23½. Creek near Missouri.—Good camp.

15. Slough near Missouri.—Good camp.

17½. Milk River.—One good camp between this and the last camp.

13½. Milk River.—Several good camps passed.

17½. Milk River.—Good camp.

19½. Milk River.—Several good camps passed.

17¾. Milk River.—At the crossing. The road follows a trail on the bluffs, and descends again to the river.

7½. Lake.—No wood; grass and water plenty.

12½. Milk River.—Second crossing. Good camp.

12. Milk River.—Good camp.

15½. Milk River.—Good camps between this and the last camp

10¾. Milk River.—Good camp.

20. Milk River.—Good camp.

16. Milk River.—Good camp.

Miles.

18. Milk River.—At the third crossing.—Good camp.

7½. Branch of Milk River.—Good camp.

17½. Branch of Milk River.—Several good camps between this and the last camp.

6. Branch of Milk River.—Good camp.

19¼. Prairie Spring.—No wood; water and grass plenty.

13¾. Teton River.—Road crosses "Marias River."

8¾. Teton River, at Fort Benton.—A trading-post.

2½. Small Creek.—Good wood, water, and grass.

18¾. Missouri River.—Good camp.

20. Missouri River.—Above the falls. Road much broken into ravines. Wood, water, and grass.

16¾. Missouri River —Road crosses first tributary above Fort Benton at ten miles.

17. Missouri River.—The road becomes very bad after fourteen miles, but is better on the north side of the Missouri.

6. Missouri River.—The road is exceedingly rough and broken; crosses the river.—Good wood, water, and grass.

11. Tributary of the Missouri.—The most difficult part of the road is passed, but the country is still hilly.

18½. Tributary of the Missouri.—The road follows up the last-mentioned stream to near its head. Good camps.

15. Near the summit of Little Blackfoot pass, on a broad Indian trail; excellent road.

14¾. Little Blackfoot River.—Road crosses the summit of the Rocky Mountains. Good road for wagons, with many camping-places.

17½ Little Blackfoot River.—Road good, descending along the river. Near the camp a large fork comes in.

28½ Little Blackfoot River.—Good road, which follows the broad open valley for fourteen miles. Good camps.

19½. Little Blackfoot River.—The valley contracts, so that wagons will be forced to take the bed of the river in some places. The river is fordable, and the trail crosses it five times during the day.

22½. Blackfoot River.—Sixteen miles from the last camp "Blackfoot" and "Hell Gate" Rivers enter, and about one mile of this distance is impassable for wagons; they would have to cross the river, which is fordable. Good camps.

27½. Fort Owen.—Road runs up the St. Mary's River to Fort Owen over a broad, good trail in the valley.

40. St. Mary's River.—The south Nez Percés trail leaves the main trail, which ascends the St. Mary's Valley to the Forks, and follows the south-west fork to its source. To the Forks, the valley of the St. Mary's is open, and admits wagons.

24. South-west Fork of St. Mary's River.—The road follows a narrow trail, crossing the river frequently, and is not passable for wagons. The valley is narrow and shut in by hills.

Miles.

5½. Kooskooskia River.—Road leaves the St. Mary's River, passing over a high ridge to the Kooskooskia River.

10. Branch.—Road runs over wooded hills.

14. Creek.—Road runs over wooded hills.

9. Small Creek.—This is the best camp between the St. Mary's River and the Nez Percés country.

15. Small Creek.—Road passes over wooded hills.

9. Small Branch.—Road passes over wooded hills, is very rough and difficult. Poor camp.

14. Small Creek.—Ten miles from last camp, the road passes a high divide, ascending rapidly, though not difficult. Good grass on the summit, but no water.

13. Small Creek.—Good camp where the trail emerges from the woods on to the high plateau.

7. Clear Water River.—Large tributary. Road runs over high table-land, and descends to the valley of the river.

43. Lapwai River.—The road follows a broad trail down the river six miles, when it leaves the river bottom and ascends the plateau, which extends to Craig's house, on the Lapwai, fifteen miles from the river.

23. Tributary Snake River.—The trail runs over high ground from Craig's to Lapwai River, fifteen miles. This river is 450 feet wide. No wood. Indians are generally found here, who ferry over travelers. The trail follows Snake River for several miles.

26¼. Tchannon River.—The trail passes 5½ miles up the bottom of a small creek; then runs over a steep hill to another small creek, 8 miles; then along the valley of this stream 10½ miles; thence over a high hill to camp on Tchannon River, 3 miles.

11½. Touchet River.—The trail crosses the Tchannon River, and ascends to a high plain, which continues to camp.

32½. Touchet River.—Road follows a good trail along the valley, where good camps are found anywhere, with wood, water, and grass.

19½. Fort Wallah Wallah.—Leaving Touchet River, the trail passes over again to the plains, where there is neither wood, water, or grass to Fort Wallah Wallah.

Total distance from St. Paul's to Fort Union	712½	miles.
„ „ Fort Union to Fort Benton.........	377½	„
„ „ Fort Benton to Fort Owen	255	„
„ „ Fort Owen to Fort Wallah Wallah	340¾	„
Total distance from St. Paul's, Min., to Fort Wallah Wallah, Oregon	1685¾	„

XXI.—*Lieutenant* E. F. Beale's *route from Albuquerque to the Colorado River.*

[Distances in miles and hundredths of a mile.]

Miles.

Albuquerque to—

2·10. Atrisco.—Wood, water, and grass.
20·63. Rio Puerco.—Water in pools; wood and grass.
19·41. Near Puta.—Abundance of wood, water, and grass.
13·12. Covera.—Water and grass abundant; wood scarce.
13·06. Hay Camp.—Wood, water, and grass plenty.
25·37. Agua Frio.—Wood, water, and grass plenty.
16·28. Inscription Rock.—Small spring; grass and wood plenty.
16·32. Ojo del Pescado.—Water and grass plenty; wood for camp.
15·13. Zuñi.—Grass and water plenty; wood scarce.
6·19. Indian Well.—Wood, water, and grass.
14·43. No. 1.—Wood and grass; no water.
11·93. Jacob's Well.—Wood, water, and grass.
6·57. No. 2, Navajo Spring,—Wood, water, and grass.
13·62. Noon Halt.—Water by digging; grass and wood scarce.
6·13. No. 3.—Grass abundant.
7·75. Noon Halt.—Water, wood, and grass abundant.
7·25. No. 4.—Water in holes; grass and fuel plenty.
3·60. Three Lakes.—Wood, water, and grass.
1·75. Crossing Puerco.—Wood, water, and grass abundant as far as Leroux Spring.
11·25. No. 5.
18·50. No. 6.
10·17. No. 7.
13·25. No. 8.
19·35. Cañon Diablo.
14·75. No. 10.
13·50. Near Cosnino (Colinino) Caves.
17·32. San Francisco Spring.
9·06. Leroux Spring.
8·48. No. 13.—Wood and grass, but no water.
11·13. Breckenridge Spring.—Wood, water, and grass abundant.
8·07. No. 14.—Wood, water and grass abundant.
6·50. Cedar Spring.—Wood, water, and grass abundant.
10·50. No. 15.—Wood, water, and grass abundant.
19·75. Alexander's Cañon.—Wood and grass plenty; not much water.
8·05. Smith's Spring.—Wood, water, and grass abundant.
8·75. Pass Dornin.—Wood and grass abundant; no water.
13·50. No. 19.—Wood and grass abundant; no water.
16·35. No. 20.—Water two miles from camp; wood and grass plenty.
4·06. Hemphill's Spring.—Wood, water, and grass abundant.

Miles.
21·25. No. 21.—Wood, water, and grass abundant.
9·75. No. 22.—Wood and grass; spring one mile distant.
5·50. No. 23.—Wood and grass plenty; no water.
8·45. No. 24.—Wood and grass; spring three miles off.
16·75. No. 25.—Wood and grass; no water.
7·25. Sabadras Spring.—Wood, water, and grass.
13·25. No. 26.—Wood; no grass or water.
8·75. Spring.—Wood, water, and grass.
1·25. No. 27.—Wood, water, and grass.
3·17. No. 28.—Wood, water, and grass.
1·25. No. 29.—Wood, water, and grass.
3·11. No. 30.—Wood, water, and grass.
2·25. No. 31.—East bank of Colorado River; wood.
No. 32.—West bank; water and Grass abundant.

XXII.—*Captain* Whipple's *Route from Albuquerque, New Mexico, to San Pedro, California.*

[Distances in Miles and hundredths of a mile.]

Miles.
Albuquerque to—
0·88. Atrisco.—Permanent running water.
12·16. Isleta.—Permanent running water.
22·78. Rio Puerco.—Water in holes.
18·30. Rio Rita.—Permanent running water.
13·17. Covera.— " "
14·66. Hay Camp.— " "
17·71. Sierra Madre.—No Water.
8·06. Agua Frio.—Permanent running water.
17·49 Inscription Rock.—El Moro. Permanent springs.
14·23. Ojo del Pescado.—Permanent springs.
11·74. Zuni.—Permanent running water.
8·83. Arch Spring.—Permanent spring.
10·77. ....—No water.
19·69. Jacob's Well.—Permanent water-hole.
7·04. Navajo Spring.—Permanent Springs.
12·13. Willow Creek.—Rio de la Jara. Water in holes.
10·87. Rio Puerco of the West.—Water in holes.
11·59. Lithodendron Creek.—Permanent running water.
11·99. Colorado Chiquito.— " "
14·42. " — " "
8·63. " — " "
4·94. " — " "
1·35. " — " "

Miles.
4·90. Colorado Chiquito.—Permanent running water.
10·99. " — " "
15·88. " — " "
4·44. " — " "
1·51. " — " "
29·72. Colinino (Cosnino) Caves.—Permanent water-holes.
11·81. Near San Francisco Spring.—No water; water 4 miles from camp.
10·46. Leroux's Spring.—Permanent water.
8·23. ... .—No water.
6·17. ....—No water.
8·54. New Year's Spring.—Permanent spring.
9·77. Lava Creek.—Water in hole.
9·89. Cedar Creek.—Water in holes.
13·26. Partridge Creek.—Water in holes.
3·89. " — "
15·52. " — "
0·87. Picacho Creek.— "
7·45. ....—No water.
8·69. Turkey Creek.—Permanent running water.
5·71. Pueblo Creek.— " "
6·67. " — " water in holes.
5·98. " — " "
5·80. Cañon Creek.— " "
12·16. " — " "
0·30. " —Water in holes.
11·29. " — "
9·64. Cactus Pass.—Permanent running water.
7·97. White Cliff Creek.—Permanent running water.
11·60. Big Horn Springs.—Permanent spring.
12·83. Mouth of Cañon Creek.—Permanent running water.
9·21. "Big Sandy" Creek.— " "
4·35. " — " "
6·21. " — " "
4·08. " — " "
6·10. " — " "
5·56. " — " "
4·64. Mouth of Big Sandy Creek.—Permanent running water as far as the Colorado River.
6·52. Rio Santa Maria (Bill Williams Creek).
8·97 "
6·85. "
7·22. "
3·90. "
8·69. "
4·33. Mouth of Rio Santa Maria.
4·74. On Colorado River.

Miles.
5·02. On Colorado River.
9·06. ”
11·39. ”
29·87. ”
1·02. Mojave Villages.
9·46. Crossing of the Colorado River.
0·33. On Colorado River.
2·78, On Colorado River.
29·71. ....—The road, on leaving the Colorado, runs up over a gravelly ridge to a barren niesa, and descends the bed of the Mojave 4 or 5 miles above its mouth, and at 9½ miles it passes springs near the point where the road turns around the western base of a mountain. There is no water at the camp, but grass in an arroyo.
9·00. Pai-Uté-Creek.—This is a fine stream, with good water and grass.
13·00. Arroyo.—Grass and wood; water is found by digging.
7·00. Fine Spring.—Good water and grass. The wagon-road passes around the hills, but an Indian trail leads through the ravine where the spring is.
19·00. Marl Spring.—This is a small but constant spring; excellent grass, and greasewood for fuel.
30·00. Lake.—The road follows a ridge for some distance, then descends to an arroyo, and in a few miles emerges into a sandy plain, where there is the dry bed of a lake, which is firm, and makes a smooth, good road. The camp is at some marshy pools of water. Good grass, and greasewood for fuel.
12·00. Mojave River.—Road passes through a valley of drifted sand, and at the camp strikes the river, which is here a beautiful stream of fresh water, 10 to 12 feet wide and a foot deep, with a hard, gravelly bottom. Grass in the hills near.
13·00. Mojave River.—The road ascends the river, the banks of which are covered with fine grass and mesquite wood. Good camps along here.
20·00. Mojave River.—The road leads up the river for a short distance, when it turns into an arroyo, and ascends to a low mésa, and continues along the border of a level prairie covered with fine bunch-grass. It then enters the river bottom again, which is here several miles wide, and well wooded. Grass good.
20·00. Mojave River.—Six miles from camp, the road strikes the Mormon road, and crosses the stream near a Mormon camping-place. The trail runs along the river, which gets larger and has more timber on its bank as it is ascended. Good grass, wood, and water.
22·00. Mojave River.—A short distance from camp the valley con-

Miles.

tracts, but the road is good. It leaves the valley and crosses a gravelly ridge, but enters it again. Good grass, wood, and water.

15·00. Mojave River.—Road continues along the right bank of the river, in a south-west course, and crosses the river at camp. Good wood, water, and grass.

29·50. Cajou Creek.—The road leaves the river at the crossing, and runs toward a break in the San Bernadino Mountains; it ascends a sharp hill and enters a cedar thicket; it then ascends to the summit of the Cajou Pass; thence over a spur of the mountains into an arroyo or creek in a ravine; thence along the dry channel of the Cajou Creek for two miles, where the water begins to run, and from thence the road is rough to camp.

7·00. Cajou Creek.—Road continues along the creek to camp, and is rough. Wood, water, and grass at camp.

20·00. Cocomouga's Ranch.—On a pretty stream of running water. The road runs for six miles down the Cajou Creek, along its steep and rocky bed. It is here a good-sized stream. Captain Whipple's road here leaves the San Bernadino road, and turns to the west along the base of the mountains towards Los Angeles; it then crosses a prairie, and strikes the ranch of Cocomouga. Wood, water, and grass.

24·00. Town of El Monté.—The road runs upon the northern border of a basin which is watered by many small streams, and is settled. The camp on the pretty stream of San Gabriel, where there is a good camping-place.

14·25. City of Los Angelos.—The road passes the Mission of San Gabriel, then enters a ravine among hills and broken ground; it then descends and crosses the river which waters the valley, and enters the city. There is a good camp upon the point of a ridge on the left bank of the river.

23·00. San Pedro.—Good camp.

XXIII.—*From Fort Yuma to Benicia, California.*
From Lientenant R. S. Williamson's Report.

[Distances in miles and hundredths of a mile.]

Miles.

Fort Yuma, on Rio Colorado, to—

6·61. Pilot Knob.
5·06. Algodones.
11·18. Cook's Wells.
21·11. Alamo Mocho.
14·16. Little Laguna.

Miles.

10·29. Big Laguna.

12·92. Forks of Road.—The left-hand road leads to San Diego, 139·94 miles ; the right-hand to San Francisco.

17·62. Salt Creek.

28·94. Water in the Desert.—Below point of rocks.

12·60. Cohuilla Village.

15·82. Deep Well.

10·62. Hot Spring.

7·36. East base of San Gorgonio Pass.

18·29. Summit of Pass.

27·10. San Bernadino.—Mormon town.

17·60. Sycamore Grove.

14·00. Qui-qual-mun-go Ranch.

26·60. San Gabriel River.—At crossing.

6·70. Mission of San Gabriel.

9·00. Los Angelos.

10·20. Cahuengo Ranch.—At the crossing of a branch of Los Angelos River.

10·70. Mission of San Fernando.

5·90. Summit of San Fernando Pass.

7·15. Santa Clara River, south-east fork.

15·80. Summit of Coast Range.—In San Francisquito Pass.

18·00. Eastern base of Sierra Nevada.

6·70. Summit of Tejon Pass.

13·10. Dépôt Camp in the Tejon.

31·00. Kern River.—At the crossing.

10·80. Dépôt Camp on Pose Creek, or "O-co-ya."

24·30. White Creek.

14·90. More's Creek.

5·10. Tulé River.

22·00. Deep Creek.—Deep Creek is the first of four creeks, crossed by the wagon-road into which the "Pi-pi-yu-na" divides itself after emerging from the Sierra. These streams are commonly known as the "Four Creeks."

0·29. Cameron Creek.—The second of the "Four Creeks."

3·30. Kah-wee-ya River.—The third and principal one of the "Four Creeks."

0·89. St. John's Creek.—The last of the "Four Creeks." At the crossing.

28·13. Pool's Ferry.—On King's River.

12·32. Slough of King's River.

25·73. Fort Miller.—On San Joaquin River, in the foot-hills of the Sierra Nevada.

9·40. Cottonwood Creek.

7·72. Fresno River.

12·15. Chowchilla River.—Sometimes known as "Big Mariposa."

10·39. Mariposa River.

Miles.

6·03. Bear Creek.
18·33. Merced River.
18·87. Davis' Ferry.—Tuolumne River.
28·85. Grayson.—A ferry on the San Joaquin River.
27·54. Elk Horn.—The distance is by the wagon-road, and is circuitous.
6·90. Summit of Livermore Pass.
7·20. Egress from Livermore Pass.
40·42. Martinez.—On the Straits of Carquives, opposite Benicia, California.

Total distance from Fort Yuma to Benicia, 800.45 miles.

XXIV.—*A new route from Fort Bridger to Camp Floyd, opened by Captain* J. H. Simpson, U.S.A., *in* 1858.

Miles.

Fort Bridger to—
6. Branch of Black's Fork.—Wood water, and grass.
7¼. Cedar on Bluffs of Muddy.—Grass and wood all the way up the ravine from the Muddy, and water at intervals.
5½. Last water in ravine after leaving the Muddy.—Wood, water, and grass.
5¾. East Branch of Sulphur Creek.—Wood, water, and grass. Junction of Fort Supply Road.
½. Middle Branch of Sulphur Creek.—Sage, water, and grass.
3. West Branch of Sulphur Creek.—Willow, water, and grass; spring a mile below.
5¼. East Branch of Bear River.—Wood, water, and grass.
¼. Middle Branch of Bear River.—Wood, water, and grass.
2¾. Main Branch of Bear River.—Wood, water, and grass.
9¾. First Camp on White Clay Creek.—Wood, water, and grass.
5¼. White Clay Creek.—Wood, water, and grass.
15. White Clay Creek.—Good camps all along the valley of White Clay Creek.
¾. Commencement of Cañon.—Wood, water, and grass.
½. White Clay Creek.—Good camps all along the valley of White Clay Creek to the end of the lower Cañon.
12. Weber River.—Wood, water, and grass.
6. Parley's Park Road.—Wood, water, and grass. Pass over the divide.
3¾. Silver Creek.—Willows, water, and grass.
6. Timpanogos Creek.—Wood, water, and grass. Cross over the divide.
1. Commencement of Cañon.—Wood, water, and grass.

Miles.

24½. Cascade in Cañon.—Good camps at short intervals all along Timpanogos Cañon.

4¼. Mouth of Cañon.—Wood and water.

6¼. Battle Creek Settlement.—Purchase forage.

3¼. American Fork Settlement.—Purchase forage.

3. Lehi (town).—Purchase forage. Grass near.

2¾. Bridge over Jordan.—Grass and water; wood in the hills 1½ miles distant.

14. Camp Floyd.—Wood, water, and grass.

Total distance from Fort Bridger to Camp Floyd, 155 miles.

NOTE.—Captain Simpson says this wagon-route is far superior to the old one in respect to the grade, wood, water, and grass, and in distance about the same.

XXV.—*From Fort Thorne, New Mexico, to Fort Yuma, California.*

[Distances in miles and hundredths of a mile.]

Miles.

Fort Thorne, N. M., to—

14·30 Water Holes.—One mile west of hole in rock. Water uncertain; no wood.

9·19. Mule Creek.—Water at all seasons a little up the creek; wood plenty.

12·00. Cook's Spring.—Water sufficient for camping; mesquite bushes on the hills.

19·50. Rio Mimbres.—Water and wood abundant.

16·30. Ojo de la Vaca.—Water and wood.

12·00. Spring—Constant small streams two miles up the cañon; water at the road uncertain.

44·40. Rancho.—Pond of brackish water one mile to the right, four miles before reaching here.

13·90. Rio St. Simon.—Constant water a few miles up, and mesquite wood.

18·40. Pass in the Mountains.—Water on the left about two miles after entering the Pass.

6·40. Arroyo.—Wood one mile up; water uncertain; small stream crossing the road 1¼ miles from last camp.

26·30. Nugent's Spring.—Large Spring.—Excellent water one mile south, at Playa St. Domingo.

17·20. Cañon.—To the left of the road.—Water 1½ miles up the cañon, two miles from the road.

17·00. Rio San Pedro.—Water and wood abundant.

16·30. San Pedro.—Water abundant; wood distant.

Miles.

20·80. Cienequilla.—Water and wood abundant.

7·30. Along Cienequilla.—Water and wood abundant; road rough.

21·80. Mission of San Xavier.—Large mesquite, and water plenty in Santa Cruz River.

8·00. Tucson.—Village on Santa Cruz River. Tucson is the last green spot on the Santa Cruz River. The best camping-ground is two miles beyond the village, where the valley widens, and good grass and water are abundant.

7·20. Mud Holes.—The road passes over arroyas, but is rather level.

65·00. Agua Hermal.—Road passes over a desert section, and is hard and level. Water is found in most seasons, except in early summer, in natural reservoirs on an isolated mountain about midway, called "Picapo;" poor water, and tall coarse grass at the mud-holes. Road here strikes the Rio Gila.

15·10. Los Pimos.—Road follows the river bottom. Lagoon of bad water near camp. Grass good; plenty of cottonwood and mesquite.

13·20. Los Maricopas.—Road takes the river bottom, and passes through cultivated fields; soil and grass good. The Indian village is on a gravelly hill. The road is good.

40·00. El Tezotal.—The road leaves the river and crosses the desert. No water between this and the last camp at the Maricopas' village. Road is good. The calita abounds here, and the mules are fond of it.

10·50. Pega del Rio.—Road runs in the river bottom, and is level.

Rincon de Vega.—Road runs in the river bottom, and is level. Good grass.

10·50. Mal Pais.—Road continues near the river, but over low gravel-hills and through a short cañon of deep sand.

9·50. Mil Flores.—Pass over a very steep precipice to an elevated plateau, thence over gravel-hills 4½ miles to camp, where there is excellent grass and wood.

13·70. Santado.—Road keeps the river bottom until within four miles of camp, when it turns over the plateau. Good grass.

16·70. Las Lonas.—Road follows the river bottom. Scattered bunch-grass on the hills.

11·40. Vegas.—Road follows along the river bottom. Grass poor.

16·80. Metate.—Road runs along at the foot of a rugged mountain. Excellent grass at the camp.

14·70. El Horral.—Road ascends to the plateau, which it follows for seven miles over a level country, then descends over gravelly hills to the river. Camp on the river bank near the desert. Wood plenty.

20·80. Los Algodones.—Road runs along at the foot of the hills or spurs of the desert; small rugged hills, vegetation, dwarf mesquit, cacti, etc. Good grass at camp.

Miles.
7·40. Fort Yuma, on the Rio Colorado.

Total distance from Fort Thorne, N.M., to Fort Yuma, 571 miles.

XXVI.—*Lieutenant* BRYAN'S *Route from the Laramie Crossing of the South Platte to Fort Bridger*, via *Bridger's Pass.*

Miles.
Laramie crossing to—

14. Bryan's Crossing.—Road runs on the south side of the Platte. Good grass and water.
12. First Crossing of Pole Creek.—Pole Creek is a rapid stream, sandy bed, 15 feet wide, and 2 feet deep. Good grass on the creek, and wood three miles off on the bluffs.
37. Second Crossing of Pole Creek.—Road runs along the creek. Good grass and good camps at any point. Good road.
17¼. Third Crossing of Pole Creek.—Good camp. Wood on the bluffs.
20½. Fourth Crossing of Pole Creek.—Creek dry for three miles. Good grass.
20¼. Bluffs covered with dead pines.—Creek is crossed several times. Road runs over a rough broken country. Good grass.
14½. Road from Fort Laramie to New Mexico.—Road rather rough. The valley opens out into a wide plain. Plenty of grass.
10½. On Pole Creek.—Good road; good camp.
20. On Pole Creek.—Road crosses several ravines, most of which can be avoided by keeping on the bluffs; the valley is narrow Grass is not very good.
17½. Cheyenne Pass.—Road passes over a rolling country. Good grass; willows for fuel. Military post established here.
4½. Summit of Black Hills.—Source of Pole Creek. Grass poor.
10¼. East Fork of Laramie River.—Good camp.
16. West Fork of Laramie River.—Good camp. Cherokee trail comes in here.
14. Cooper's Creek.—Wood and grass.
10½. East Fork of Medicine Bow Creek.—Wood and grass as far as Pass Creek.
2½. Small Creek.
6. Birch Creek.
5¼. West Fork of Medicine Bow Creek.
2. Flint's Creek.

Miles.

3. Elm Creek.

7. Rattlesnake Creek.

5. Pass Creek.

14½. North Fork of the Platte.—Good road over high prairie. Five miles before reaching the river, the Cherokee trail turns to the left, and crosses three miles above. Good camps on the river.

3½. First Crossing of Sage Creek.—Good road. Grass not plenty.

10½. Second Crossing of Sage Creek.—Road runs through Sage Creek Valley; hilly, broken, and sterile country, covered with sage-brush. Grass not abundant. Cherokee trail leaves three miles back.

4. Third Crossing of Sage Creek.—Road continues through sage-brush. Grass gets better.

3. Fourth Crossing of Sage Creek.—Good grass, wood, and water.

9. Bridger's Pass.—Road runs over a hilly country, crossing several small branches, with a little grass upon their banks; country covered with sage.

3½. Muddy Creek.—The valley of the "Muddy" is deep and narrow at first, and afterward opens out. The crossings of this creek were either bridged or paved by the troops in 1858. But little grass in this valley.

20½. Near Muddy Creek.—Very little grass; poor camp.

16½. Bridger's Fork of the Muddy Creek.—The road for thirteen miles runs over a rolling country. then over a rough, broken country, with deep ravines. No water in this fork in a dry season; small springs of brackish water near the crossing. Grass poor.

4. Small Spring.—Water bad; grass poor.

2½. Small Spring.—In the bluff. Water bad; grass poor.

1. Haystack.—Clay Butte. Spring in the dry bed of the creek. Bunch-grass.

5½. Small Springs.—In bluffs on the right of the road. Grass poor and water bad.

7½. Springs.—There is a fine spring at the foot of a steep hill on the south side of the road. Very little grass; rushes on the creek.

3½. South Fork of Bitter Creek.—Good grass and water.

14¾. On Bitter Creek.—Country hilly, and intersected with deep ravines. South Fork is a fine stream of good water.

16. Sulphur Springs.—Road very hilly, crossing many deep ravines. Grass and sage plenty.

9. Bitter Creek Crossing.—No grass at the crossing. Water bitter when the creek is down, but tolerable in high water. Road rough, with numerous ravines.

18½. North Fork of Bitter Creek.—Cherokee trail enters near the crossing. Road good, but little grass except in spots. Sage for fuel.

Miles.
4. Bluffs.—Springs of good water in the elevated bluffs on the right of the road in the cottonwood groves. Grass good and abundant at the base of the bluffs.

11¾. Green River.—Road is very rough and hilly, and winds along the valley of the creek. Good camp on the river, with plenty of wood and grass.

15¾. Crossing of Black's Fork.—Road runs up through Rabbit Hollow, which is steep and sandy; it then passes over rolling prairie to Black's Fork. Bunch-grass on the hills, and good camp at the crossing.

11¼. Fort Laramie Road.—Rolling country; good road through sage bushes. Good camps along the creek.

5¾. Ham's Fork.—Good camp on either side of the creek. United States bridge here; good road.

¾. Black's Fork crossing.—Good ford except in high water, when the right-hand road on the north bank of the creek is generally traveled.

14½. Fourth Crossing of Black's Fork.—Good road; fine camp; plenty of wood, water, and grass.

2¾. Fifth Crossing of Black's Fork.—Good camp; good road.

2¾. Smith's Fork.—Good camp; good road.

11¾. Fort Bridger.—Good camp near; good road.

Total distance from the Laramie Crossing of the South Platte to Fort Bridger, 520½ miles. By the Fort Laramie road the distance is 569 miles.

XXVII.—*Wagon-route from Denver City, at the Mouth of Cherry Creek, to Fort Bridger, Utah.*

Miles.
Denver City to—

5. Vasquez Fork.—Good road, and fine camp.

19½. Thompson's Fork.—Road crosses three creeks about five miles apart, is good, and the camp is well supplied with water and grass, but wood is scarce.

16½. Bent's Fork.—Road crosses two streams about five miles apart; no wood on the first. Good camp.

26. Cashe la Poudre River.—Excellent road crossing two streams at ten and twenty-three miles from the last camp; good camps on both. Cashe la Poudre is a fine large stream which issues from the mountains near the road, and is difficult to cross in high water. It has a firm bottom. Good camps along this stream, with plenty of wood and grass.

Miles.

16. Beaver Creek.—Road turns to the left and enters the hills, ascending very gradually between two lines of bluffs, and is good except in wet weather. Good camp.

19. Small Branch.—Road crosses Beaver Creek three times, affording good camps. Road is hilly, but not very rough, passing for a portion of the distance through a timbered region. Elk and mountain sheep are abundant in this section. The camp is near the summit of the divide. Grass short.

17½. Tributary of Laramie River.—Good road on the divide. Grass and water plenty, but wood not abundant.

18½. Tributary of Laramie River.—Road passes Laramie Fork three miles from the last camp. Good camp.

21. Tributary of Laramie River.—Road crosses a small creek at 14 miles from the last camp. Fine camp.

17. Medicine Bow Creek.—At twelve miles the road crosses Sulphur Spring Creek, and at the West Fork of the Laramie, Lieutenant Bryan's road enters. At ten miles from the last camp there are two roads—one, Bryan's, leading north of the Medicine Bow Butte, and the other to the south of it. The former is the best. Good camp.

17½. Prairie Creek.—Fine Camp. A portion of the road is very rough. It crosses several small branches, upon which good camps may be had. Fine game section, with bear, elk, etc., in great abundance.

12½. North Fork of the Platte.—Excellent camp. Leaving Bryan's road, four miles back, taking the left, which is altogether the best of the two. The crossing of the Platte is good except in high water, when it is very rapid. A flat-boat was left here by Colonel Loring's command in 1858.

12½. Clear Creek.—Sage for fuel; grass short.

23. Dry Creek.—Road leaves Bryan's trail to Bridger's Pass, and bears to the right, passing over a smooth country covered with sage, and poorly watered; passes a pond of milky water at thirteen miles. There is water in Dry Creek, except in a very dry season. Two miles from the creek, on the old trail, there is a fine spring on the left of the road, which runs down into the road, and here is the best grass after leaving the Platte, with plenty of fuel.

10½. Muddy Creek.—Road leaves the old Cherokee trail at Dry Creek, and bears to the left. Good camp for a limited number of animals; fine grass along near the bank of the creek. Bad crossing. Buffalo seen here.

19½. Lake.—Old trail enters near this camp. Road passes a brackish spring four miles back. The road may be shortened by bearing to the left, and skirting the hills for about six miles before reaching the lake. The water in the lake is not good, but drinkable, and will be abundant, except in the very dryest

Miles.

part of the summer. Grass is good on the hills. The road from Dry Creek is shorter than the old road by 30 miles.

24½. Red Lakes.—Road is good, but traverses a very dry and sterile region. The water is not good in the lakes, but drinkable, and may go dry in midsummer. Grass tolerable.

22. Seminoes Spring.—After passing the flats at the Red Lakes, the road is smooth and good, and there is a good camp at Seminoes Spring.

12½. Bitter Creek.—New road to the left, cutting off ten or twelve miles. Good camp; water a little saline, but drinkable.

25. Sulphur Spring.—Road runs along the valley of Bitter Creek, where there is but little grass until reaching camp. Animals should be driven across the creek into the hills, where the best grass is found.

17. Green River.—Road leaves Bitter Creek at Sulphur spring, and passes near some high bluffs, where there are small springs and good grass. Excellent camp at Green River. From here the road runs over the same track as Bryan's road to Fort Bridger. From all the information I have been able to obtain regarding Lieutenant Bryan's road from Sage Creek through Bridger's Pass, and thence down the Muddy Creek, I am inclined to believe that the road we traveled is much the best. It is said that Lieutenant Bryan's route from Bridger's Pass to Green River has a scarcity of grass. The water is brackish, and the supply limited, and may fail altogether in a dry season. The road passes through deep valleys and cañons, crossing muddy creeks and deep ravines. The creeks have been bridged, and the ravines cut down so as to form a practicable road; but freshets will probably occur in the spring, which will destroy a great deal of the work, and may render the road impassable.—*Lieutenant Duane's Notes.*

The other road is for the greater part of the distance smooth, and has a sufficiency of grass in places, and may become scarce in a very dry season.

XXVIII.—*From Nebraska City, on the Missouri, to Fort Kearney.*

Nebraska City, on the Missouri River, is a point from which a large amount of the supplies for the army in Utah are sent, and one of the contractors—Mr. Alexander Majors, speaks of this route in the following terms: "The military road from Fort Leavenworth crosses very many tributaries of the Kansas River, the Soldier, the Grasshopper, etc., etc., which are at all times difficult of passage.

There are no bridges, or but few, and those of but little service. From Nebraska City to Fort Kearney, which is a fixed point for the junction of all roads passing up the Platte, we have but one stream of any moment to cross. That one is Salt Creek, a stream which is now paved at a shallow ford with solid rock.

"There is no other stream which, even in a high freshet, would stop a train a single day. Again, upon this route we have an abundance of good grazing every foot of the way to Fort Kearney. The route from Nebraska City is about 100 miles shorter to Fort Kearney than that from Fort Leavenworth, the former being less than 200 miles, and the latter about 300 miles."

From Nebraska City to Salt Creek is . . . . 40 miles.
„ Salt Creek to Elm Creek is . . . . . 60 „
„ Elm Creek to Fort Kearney is . . . . 100 „

Upon the entire route there is an abundance of wood, water, and grass, and camping-places frequent.

XXIX.—*From Camp Floyd, Utah, to Fort Union, New Mexico.* By Colonel W. W. Loring, U.S.A.

Miles.

Camp Floyd to—

23. Goshen.—The road runs through Cedar Valley; is level and good for 11 miles, to where the road forks. The left runs near the lake, and has good camps upon it. Thence to a fine spring, where there is a good camp, is 3 miles. Grass continues good to the camp near Goshen. Wood, water, and grass abundant.

14. Salt Creek.—Road runs over a mountain in direct course to a fine spring branch, which runs into Salt Creek at 3½ miles, where is a good camp; thence through a meadow to a small branch 3 miles, striking the old Mormon road again opposite a mud fort, where there is a fine spring and good camp; thence into the valley of Salt Creek, where there are good camps.

18. Pleasant Creek.—Near the last camp the road forks, one running to Nephi, a small Mormon village, the other to Salt Creek Cañon, which is the one to be taken. The road runs up the cañon 5 miles; thence up its small right-hand fork to a spring, 3 miles; thence to camp. Good camps can be found anywhere after crossing Salt Creek, with abundance of wood, water, and grass.

19½. Willow Creek.—Road at 6½ miles passes a fine spring; half a mile farther is another spring, where the road forks. Take the

Miles.

right through a meadow; it is 3 or 4 miles shorter. To the crossing is 3 miles; thence to the main road again 3 miles; to the village of Ephraim 5 miles. Good camp.

12. Lediniquint Creek.—At 6 miles pass Manti; thence to Salt and Sulphur Springs is 3 miles. Good camp with a fine spring, wood, and grass.

15. Lediniquint Creek.—Road passes over a rugged country for 4 miles, to a creek; thence 1 mile it crosses another creek; thence 2½ miles up the creek, where there is a good camp. The road improves, and for 8 or 9 miles camps can be found by leaving the creek a short distance. The creek on which the camp is is muddy, with narrow channel.

18. Onapah Creek, or Salt Creek.—Road is good over a barren country to the pointed red hills near the entrance to Wasatch Pass, 7 miles. From the red hills across Salt Creek 3 times in 4 miles; grass fair at 2nd crossing; very good at 3rd crossing, and a good camp. Road rough for 3 miles after leaving the creek. The road then enters a fine valley, with plenty of blue and bunch grass. Road is level to within a mile of the camp. Wood, water, and grass abundant at camp.

7½. Head of Branch of Salt Creek.—Road runs over a ridge at 2 miles, thence 1 mile to a small branch. Grass abundant. Road runs along the branch 3 miles; in places very rough, with some sand; ascends the entire distance, and the camp is very elevated. Good spring at camp.

5¾. Salt Creek.—Road passes over a ridge 2½ miles to a spring. Good camp at this spring. Colonel Loring worked the road at this place. It crosses the creek 6 times within 5¾ miles. Good camp, with abundance of wood, water, and grass.

6½. Silver Creek.—Road traverses a rolling section, is good, passes several springs, where there are good camps, and crosses several trails which lead from California to New Mexico.

17½. Media Creek.—At 2 miles the road passes the dividing ridge between the waters of Salt Lake and Green River; thence 2 miles' descent to Shipley Creek, where is a good camp. For about a mile the road is rough, but then descends into an open plain, where the road is good. The ground is rough about the camp, and covered with sage and greasewood. Two miles up the creek, near the cañon, is some grass, but it is not abundant here.

19¾. St. Raphael Creek.—Road passes a rolling section for 5 miles; thence 1½ mile to Garamboyer Creek, where there is a good camp; thence, with the exception of a short distance, the road is good to the Knobs, 9 miles, when it is broken for 4½ miles. Good camp.

11¾. San Matio Creek.—For 3 miles the road is over a rolling section, with steep hills, to a creek, where is a good camp;

Miles.

thence for 3 miles along the creek, soft soil and heavy road; thence 5 miles to another creek, some grass, but not plenty; thence to camp the road is rough in places. Good camp.

14¼. In the Hills.—Road runs over a rolling country 2½ miles to San Marcos, or Tanoje Creek, where there is good grass and water, with sage. Two miles farther over a gravelly road, then a good plain road for 9¾ miles to camp. Good wood, water, and grass.

23. Spring.—Road for the first 10 miles is rocky, when it strikes a spring, where there is a good camp; thence 2 miles to water in a tank, not permanent; thence the road is on a ridge for 6 miles, and is good; thence 3 miles the road is sandy. The spring at camp is large, with plenty of wood, but the grass is scarce. Down the creek it is more abundant.

18. Green River.—For 5 miles the road is sandy; thence the road is good for the remainder of the distance to camp, where there is plenty of wood, water, and grass.

13. 13-Mile Spring.—Green River can be forded at ordinary stages. Road runs among several arroyas for a few miles, and is then straight and good to camp. Good grass a mile to the east of camp.

An Arroya.—Road runs between two rocky buttes, and strikes the Mormon trail, which leaves Green River at the same place, but is very tortuous. Water not permanent here; good grass three-fourths of a mile from camp.

20¼. Cottonwood Creek.—Road passes over a broken country to a water-hole, 9 miles; grass abundant; thence there is sand in places; crosses several arroyas. Camp is between two mountains. Water, wood, and grass abundant.

12. Grand River.—Road is over a rolling country; in places light sand and heavy for wagons. Good camp.

13. Grand River.—Road is rolling and sandy. The Mormon road runs nearer the mountains, and Colonel Loring thinks it is better than the one he traveled. Good camp.

16¾. 1½ mile from Grand River.—The first three miles is level, then the road passes over a very elevated ridge, and descends into the valley. Grand River runs through a cañon, and cannot be reached with the animals. Road in places sandy. Camp good.

9½. Grand River.—At 2 miles strike Salt Creek, where the Mormon road passes up a dry creek toward Gray Mountain. Road skirts the mountains along Grand River, and is rough in places, passing over abrupt hills. Good camp.

16¾. Grand River.—Road runs over a level and firm section, with good camps at any point along the river. Cross the Mormon and other trails. Good ford at the crossing, except in high water. Good camp.

Miles.

18½. On an Arroya —Road runs over an undulating surface, crossing several small streams issuing from Elk Mountain, affording good camps at almost any place, and strikes Marcy's and Gunnison's trails. Good camp.

15¼. Grand River.—Rolling country ; high ridges with abrupt slopes for 6¼ miles ; thence into a plain for 7¼ miles to Double Creek. Good camps.

12. Oncompagre River.—Good ford, except in high water. At 6 miles cross a dry creek ; thence 3 miles over a high, level, and firm road ; strike a large trail ; descend a hill with gentle slope into the Valley of Oncompagre, where there are fine camps. Winter resort for Uté Indians.

14½. Oncompagre River.—Road runs along the valley of the Oncompagre, is good, and camp may be found at any point, with plenty of wood, water, and grass.

13. Cedar Creek.—Road leaves the Oncompagre, and bears to the east up Cedar Creek to the gap in the mountain, 6 miles ; thence up the valley of Cedar Creek to camp, where are wood, water, and grass. The Gap is the first opening in the mountains above the mouth of the Oncompagre.

8¾. Devil's Creek.—Road runs to the head of Cedar Creek, over the divide, into the valley of Devil's Creek, and is rough, with a steep descent. Camp is near a narrow cañon, called Devil's Gate, with high perpendicular bluffs. Good camp.

3. North Fork of Devil's Creek.—Road very rocky, and worked by Colonel Loring. Marcy's and Gunnison's trails pass here. Good camp.

7¾. Cebola Creek.—Road passes over abrupt hills covered with pine. Good Camp.

5½. Ruidos Creek.—Road rough, with abrupt ascents and descents. Fine creek 5 feet wide, and good camp.

13. Grand River.—Road rather smooth for the first 3 miles, then rough and rocky, crossing several creeks, and descending into the valley of the Grand or Eagle-tail River, where is a good Camp. Plenty of brook trout in all the streams in this section.

14½. Grand River.—Road crosses the river three times; bottom wide; grass and wood abundant. Cross several beautiful streams, upon which are good camps. Some sand, and rough places, but generally good road. Game and brook trout abundant in this region. Indians resort to this section a great deal.

18. Cutebetope Creek.—At about 5 miles the Cutebetope Creek enters, forming at the confluence a beautiful valley, which the road crosses, and strikes the creek near the Point of Rocks, where the valley is only 40 yards wide, but after passing the Point it opens again. The course of the creek is nearly north. Good camps.

Miles.

20. Spring near Beaver Creek.—Road crosses several small creeks, where are several good camping-places. Camp good.

16¾. Sawatch Creek.—Road runs over a very rough and mountainous section for 14 miles, to the summit of the Rocky Mountains, Chochetope Pass; thence it descends to camp, where grass, wood, and water are abundant.

21½. Sawatch Creek.—Road rough and rocky in places; strikes the main Sawatch Creek at 9½ miles; crosses numerous small branches, where are grass, wood, and good water in abundance.

25½. Camero Creek.—Road for 7 miles, to Sawatch Buttes, is good; thence 1½ mile to the last crossing of the Sawatch, where is a good camping-place. Good camp at Camero Creek.

3½. Garita Creek.—Good road and good camp.

16½. Rio Grande.—Road level and good. Good camps along the river at almost any point.

6. Rio Grande.—Good road and camp.

17½. Fort Garland, Hay Camp.—Road continues down the river, and is good. For 6 miles there is timber; but, after this, willow is the only wood to camp. Good road. Hay is cut at this place for Forts Massachusetts and Garland.

16. Culebra Creek.—At 4½ miles cross Trinchera Creek, where is a good camp. Road rather sandy. Good camps any where on Culebra Creek.

24¾. Latos Creek.—Road tolerable to Costilla Creek, 10¾ miles. Camp good.

14. Ascequia, near Lama Creek.—Road crosses several small branches. At 9½ miles strike Red River. Grass at camp good, but not abundant.

19¾. Meadow, near Indian Pueblo.—At 6 miles the road crosses the San Christobal; thence over another ridge into the valley of the Rio Hondo. Camp 2 miles from Taos.

2. Taos, New Mexico.—Good road. At Taos are several stores, where goods of all descriptions can be had at fair prices.

13. Taos Creek Cañon.—Road passes through the settlement, where grain and vegetables can be obtained. It then enters the Taos Cañon at 3 miles, and crosses the Cañon Creek frequently to camp. Good camp.

29. Gaudelapepita.—At 5 miles the road ascends to the dividing ridge, and is tolerable; thence in 4 miles cross the mountain, and reach a fine spring branch, where is a fine camp. Thence the road passes short ridges for 9 miles to Black Lake. Good camp.

Fort Union.—Road follows Coyote Cañon 3 miles; thence 1 mile to Mexican settlement; thence 19½ miles over the prairie to the fort.

Colonel Loring came over the route from Camp Floyd to Fort Union with a large train of wagons. He, however, found the road in many places upon the mountains very rough, and it will require working before it will be suitable for general travel with loaded wagons. It is an excellent route for summer travel with pack-trains, and is well supplied with the requisites for encamping.

From Fort Union to Fort Garland, the road passes through a settled country, where supplies of grain and vegetables can, at all times, be purchased at reasonable prices; and there are small towns met with during almost every day's march, where small shops supply such articles of merchandise as the traveler needs.

XXX.—*Wagon-route from Guaymas, Province of Sonora, Mexico, to Tubac, Arizona.* From Captain STONE's Journal.

Miles.

Guaymas to—

10¼. Rancho del Cavallo.—Good wood, water, and grass.

9. Rancho de la Noche Buena.—Good wood and grass, but no water for animals in May and June.

19⅝. Rancho de la Cuneguinta.—Good wood, water, and grass the year round; water in tanks and wells.

15¾. Rancho del Posito.—Good wood and grass the year round; water for men at all times, and for animals except in the months of May and June.

8. Rancho de la Palma.—Wood, water, and grass at all times.

16⅝. Rancho de la Paza.—Good wood, water, and grass at all seasons.

16. Hermosillo.—This is a town of 10,000 inhabitants, on Sonora River, where all supplies may be procured.

13. Hacienda de Alamita.—Plenty of running water, wood, grass, and grain.

8. Hacienda de la Labor.—Plenty of running water, grass, and grain.

28. Rancho de Tabique.—Roughest part of the road, but not diffi- for wagons. Wood, water, and grass. From Hermosillo to this place there is water at short intervals along the road.

36. Rancho Querebabi.—Wood and grass; water in tanks.

12. Barajita.—Small mining village. Bad water; good wood and grass.

13. Santa Aña.—Village on the River San Ignacio. Plenty of wood, water, and grass.

12. La Magdalena.—Thriving town where all supplies can be procured.

5. San Ignacio.—Village on the river. Good wood, water, and grass.

Miles.
6½. Imuris.—Village on the river. Wood, water, and grass.
11½. Los Alisos Rancho.—Wood, water, and grass.
3½. La Casita.—Wood, water, and grass.
3½. Cíbuta.—Wood, water, and grass.
11¼. Agua Zarca.—Wood, water, and grass.
23¼. Rancho de las Calabasas.—Wood, water, and grass.
13. Tubac.—Silver mines at this place.
Total distance from Guaymas to Tubac, 295 miles.

NOTE.—During the months of July, August, and September, water will be found at almost any part of the road from La Casita to Hermosillo. There is no lack of wood or grass on any part of the road from Guaymas to the frontier. The only difficulty in encamping at almost any point upon the road is that of obtaining water in the dry season, *i.e.*, from February to the first of July. The remarks for each place apply to the most unfavorable seasons.

XXXI.—*From Fort Hope, Fraser River, to Fort Colville on the Columbia.* According to Lieutenant PALMER, R.E. (Contributed by Mr. RAVENSTEIN, F.R.G.S.).

(Fort Hope is situated under 49° 22′ N. lat., 121° 25′ W. long. 85 miles above New Westminster, the capital of British Columbia Communication between the two places is kept up by steamers during the season).

Miles.
From Fort Hope (140 feet above the level of the sea) to—
15. Mason's Mountain (1890 feet).—Road ascends the level and lightly timbered Coquahalla valley. Steep and difficult ascent, between two spurs of the Mason's Range, begins after 9 miles. At camp wood and water plentiful, but no grass.
19. Camp du Chevreuil (3,640 feet).—After 1½ hours' travelling reach summit of pass by a steep and rocky zig-zag trail, in many places encumbered with mud. (Mason's Pass is impracticable for seven months in the year. Snow falls to the depth of 25 to 30 feet, and travelling before the 1st of June or after the 1st of October is dangerous). After a steep and dangerous descent of 1,100 feet on western slope reach a muddy bottom, densely wooded, follow trail through forest for 5 miles, ford a tributary of the Coquahalla, climb steep slope on opposite bank to camp, near mountain Stuchd-a-choiré. Wood and water abundant; grass sufficient for horses. Deer scarce, but ptarmigans abound.
15. Camp on bend of Tulameen (3,260 feet).—Strike head-waters of Tulameen 3 miles from last camp, and 800 feet below

Miles.

summit of range, follow its left bank for 12 miles ford the river to camp. Road easy. Wood and water plentiful. Very little grass.

12. Camp on Tulameen Range (about 4,200 feet).—Leave river and ascend for 4 miles through a steep and narrow defile to an undulating plateau, slightly timbered, and covered with yellow furze and heath. High grass near the numerous ponds and marshes. Camp near small circular lake. Wood in plenty; little grass.

12. Campement des Femmes (2,170 feet).—Descend to Tulameen, and ford opposite camp. Country lightly timbered and grassy on uplands, heavily timbered in valleys; at camp, wood, water and grass plentiful and good.

59. Big Bend of Similkameen (775 feet).—Along left bank of Tulameen and Similkameen. Fine prairie country. Timber near river and at foot of mountains. Water and excellent bunch-grass plentiful.

18. Osoyoos Lake (630 feet).—Leave Similkameen and cross divide to Osoyoos lake; follow its western shore to where it contracts and is fordable. Brush and grass plentiful; timber scarce. Water-fowl abound.

10. Divide, Colville Range (2,390 feet).—Ford lake and follow its eastern shore for 5 miles, then along small stream up divide. Road good, ascent gradual. Wood, water, and grass abundant.

19. Siyakin Forks (1,570 feet).—Summit of divide, 2850 feet. Descend to head waters of Siyakin, follow its left bank, and camp at Forks with N-whoy-al-pit-kwu (Colville River). Road easy. Slopes gradual. Excellent bunch-grass, wood and water abundant.

56. Grande Prairie (1,360 feet).—Along Colville River, which has to be forded at several places. Park-like country. First-rate camping places abundant. Wood, water and grass plentiful. Wild fowl.

47. On the Columbia, opposite Fort Colville (48° 38′ N., 118° 4 W., of Greenwich, Altitude 830 feet).—Continue down narrow valley of the Colville, which has to be forded repeatedly. Dense forests of fir cover mountain slopes. Water and grass generally abundant.

(An excellent waggon-road has been constructed by the American Government between Colville and Walla-Walla. Distance about 235 miles. The road as far as the Spokan (60 miles), leads through a magnificent forest of Pines. It then crosses the Columbian Desert to the Snake River, about 10 miles from Walla-Walla. In this desert the soil is loose sand, and there is a very scarce growth of bunch-grass. Water is found at long intervals only).

THE END.

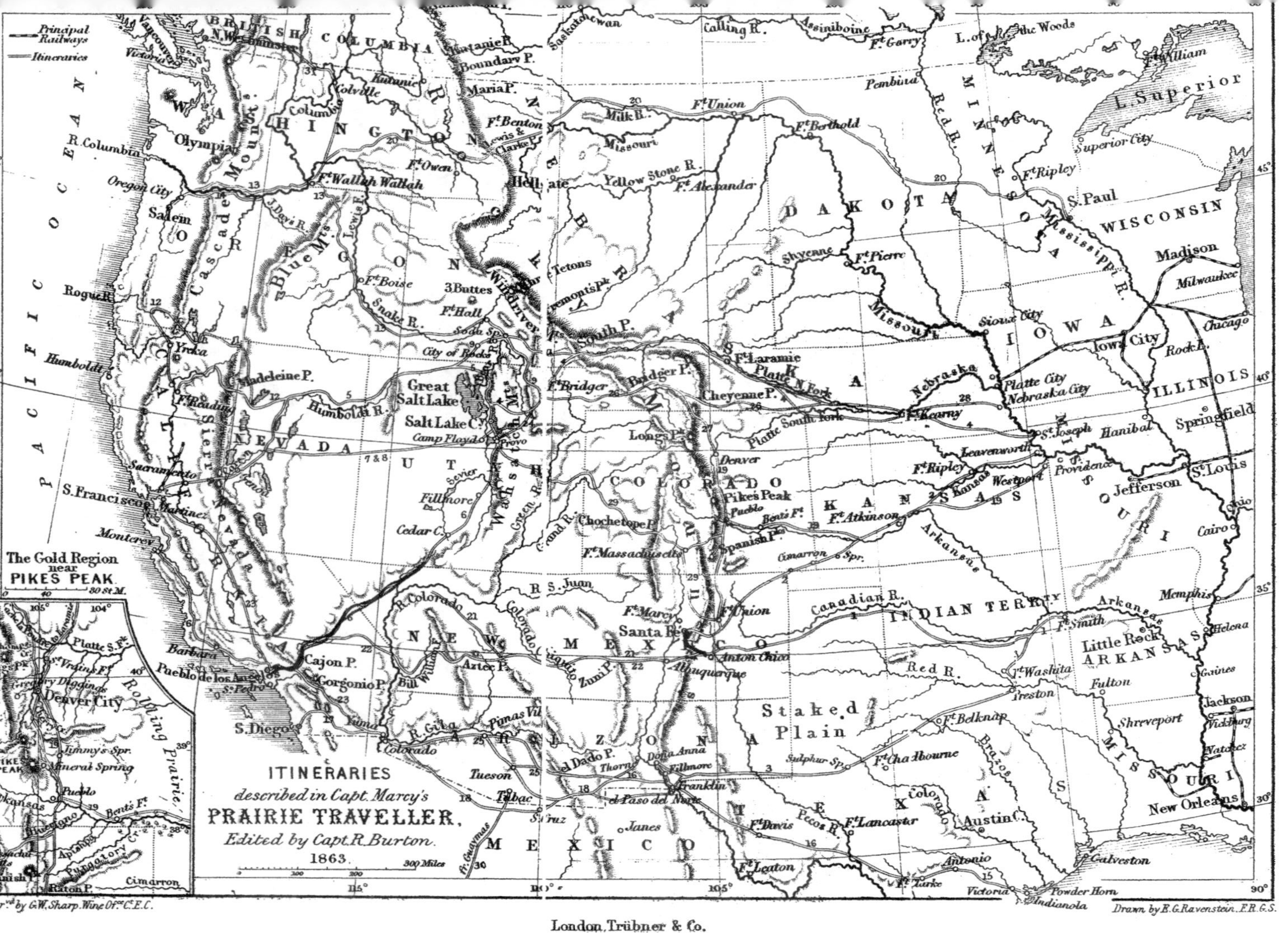
ITINERARIES
described in Capt. Marcy's
PRAIRIE TRAVELLER.
Edited by Capt. R. Burton.
1863.
The Gold Region near PIKES PEAK.
Principal Railways
Itineraries
PACIFIC OCEAN
BRITISH COLUMBIA
WASHINGTON
OREGON
CALIFORNIA
NEVADA
UTAH
NEBRASKA
DAKOTA
MINNESOTA
WISCONSIN
IOWA
ILLINOIS
MISSOURI
KANSAS
COLORADO
NEW MEXICO
INDIAN TERRY
ARKANSAS
TEXAS
MEXICO
L. Superior
Great Salt Lake
Salt Lake C.
S. Francisco
Sacramento
Santa Fe
Denver
Pikes Peak
St. Louis
New Orleans
Staked Plain
Engrd. by G.W. Sharp. Wine Offce. C.E.C.
Drawn by E.G. Ravenstein. F.R.G.S.
London, Trübner & Co.

Has Man a Soul?—A verbatim report of two nights' debate at Burnley, between the Rev. W. M. WESTERBY and C. BRADLAUGH. 1s.

Christianity in relation to Freethought, Scepticism and Faith.—Three Discourses by the BISHOP OF PETERBOROUGH, with Special Replies by CHARLES BRADLAUGH. 6d.

Secularism Unphilosophical, Unsocial and Immoral.—Three nights' debate between CHARLES BRADLAUGH and the Rev. Dr. McCANN. 1s.

Is it Reasonable to Worship God?—A verbatim report of two nights' debate at Nottingham between the Rev. R. A. ARMSTRONG and C. BRADLAUGH. 1s.

My Path to Atheism.—Collected Essays of ANNIE BESANT.—The Deity of Jesus—Inspiration—Atonement—Eternal Punishment—Prayer—Revealed Religion—and the Existence of God, all examined and rejected; together with some Essays on the Book of Common Prayer. Cloth, gilt lettered, 4s.

Marriage: as it was, as it is, and as it should be. By ANNIE BESANT. Second Edition. In limp cloth, 1s.

Verbatim Report of the Trial, The Queen against Bradlaugh and Besant.—Neatly bound in cloth, price 5s., post free. With Portraits and Autographs of the two Defendants.

Second Edition, with Appendix, containing the judgments of Lords Justices Bramwell, Brett, and Cotton.

The Jesus of the Gospels and **The Influence of Christianity on the World.** Two nights' Debate between the Rev. A. HATCHARD and ANNIE BESANT. 1s.

PAMPHLETS BY ANNIE BESANT.

	s.	d.
The Physiology of Home—No. 1. "Digestion"; No. 2, "Organs of Digestion"; No. 3, "Circulation"; No. 4, "Respiration"; 1d. each. Together, in neat wrapper	0	4
Free Trade *v.* "Fair" Trade—No. 1, "England before the Repeal of the Corn Laws"; No. 2, "The History of the Anti-Corn Law Struggle"; No. 3, "Labor and Land: their burdens, duties and rights"; No. 4, "What is Really Free Trade"; No. 5, "The Landlords' Attempt to Mislead the Landless"; 1d. each. In neat wrapper with Appendix ...	0	6
Electricity and its modern applications. Four lectures. 1d. each. Together, in wrapper	0	4
Light, Heat and Sound. Limp cloth	1	6
God's Views on Marriage...	0	2
The True Basis of Morality. A Plea for Utility as the Standard of Morality. Seventh Thousand	0	2
Auguste Comte. Biography of the great French Thinker, with Sketches of his Philosophy, his Religion, and his Sociology. Being a short and convenient *résumé* of Positivism for the general reader. Third Thousand	0	6

	s.	d.
Giordano Bruno, the Freethought Martyr of the Sixteenth Century. His Life and Works. Third Thousand	0	1
The Political Status of Women. A Plea for Women's Rights. Fourth Thousand	0	2
Civil and Religious Liberty, with some Hints taken from the French Revolution. Third Thousand	0	3
The Gospel of Atheism. Fifth Thousand	0	2
Is the Bible Indictable?	0	2
England, India, and Afghanistan	0	9
The Story of Afghanistan...	0	2
The preceding two pamphlets bound together in limp cloth, 1s.		
The Law of Population: Its consequences, and its Bearing upon Human Conduct and Morals. Seventieth thousand ...	0	6
Liberty, Equality, and Fraternity	0	1
The Influence of Heredity on Free Will, from the German of Ludwig Büchner	0	2
The Ethics of Punishment. Third Thousand	0	1
Landlords, Tenant Farmers, and Laborers. Third Thousand ...	0	1
The God Idea in the Revolution	0	1
The Gospel of Christianity and the Gospel of Freethought ...	0	2
English Marseillaise, with Music. Second Thousand... ...	0	1
English Republicanism	0	1
Christian Progress	0	2
The English Land System	0	1
The Transvaal	0	1
Vivisection	0	1
Fruits of Christianity	0	2

Or bound in cloth,

Social and Political Essays.—By Annie Besant. 3s. 6d.

Theological Essays and Debate.—By Annie Besant. 2s. 6d.

PAMPHLETS BY C. BRADLAUGH.

	s.	d.
Anthropology. In neat wrapper	0	4
Hints to Emigrants, containing important information on the United States, Canada, and New Zealand	1	0
Cromwell and Washington: a Contrast	0	6
A Lecture delivered to large audiences throughout the United States.		
Five Dead Men whom I Knew when Living. Sketches of Robert Owen, Joseph Mazzini, John Stuart Mill, Charles Sumner, and Ledru Rollin	0	4
Jesus, Shelley, and Malthus, an Essay on the Population Question	0	2
Life of George, Prince of Wales, with Recent Contrasts and Coincidences	0	2
Real Representation of the People...	0	2
Letter to Albert Edward Prince of Wales, on Freemasonry ...	0	1
Why do Men Starve?	0	1
Poverty and its effect upon the People	0	1
Labor's Prayer	0	1

	s.	d.
The Land, the People, and the Coming Struggle	0	2
Plea for Atheism	0	3
Has Man a Soul?	0	2
Is there a God?	0	1
Who was Jesus?	0	1
What did Jesus Teach?	0	1
The Twelve Apostles	0	1
The Atonement	0	1
Life of David	0	2
Life of Jacob	0	1
Life of Abraham	0	1
Life of Moses	0	1
Life of Jonah	0	1
A Few Words about the Devil	0	1
Were Adam and Eve our First Parents?	0	1
Perpetual Pensions. Thirtieth thousand	0	2
The Laws Relating to Blasphemy and Heresy	0	6

Or to be obtained in volumes.

Political Essays.—By C. Bradlaugh. Bound in cloth, 2s. 6d

Theological Essays.—By C. Bradlaugh. Bound in cloth, 3s.

Four Debates between C. Bradlaugh and Rev. Dr. Baylee, in Liverpool; the Rev. Dr. Harrison, in London; Thomas Cooper, in London; the Rev. R. A. Armstrong, in Nottingham; with Three Discourses by the Bishop of Peterborough and replies by C. Bradlaugh. Bound in one volume, cloth. Price 3s.

Large Photograph of Mr. Bradlaugh for Framing, 2s. 6d.

Large Portrait of Mrs. Besant, fit for Framing, 2s. 6d.

A splendidly executed Steel Engraving of Mrs. Besant, price 2d.

Chromo-litho of Mr. Bradlaugh.—Cabinet size, 1d. In Letts's protecting case, post free 2d.

Splendid Chromo-litho of Mr. Bradlaugh.—Large size, 6d. In Letts's protecting case, post free 7d.

Cabinet Photographs of Mr. Bradlaugh and Mrs. Besant.—By the Stereoscopic Company. 2s. each.

Past and Present of the Heresy Laws.—By W. A. Hunter, M.A. 3d.

The Soil of Great Britain and Ireland. Being a series of Articles contributed to the "National Reformer." By Charles Ellershaw. In neat wrapper, 6d.

Man and God: a physiological meditation on man, his origin and nature. With philosophical meditations. By J. M. A. Perot, Corresponding Member of many Learned Societies in France and Belgium. Translated from the French (by the author's desire). Bound in cloth, 4s.

Pamphlets by Edward B. Aveling, D.Sc., Fellow of University College, London.—"The Value of this Earthly Life," 1s. "Biological Discoveries and Problems," 1s. "Science and Secularism," 2d. "Science and Religion," 1d. "The Sermon on the Mount," 1d. "Superstition," 1d. "Creed of an Atheist," 1d. "Wickedness of God," 1d. "Irreligion of Science," 1d. "Why I dare not be a Christian," 1d. "God dies: Nature remains," 1d. "Plays of Shakspere," 4d. "Macbeth," 4d. "A Godless Life the Happiest and Most Useful," 1d.

Wealthy and Wise. A lecture introductory to the Study of Political Economy. By J. Hiam Levy. 6d.

Pamphlets by Geo. Standring.—"Life of C. Bradlaugh," with portrait and autograph, 12 pages, 1d. "Life of Colonel R. G. Ingersoll," with portrait and autograph, and extracts from his Orations, in wrapper, 1d. "Court Flunkeys; their Work and Wages," 1d.

The Education of Girls.—By Henry R. S. Dalton, B.A., Oxon. Second Edition. Price 6d.

Ish's Charge to Women. By H. R. S. Dalton. 4d.

Religion and Priestcraft. By H. R. S. Dalton. 2d.

On the Connection of Christianity with Solar Worship. By T. E. Partridge. 1s. (Translated from Dupuis.)

Clericalism in France.—By Prince Napoleon Bonaparte (Jerome). Translated by Annie Besant. Price 6d.

The Cause of Woman.—From the Italian of Louisa To-Sko. By Ben W. Elmy. Price 6d.

Studies in Materialism.—By Ben. W. Elmy. Price 4d.

Lectures of Colonel Robert Ingersoll.—"Oration on the Gods." Price 6d.—"Oration on Thomas Paine." Price 4d.—"Heretics and Heresies." Price 4d.—"Oration on Humboldt." Price 2d.—"Arraignment of the Church." Price 2d. These can be supplied in one volume neatly bound in limp cloth. Price 1s. 6d. Also, by same author, "The Ghosts." Price 4d.—"Religion of the Future." Price 2d.—"Farm Life in America." Price 1d.—"Mistakes of Moses." Price 3d.—"Tilt with Talmage." Price 2d.

The Ten Commandments.—By W. P. Ball. Price 1d.

Religion in Board Schools.—By W. P. Ball. 2d.

The Devil's Pulpit, being Astronomico-Theological Discourses.—By the Rev. Robert Taylor, B.A., of St. John's College, Cambridge. (Reprinted verbatim from Richard Carlile's original edition.) In two vols., neatly bound in cloth, 8s. Or in forty-six numbers, 2d. each. Also, by same author, "The Diegesis," 3s. 6d., cloth, and "The Syntagma," 1s., both dealing with the origin and evidences of Christianity.

Facts and Figures for Working Men. An analysis of the Drink Question in relation to commerce, foreign competition, our food supply, strikes, the death rate, and prosperity of the country, etc. By Frederick Leary. 1d.

Pamphlets by Hypatia Bradlaugh.—Four Lectures on "The Chemistry of Home:" "Air, I." "Air, II.," "Water, I.," "Water, II." 1d. each, or the whole, in neat wrapper, 4d. Four Lectures on "The Slave Struggle in America." 1d. each, or in wrapper complete, 4d.

City Missionaries and Pious Frauds.—By W. R. CROFTS. 1d.

Natural Reason versus Divine Revelation.—An appeal for Freethought. By JULIAN. Edited by ROBERT LEWINS, M.D. 6d.

Pamphlets by J. Symes. — "The Methodist Conference and Eternal Punishment: Do its Defenders Believe the Doctrine," 3d. "Hospitals and Dispensaries, are they of Christian Growth?" new and revised edition, 1d. "Man's Place in Nature, or Man an Animal amongst Animals," 4d. "Philosophic Atheism," 4d. "Christianity and Slavery," 2d. "Christianity at the Bar of Science," 3d. "Debate on Atheism with Mr. St. Clair," 1s.

Robert Cooper's Holy Scriptures Analysed, with Sketch of his Life. By C. BRADLAUGH. 6d.

Thomas Paine's Common Sense.—With New Introduction. By CHARLES BRADLAUGH. 6d.

New Theory of Poverty.—By H. AULA. 1d.

Liberty and Morality. By M. D. CONWAY. 3d.

Shelley's Works, reprinted from the original MSS.—The Poet of Atheism and Democracy.—In four handsome volumes, each complete in itself. Vol. 1, Early Poems. Volume 2, Later Poems. Vol. 3, Posthumous Poems. Vol. 4, Prose Writings. 2s. each.

Pamphlets by C. R. Drysdale, M.D.—"The Population Question," 1s. "Tobacco, and the Diseases it Produces," 2d. "Alcohol," 6d.

Paine's Theological Works; including the "Age of Reason," and all his Miscellaneous Pieces and Poetical Works; his last Will and Testament, and a Steel Portrait. Cloth. 3s.

The Age of Reason. By THOMAS PAINE. Complete, with Preface by C. Bradlaugh. A new edition, the best ever issued, printed in large type on good paper, 1s.; cloth gilt, 1s. 6d.

Paine's Rights of Man. A Reply to Burke on the French Revolution. 1s.

The Immortality of the Soul Philosophically Considered. Seven Lectures by ROBERT COOPER. 1s.

Voltaire's Philosophical Dictionary. The edition in six, re-printed in two thick volumes. Two portraits and a memoir. 8s.

Analysis of the Influence of Natural Religion on the temporal Happiness of Mankind. By PHILIP BEAUCHAMP (G. Grote, the historian of Greece). Pp. 123. 1s.

Shelley's Song to the Men of England. Set to Music for four voices. By HERR TROUSSELLE. 2d.

A Manual of Political Questions of the Day, with the arguments on either side. By SYDNEY BUXTON. 130 pp. 6d.

Pamphlets by G. W. Foote.—"Secularism the True Philosophy of Life," 4d. "Futility of Prayer," 2d. "Atheism and Morality," 2d. "Death's Test, or Christian Lies about Dying Infidels," 2d. "The God Christians Swear By," 2d. "Was Jesus Insane?" 1d. "Atheism and Suicide," 1d. Bible Romances, 1d. each: "Noah's Flood," "Creation Story," "Eve and the Apple," "The Bible Devil," "Jonah and the Whale," "The Ten Plagues," "The Wandering Jews," "The Tower of Babel," "Balaam's Ass," "God's Thieves in Canaan," "Cain and Abel," "Lot's Wife." Or the 12, in colored wrapper, 1s.

The Life of Jesus. By Ernest Renan. Authorised English Translation. Crown 8vo, pp. xii.—312, cloth, 2s. 6d.; stitched in wrapper, 1s. 6d.

The Crisis in Farming; its Radical Causes and their only Remedies. Twenty-two evils arising from Landlord, thirteen from Tenant. By the Author of "Hints to Landlords and Tenants." 6d.

The First Seven Alleged Persecutions, A.D. 64 to A.D. 235. By Thos. L'Estrange. 6d.

The Eucharist. By the same Author. 6d.

These two pamphlets are highly recommended as able contributions to Freethought enquiry.

Volney's Ruins of Empires, with Plates of the Ancient Zodiac, etc., carefully reprinted from the best edition, cloth, lettered, 2s.

The Three Trials of William Hone, for Publishing Three Parodies; viz., The late John Wilkes's Catechism, The Political Litany, and The Sinecurists' Creed; on three ex-officio informations, at Guildhall, London, during three successive days—December 18th, 19th, and 20th, 1817—before three special juries, and Mr. Justice Abbot, on the first day, and Lord Chief Justice Ellenborough, on the last two days. 2s.

Land Law Reform, and its relation to Work, Wages, and Population. 2d.

The True Principle of Population, Trade Profits, &c., and the Land Laws. By T. R. 2d.

The True Source of Christianity; or, a Voice from the Ganges. By an Indian Officer. Originally published at 5s. This work is now republished verbatim, in paper covers, 1s.; cloth gilt, 1s. 6d.

The Roll Call: a Political Record of the years 1775 to 1880. Commencing with the great wars of the last century, and brought down to the close of 1880, with full Index. In paper covers, 78 pp., 6d.

Under which Lord? By the author of "Joshua Davidson." Originally published in 3 vols. at £1 11s. 6d., now issued complete in 1 vol., cloth gilt, 2s. 6d.

The Rev. Joseph Cook: A Critical Examination. By Professor Fiske. 1d.

The Jewish Sabbath and the Christian Lords. By Professor BLACKIE. 2d.

Religion in the Heavens; or, Mythology Unveiled. In a Series of Lectures. By LOGAN MITCHELL. Uniform with International Series. Cloth, gilt, 5s.

The Land Agitation in Ireland. Letter of the Most Reverend Dr. NULTY to the Clergy and Laity of the Diocese of Meath. 1d.

Gospel Contradictions. Arranged in the form of a Catechism. By T. L. STRANGE, late Judge in the High Court of Madras. 1d.

Hume's Essay on Miracles. A new edition, with an introduction commenting upon the views of Campbell, Paley, Mill, Greg, Mozley, Tyndall, Huxley, etc. By JOSEPH MAZZINI WHEELER. 3d.

Thursday Lectures at the Hall of Science. Containing Mr. Bradlaugh's lectures on "Anthropology," Mrs. Besant's on "The Physiology of Home," Miss Bradlaugh's on "The Chemistry of Home," and Dr. Aveling's on "The Plays of Shakspere." Complete in one vol. Cloth, 2s.

LIST B.

Special List of Remainders, in cloth, new and uncut—All the books in List B are at the lowest price, and no reduction can be made to the trade, the object being to supply readers of the *National Reformer* with literature at specially low rates.

Orders must be accompanied by cost of Postage, which is inserted after the letter P. Where no postage is mentioned, the books go by Sutton at cost of purchaser, and 2d. in addition to price must be sent for booking.

The Biography of Charles Bradlaugh.—Written by ADOLPHE S. HEADINGLEY. Crown 8vo., cloth, 332 pages (published at 7s.), reduced to 2s. 6d. P. 4½d.

Eminent Radicals in and out of Parliament. By J. MORRISON DAVIDSON, Barrister-at-law. Being sketches of W. E. Gladstone, John Bright, P. A. Taylor, Sir C. Dilke, J. Cowen, Sir W. Lawson, H. Fawcett, J. Chamberlain, T. Burt, H. Richards, L. H. Courtney, A. J. Mundella, John Morley, Robert William Dale, Joseph Arch, Edward Spencer Beesly, Charles Haddon Spurgeon, Charles Bradlaugh, Frederic Augustus Maxse, James Beal, Moncure Daniel Conway, James Allanson Picton, The Hon. Auberon Herbert, Edward Augustus Freeman. Demy 8vo., 262 pp. Published at 10s. 6d. 2s. 6d. P. 7d.

The Outcast.—By WINWOOD READE. Handsomely bound, pp. 262., 1s. 6d. P. 3½d.

The Apocryphal New Testament, being all the Gospels, Epistles, &c., attributed to Christ, his Apostles, and their companions in the first four centuries of the Christian Era. By W. HONE. 2s. 6d. P. 6d.

Ancient Mysteries described, by WILLIAM HONE. With Engravings on Copper and Wood. 2s. 6d. P. 6d.

Morley (Henry, author of "English Literature," &c., &c.), Clement Marot, and other studies. 2 vols. in 1, thick crown 8vo, (pub. at 21s.), 4s. P. 8d.

Correspondence of Charles Lamb, with an Essay on his Life and Genius. By THOMAS PURCELL. pp. 537, gilt lettered, 2s. 6d. P. 8d.

Voltaire: his Life and Times. By F. ESPINASSE. 1694 to 1726. 620 pp. (published at 14s.), 2s. 6d. P. 8d.

Rousseau.—By JOHN MORLEY. 2 vols., 7s. 6d. Published at 24s.

The Upas: a Vision of the Past, Present, and Future.—By Capt. R. H. DYAS. This book traces the rise, reign, and decay of Superstition. Published at 10s., reduced to 2s. 6d. P. 7d.

History of English Literature.—By H. A. TAINE, D.C.L., Translated by H. VAN LAUN. 2 vols. Vol. I., pp. 531; Vol. II., pp. 550, 12s.; published at 24s.

Ireland under British Rule.—By Lieut.-Colonel H. J. W. JERVIS, R.A., M.P. Neatly bound. Pp. 321. 2s. P. 7½d.

Views of the Deity, Traditional and Scientific.—A Contribution to the Study of Theological Science (written against the Materialist Position). By JAMES SAMUELSON. Pp. 171. 1s. 6d. P. 3½d.

Thomas Wentworth, Earl of Strafford, and Lord Lieutenant of Ireland, The Life of. By ELIZABETH COOPER. 2 vols., 8vo, (published at 30s.), 5s.

Hans Breitman's Christmas, with other Ballads, reduced to 6d. Post free.

Hans Breitman as a Politician, with other Ballads, reduced to 6d. Post free.

Story of the Commune.—By a COMMUNALIST. 6d. Post free.

Castelar's Life of Byron, and other Sketches. Translated by Mrs. ARTHUR ARNOLD. 8vo (published at 12s.), 3s. 6d. P. 7d.

The other Sketches are—Victor Hugo, Alexander Dumas, Emile Girardin, Daniel Manin, Adolphe Thiers.

The Last Days of a Condemned.—By VICTOR HUGO. With Observations on Capital Punishment, by Sir P. Hesketh Fleetwood, Bart, M.P. 1s. P. 3½d.

David Fredrich Strauss, in his Life and Writings.—By EDWARD ZELLER. Published at 5s. Pp. 160. 1s. P. 4d.

Lessing's Letters on Bibliolatry. Translated by H. H. BERNARD, Ph.Dr. Pp. 144. 1s. 6d. P. 3d. Published at 5s.

Life and Pontificate of Leo. X.—By WILLIAM ROSCOE. Neatly bound, pp. 425. 1s. P. 2½d. A standard Historical authority.

Episodes of the French Revolution, from 1789 to 1795, with an appendix embodying the Principal Events in France from 1789 to the present time, examined from a political and philosophical point of view. By V. F. BENVENUTI. Demy 8vo, 310 pp., 1s. 6d. P. 6d.

William Godwin: his friends and contemporaries. 2 vols., demy 8vo, handsomely bound in cloth, with portraits of William Godwin and Mary Wollstonecraft, and *fac-similes* of writing. The work, published at 28s., is beautifully printed on superior toned paper. 5s. 6d.

The Peasant's Home. Showing the progress in the condition of agricultural laborers from 1760 to 1865. This work was the Howard Prize Essay for 1875, the subject being "The State of the Dwellings of the Poor in the Rural Districts of England, with special regard to the improvements that have taken place since the middle of the eighteenth century and their influence on the health and morals of their inmates." Crown 8vo, 136 pp., 6d. P. 3½d.

A History of the Creation and the Patriarchs; or, Pentateuchism Analytically Treated (Genesis). 288 pp., crown 8vo. 1s. P. 3½d.

The New Nation. By JOHN MORRIS. In 5 vols., published at two guineas in 1880. This learned work is by a Deist, who brings a vast mass of philological evidence to bear on the dissection of Biblical myths. Cloth, demy 8vo, containing an aggregate of 2,362 pp. 5s. Very cheap.

Rousseau, as described by himself and others. With remarks and explanations, by THOS. CRADDOCK. Contains an outline of Rousseau's life and an account of his friends and his works, and gives the opinions of Diderot, Voltaire, Marmontel, Grimm, Barante, Morley, etc., upon the philosopher; with chronological index of the principal events in Rousseau's life. 251 pp. 1s. 6d. P. 6d.

Cousin's Philosophy of Kant. With a Sketch of Kant's Life and Writings. By A. G. HENDERSON. Pp. 194. Neatly bound. 2s. 6d. P. 5d. Published at 6s.

The True History of Joshua Davidson, Christian and Communist.—By Mrs. LYNN LYNTON. Sixth Edition. Handsomely bound, thick paper, pp. 279. Price 1s. 6d. P. 4d.

Rossel's Posthumous Papers. Pp. 294. 1s. P. 4d.

Half Hours with the Freethinkers—Lives of Lord Bolingbroke, Lord Shaftesbury, Shelley, Anthony Collins, Charles Southwell, Descartes, Heinrich Heine, Thomas Paine. 3d. P. ½d.

Republican Superstitions. By MONCURE D. CONWAY. 1s. 6d. (Published at 7s. 6d.) P. 3d.

The Survival, with an Apology for Scepticism. 471 pp. 1s. P. 7d

Australian Views of England. By HENRY PARKES. Pp. 112. 1s. P. 3½d.

Isis and Osiris, or the Origin of Christianity. By JOHN STUART GLENNIE, M.A. (New edition) 3s. 6d. P. 8½d. Published by Messrs. Longmans at 15s. 432 pages.

Parallel Lives of Ancient and Modern Heroes. By CHARLES DUKE YONGE. 270 pp. Published at 4s. 6d. 1s. 6d. P. 3½d.

Travels in the Philippines. By F. JAGOR. With numerous Illustrations and Maps. 370 pp. Handsomely bound. (Published at 16s.) 3s. P. 8d.

The Papal Conclaves, as they were and as they are. By T. ADOLPHUS TROLLOPE. 434 pp. Handsomely bound. (Published at 16s.) 3s. P. 8½d.

National Christianity; or, Cæsarism and Clericalism. By the Rev. J. B. HEARD. 2s. (Published by Messrs. Longmans at 10s. 6d.) P. 7d.

Alfieri: his Life, Adventures, and Works. By C. MITCHELL CHARLES. 6d. P. 1½d.

Richard Cobden and the Free Traders. Gilt, crown 8vo, pp. 298, with portrait, 1s. 6d. P. 4d.

Howell's Capital and Labour.—Including Chapters on the history of Guilds, Trades' Unions, Apprentices, Technical Education, Intimidation and Picketing, Restraints on Trade; Strikes—their Objects, Aims, and Results; Trade Councils, Arbitration, Co-operation, Friendly Societies, the Labor Laws, &c. By GEORGE HOWELL. 4s. P. 5d.

The Trades Unions of England. By M. LE COMTE DE PARIS. Translated by NASSAU J. SENIOR. Edited by THOMAS HUGHES, M.P. 2s. P. 3d.

This book, together with **Capital and Labour**, by GEORGE HOWELL, present views of Trade Unionism from entirely different standpoints. (Published at 7s. 6d. each.) The two supplied, post-free, for 6s.

Plutarch's Lives. Langhorne's Translation, Text and Notes complete and revised (Grecian section). 2s. P. 6d.

A Visit to the Seat of War in the North (the Crimean War). By LASCELLES WRAXALL. Pp. 106. 6d. P. 1½d.

Sketches of the Hungarian Emigration into Turkey. By A. HONVED. 6d. P. 1½d.

Pictures from the East. By JOHN CAPPER. Describing especially Ceylon. Pp. 162. 6d. P. 2d.

Montenegro and the Slavonians of Turkey. By COUNT VALERIAN KRASINSKI. This very interesting book ought, at the present time, to be most eagerly read. Pp. 152. 8d. P. 2d.

Florian and Crescenz: a Village Tale from the Black Forest. By BERTHOLD AUERBACH. Translated by META TAYLOR. 6d. P. 1½d.

Oriental Zigzag: Wanderings in Syria, Moab, Abyssinia, and Egypt. By CHARLES HAMILTON. Handsomely illustrated. 304 pp. 2s. 6d. P. 6d.

Man with the Iron Mask. By MARIUS TOPIN. Translated and edited by HENRY VIZETELLY, with fac-simile. Crown 8vo (Published at 9s.), 2s. 6d. P. 5d.

Bryant (William Cullen), Orations and Addresses. Portrait, thick crown 8vo, (Published at 7s. 6d.) 2s. 6d. P. 6d.

The Age and the Gospel: Essays on Christianity, its Friends and Opponents. By the Rev. B. FRANKLAND, B.A. A controversial book on the Christian side. 303 pp., 2s. P. 5d.

Life and Conversations of Dr. Samuel Johnson. By ALEXANDER MAIN. Preface by GEORGE HENRY LEWES. 441 pp. Published at 10s. 6d. 2s. 6d. P. 5d.

Wanderings in the Interior of New Guinea.—By CAPTAIN J. A. LAWSON. With Frontispiece and Map. Pp. 282. Handsomely bound. Published at 10s. 6d. 2s. 6d. P. 5d.

Longinus on the Sublime. A new translation, chiefly according to the improved edition of Weiske. By a Master of Arts of the University of Oxford. Pp. 92. 1s. P. 1½d.

English Life of Jesus. By THOMAS SCOTT. 2s. 6d. P. 5d.

The Book of Genesis Analytically Treated. With account of Scripture Legends and the various Commentaries. Crown 8vo, pp. 288, 1s. P. 4d.

Catéchisme du Libre Penseur. Par EDGAR MONTEIL. (Published at 3s. 6d.) Reduced to 1s. P. 3d. This has been specially attacked recently in the "Contemporary Review" and various English Conservative journals.

Unorthodox London; or, Phases of Religious Life in the Metropolis. By the Rev. D. MAURICE DAVIES. Two volumes bound in one. Contains: South Place Chapel, Finsbury—MONCURE D. CONWAY on Mazzini—Colonel WENTWORTH HIGGINSON on Buddha—Unitarianism, a Sunday Lecture, by Professor HUXLEY—Tabernacle Ranters—The Walworth Jumpers—Bible Christians—Plymouth Brethren—A Quakers' Meeting—Dr. CUMMING—Seventh Day Baptists—Christadelphians—Moravians—Father IGNATIUS at Home, &c. 465 pp. 2s. 6d. P. 6½d. (Published originally in Two Volumes at 28s.)

Orthodox London. By the same Author. Two volumes bound in one. Contains: The Rev. H. R. HAWEIS—Father STANTON—Mr. FORREST—Rev. T. TEIGNMOUTH SHORE—Mr. LLEWELLYN DAVIES—Mr. MAGUIRE—Dean STANLEY—Canon LIDDON—Canon MILLER—Mr. STOPFORD BROOKE—Midnight Mass—Archbishop of York—Bishop of London—Bishop of Manchester—Bishop of Lincoln, &c., &c. 458 pages. 2s. 6d. P. 6½d. Published originally in Two Volumes at 28s.

Chapters on Man, with the Outlines of a Science of Comparative Psychology. By C. STANILAND WAKE. Pp. 343. 2s. 6d. P. 4½d. Published at 7s. 6d.

Origines Biblicæ; or, Researches in Primeval History. By C. T. BEKE. 2s. P. 5d.

The Public Lives of W. E. Gladstone and of Earl Beaconsfield.—Large type, stiff covers, 132 pp. (Published at 1s.), 3d. Post free, 5d.

The Life and Labours of Albany Fonblanque. Neatly bound, cloth, 546 pp., quite new and uncut. Published at 16s. 4s. P. 9½d.

Foundation of Christianity: a Critical Analysis of the Pentateuch and the Theology of the Old Testament. By GEORGE B. JACKSON, A.B. "A searching and uncompromising inquiry into the origin and credibility of the religion of the patriarchs." Published at 2s., paper in perfect condition, 6d. P. 2d.

The Agricultural Laborer. By T. E. KEBBELL, Esq., of the Inner Temple. Cloth, 239 pp., 1s. P. 4d.

The History of Clerkenwell. By the late W. J. PINKS, with additions and Notes by the Editor, Edward J. Wood, complete in one vol., fully gilt, 800 pp. (published at 15s.), 7s. 6d.

Clarke's Critical Review. Pub. at 5s. 6d. 446 pp., 2s. 6d. P. 3½d.

Principles of Reform in the Suffrage. By SHADWORTH D. HODGSON. Containing the functions of government, the determination of the governing classes, and the problem of Reform. Cloth, new and uncut, 1s. P. 3d.

Harmony of Laws; or, Analysis of the Principles Common to the Laws of Civilised Nations. By G. UNDY. 6d. P. 1d. Published at 2s. 6d.

Different Significations of the Word Religion. By A. J. ELLIS, B.A. Published at 3d. **The Principles of Individual Liberty:** how far applicable to the relation of the sexes. By W. C. COUPLAND. Followed by report of Debate in the London Dialectical Society, in which Mrs. Besant, Miss Vickery, Dr. C. R. Drysdale, Mr. Moncure D. Conway, and Mr. Bradlaugh took part. Published at 6d. **The Dyer's Hand;** preceded by "The Way to God," by A. J. ELLIS. Published at 2d. The three pamphlets sent together, post free, for 6d.

Jeux d'Esprit, written and spoken by French and English wits and humorists. Collected and edited by HENRY S. LEIGH. Published at 6s.; 2s. 6d. P. 4d.

Gastronomy as a Fine Art; or, the Science of Good Living: a translation of the "Physologie du Goût" of Brillat-Savarin. By R. E. ANDERSON, M.A. Published at 6s.; 2s. 6d. P. 4½d.

The Philosophy of the Conditioned: with Criticisms on John Stuart Mill's Examination of Sir William Hamilton's Philosophy. By Professor MANSEL. 2s. P. 4d.

Utilitarianism Explained and Exemplified in Moral and Political Government, in answer to John Stuart Mill. 463 pp., cloth, 1s. 6d. P. 5d.

Thoreau: his Life and Aims: a Study. By H. A. PAGE, Author of "Life of Thomas de Quincey," "Memoirs of Hawthorne," &c. Richly gilt (published at 6s.), 2s. P. 4d.

The Science of Exchanges.—By N. A. NICHOLSON. 1s. P. 3d. Ought to be read by all interested in the currency question.

American Poets, Selected and Edited by W. M. ROSETTI. Cloth crown 8vo., gilt edges, and richly gilt and illustrated covers, 512 pp., a very handsome book. 2s. P. 5d.

Rise and Decay of Islam. By A. J. DUNN. 368 pp. 2s. P. 6d.

The Voice of the Nation, 1880. Being a Summary of the Results of Elections in the United Kingdom, showing the Number of Registered Electors, the Number of Votes actually recorded for each, the Names of all the Candidates, and Alphabetical Index for the New House of Commons. In colored wrapper, 40 pp. (Published at 6d.) Post free 1½d.

The Principles of Human Knowledge, Being Berkeley's Celebrated Treatise on the Nature of the Material Substance (and its relation to the Absolute), with a brief introduction to the doctrine and full explanations of the text; followed by an Appendix with remarks on Kant and Hume. By COLLYNS SYMON, LL.D. 1s. P. 3d.

The Rights of Tenants of Ecclesiastical Lands under the Irish Church Act, 1869. By C. H. TODD. Crown 8vo, pp. 40, paper wrapper, 1d. P. ½d.

A Practical Manual of the Law of Sales of Food, Drinks, and Medicines, with a reprint of the Act of 1875 against Adulteration, with full notes of all the cases decided on the prior statutes, and on the legal rights and obligations of Manufacturers, Sellers, and Dealers, with suggestions by a Chemical Analyst; Alphabetical Index, List of Adulterations, and Analytical Tables and Forms. To which are added the principal clauses in the Explosive Substances Act, 1875, and Petroleum Acts, with notes of the cases thereon, by a Barrister and Magistrate. Stiff paper cover, post 8vo, pp. 80. (Published at 2s.) 3d. P. 1d.

The Life and Struggles of William Lovett, in his Pursuit of Bread, Knowledge, and Freedom: an Autobiography. Demy 8vo, cloth gilt, 473 pp. (Published at 5s.) 1s. 6d. P. 6d.

Selections from the English Poets from Spencer to Shelley, with short literary notices. By HOWARD WILLIAMS, M.A. Crown 8vo, 452 pp. 2s. P. 5d.

Exotics; or, English Words from Latin Poets. By E. N. HOARE, M.A., Dean of Waterford. Post 8vo, 334 pp., with thoroughly complete index. 1s. 6d. P. 4d.

The Association of Ideas, and its Influence on the Training of the Mind. By the Rev. JAS. MCCOSH, LL.D., Professor of Logic and Metaphysics, Queen's College, Belfast. 36 pp., wrapper. (Published at 3d.) 1d. P. ½d. Six copies post free for 6d.

Who was St. Titus? The Scripture notices on the subject compared with received opinions, by A. KING, A.B. Demy 8vo, 250 pp. 1s. 6d. P. 4½d.

Ultramontanism v. Civil and Religious Liberty. By the celebrated FATHER O'KEEFE. Demy 8vo, 270 pp., 1s. P. 5d.

The Genuine Book. An Inquiry and Delicate Investigation into the conduct of Her Royal Highness the Princess of Wales, before Lords Erskine, Spencer, Grenville and Ellenborough, the four Special Commissioners of Inquiry appointed by His Majesty in the year 1806, with appendices; superintended through the press by the Right Hon. Spencer Percival. Boards (old), demy 8vo, 360 pp. (Published at 12s.) 3s. P. 6d. This book is now very rare.

The People's Blue Book. Taxation as it is and as it should be. Revised, enlarged and brought down to the present time, with a supplemental chapter on Ireland, by C. TENANT. Stiff paper wrappers, crown 8vo, 970 pp., 2s. P. 6½d.

Political Rights of the British People: How acquired, retained, or forfeited; with a sketch of such rights under ancient and modern Republics, by J. A. DEAN. Crown 8vo, 368 pp., cloth gilt, 1s. 6d., or in boards, 1s. P. 4½d.

Milton's Poetical Works. Cloth, gilt, 16mo, steel frontispiece, 420 pp., new. Post free 1s.

Oriental Customs; or, an Illustration of the Sacred Scriptures by an Explanatory Application of the Customs and Manners of the Eastern Nations, especially the Jews therein referred to. Collected from the most celebrated travellers and most eminent critics, by SAMUEL BURDEN, D.D. Boards, demy 8vo, 500 pp. 2s. 6d. P. 6d.

The Secret History of "The International" Working Men's Association. By ONSLOW YORKE. This work (published at 2s.) contains many curious facts concerning the principal actors in the socialistic and communistic movements in Europe. This book has often been referred to in debates in the House of Commons, in the Chamber of Deputies in Paris, and in the German Parliament. Crown 8vo, 166 pp., limp cloth, 6d. P. 2d.

Montenegro: its People and their History. By W. DENTON, M.A., author of "Servia," "The Christians of Turkey," etc. With map, cloth gilt, crown 8vo, 292 pp., 1s. 6d. P. 4d.

Class Despotism, as exemplified during the four years' struggle for freedom in the United States; and The Evils of Individual Wealth, considered as affecting the well-being and lives of the mass of a people Cloth gilt, 336 pp., 4d. P. 2d.

The Year Book of Facts in Science and Art. By JAMES MASON. This very useful book contains a complete record of the inventions, improvements, and all matters of interest in connexion with Chemistry, Geology, Botany, Zoology, etc., etc., in 1878, and a full report of the President's Speech at the British Association. New, cloth gilt, crown 8vo, 210 pp., 1s., or in boards 7d. P. 3½d.

The History of Co-operation in Halifax. By G. J. HOLYOAKE. 4d. P. 1d.

Theology for the People. By E. DE PENTHENY O'KELLY. Published by G. J. Holyoake. Cloth gilt, 9d. P. 3d.

Pamphlets by John Watts.—"The Christian Doctrine of Man's Depravity refuted," "Christian Theory of the Destruction of the World Refuted." The two, post free, 2d.

Lord Brougham's Speeches on Social and Political Subjects, with historical introductions. Post 8vo, cloth, 460 pp. (published at 5s.), 1s. P. 4½d.

Travels in the Slavonic Provinces of Turkey in Europe. By G. MUIR MACKENZIE and A. P. IRBEY, with a preface by the Right Hon. W. E. GLADSTONE. This splendid work, published in 1877, is the most complete ever issued on the subject, contains 21 full-page illustrations with other views, and an excellent colored map. Published in 2 vols. at 28s. Now offered, handsomely bound in 1 vol., 3s. 6d.

Curtis's Theology Displayed: a Review of the Origin and Utility of the Christian Religion. Cloth, 9d. P. 1½d.—Paper covers, 6d. P. 1d.

How did England become an Oligarchy? Addressed to Parliamentary Reformers, with a Short Treatise on the First Principles of Political Government. By J. DUNCAN, Esq. Limp cloth, 3d. P. 1d.

The Inherent Evils of all State Governments Demonstrated, being a reprint of EDMUND BURKE'S celebrated essay entitled "A Vindication of Natural Society," with notes; and an appendix briefly enunciating the principles through which "Natural Society" may be gradually realised. 66 pp., 3d. P. 1d. Published at 1s.

Essay on the Human Mind. By E. BUSHBY, B.D. Stiff paper covers, 76 pp. 3d. P. 1d. (Published at 2s. 6d.)

Modern Protestantism: a few words on Essays and Reviews. By G. J. HOLYOAKE. Published at 6d. Post free 1½d.

Thomas Cooper's Celebrated Eight Letters to the Young Men of the Working Classes. Post free 3d.

Horatio Prater's Letters to the American People on Christianity and the Sabbath. (Published by G. J. Holyoake, Fleet Street.) Cloth, new, 8d. P. 2½d. Paper covers 6d. P. 2d.

Political Poems. By VICTOR HUGO and GARIBALDI. 1d. P. ½d.

The National Inheritance: an Exhaustive Treatise on the Land Question. By JAMES WALKER. 16 pp., demy 8vo, stitched, 1d. P. ½d.

Address to Socialists on the Rational System of Society, and the measures required for the successful operation of the Universal Community Society. By ROBERT OWEN. Free 1½d.

Lord Byron's "Vision of Judgment." 24 pp., stitched, in wrapper, free 2d.

"Notre Dame!" A Freethinker's address to the Hierarchy of the Church of Rome. By R. H. DALTON, author of "Education of Girls," etc. (Published at 1s.) Post free, 1½d.

Vol. 1 of "Health." A Monthly Magazine, edited by G. DREWRY, M.D. Containing the whole issues for 1878, full of interesting articles on food, dress, diseases, sanitary matters, &c., &c. (Published at 2s.) Cloth, new, 6d. P. 4d.

An Essay on the Functions of the Brain. In paper wrapper, 1d. P. ½d.

The complete Works of Shakspere, with a Memoir. By ALEXANDER CHALMERS. Handsomely bound, richly gilt covers, 708 pp., Diprose's diamond edition, 1s. 6d. P. 5d. Very suitable for presentation.

Russian and Turk from a Geographical, Ethnological, and Historical point of view. By R. G. LATHAM, M.A., M.D. Royal 8vo, 435 pp., 3s. 6d. P. 8d.

An Inquiry into the Theories of History, with special reference to the principles of the Positive Philosophy. By W. ADAM. Dealing with the philosophy of Comte with great care and critical ability. This work was favorably noticed by J. S. Mill. Demy 8vo, 441 pp., 3s. P. 7d.

Brief Biographies of German Political Leaders, including Bismarck, Arnim, Camphausen, Lasker, Jacoby, Sonneman, Gueist, Virchow, etc., etc., in all nineteen principal men in the country. Crown 8vo, 264 pp., 2s. P. 4d.

Political Pamphlets by Thomas Paine—"Decline and Fall of the English System of Finance;" "Public Good;" "Letters to the Citizens of America;" "Agrarian Justice opposed to Agrarian Law and Agrarian Monopoly, with a plan for creating a National Fund;" "Dissertations on the First Principles of Government." The five free for 6d.

Pamphlets by R. D. Owen—"A Lecture on Consistency;" "Situations—Lawyers, Clergy, Physicians, Men and Women;" "Darby and Susan: a Tale of Old England;" "Wealth and Misery;" "Neurology: an Account of some Experiments in Cerebral Physiology;" "Sermon on Free Enquiry," etc. 1d. each. P. ½d. Or the whole free for 6d.

Letter to the Abbe Raynal, in correction of his Account of the Revolution in America. By THOMAS PAINE, with correspondence between the writer and George Washington. 54 pp., stitched in wrapper (published at 6d.), free 3d.

Address delivered by Robert Owen on the Opening of the Institution for the Formation of Character at New Lanark, on January 1st, 1816, being the first public announcement of the discovery of the Infant School System. Demy 8vo, 32 pp., stitched in wrapper, free 2d.

Indian Infanticide: its Origin, Progress and Suppression. Containing a large amount of information respecting the Social Life of the Hindus. 250 pp., 1s. 6d. P. 4d.

An Inquiry into the Nature of Responsibility, as deduced from Savage Justice, Civil Justice, and Social Justice; with some Remarks upon the Doctrine of Irresponsibility as taught by Jesus Christ and Robert Owen; also upon the Responsibility of Man to God. By T. SIMMONS MACINTOSH, author of "The Electrical Theory of the Universe." 124 pp., 6d. P. 1½d.

The Life and Writings of Joseph Priestley. Paper covers, 1d.

Personal Narrative of Travels in Eastern Lands, principally Turkish, in 1833, in a Series of Letters, 67 in all. By Professor F. W. NEWMAN. The letters are full of most interesting matter concerning Eastern Social and Political Life. Crown 8vo, paper covers, 120 pages of close print, 6d. P. 1½d.

Household Words.—Conducted by CHARLES DICKENS. Strongly bound. Each volume, 2s.; published at 5s. 6d.

Vol. 9 contains the whole of the essays on Turkey and Greece, by G. A. SALA, under the title "A Roving Englishman," written at the close of the Crimean War.

Vol. 14 contains the story of "The Wreck of the Golden Mary," also the famous papers by G. A. SALA, "A Journey due North," and "A Journey to Russia.'

Pamphlets by G. J. Holyoake.—"Working-class Representation and its Conditions and Consequences;" "Outlaws of Freethought;" "The Limits of Atheism; or, Why Should Sceptics be Outlaws;" "The Social Means of Promoting Temperance," with remarks on errors in its advocacy; "A New Defence of the Ballot;" "Life and Last Days of Robert Owen, of New Lanark;" "The Suppressed Lecture at Cheltenham;" "Public Lessons of the Hangman." The lot, post free, 8d.

Credibility of the Gospel Narratives of the Birth and Infancy of Christ, with an Introduction on the Acts of the Apostles. A critical analysis of the contradictions of the Gospel Writers. 91 pp. (published at 1s. 6d. by Thomas Scott), 6d. P. 1d.

Biographies of John Wilkes and William Cobbett, with steel engravings. By the Rev. J. S. WATSON, M.A. Good index, 410 pp., 2s. 6d. P. 6d.

Historical Studies and Recreations. By SHOSHEE CHUNDER DUTT (J. A. G. Barton), author of "Bengaliana," etc. Containing the World's History retold, in two parts: the Ancient World and the Modern World. Also Bengal, an account of the Country from the earliest times, the Great Wars of India, the Ruins of the Old World, read as Milestones of Civilisation. 2 vols, 8vo, cloth, new, uncut. Vol. I. pp. 470; vol. II. pp. 600. (Published at 32s.) 5s. 6d.

The Eternal Gospel; or, the Idea of Christian Perfectibility. By N. W. MACKAY, M.A. (Published at 2s. by Thomas Scott.) In two Parts, 200 pp. in all, 6d. P. 2d.

Phraseological Notes on the Hebrew Text of the Book of Genesis. By THEODORE PRESTON, M.A. Illustrating the remarkable peculiarities and anomalies of matter, style, and phrase in the Book of Genesis, with references to Rashi, Aben Ezra, Gesenius, etc., etc. Crown 8vo, pp. 290, 2s. P. 4½d.

THE GOLDEN LIBRARY SERIES.—Bayard Taylor's Diversions of the Echo Club—The Book of Clerical Anecdotes—Byron's Don Juan—Emerson's Letters and Social Aims—Godwin's (William) Lives of the Necromancers—Holmes's Professor at the Breakfast Table—Hood's Whims and Oddities, complete, with all the original illustrations—Irving's (Washington) Tales of a Traveller—Irving's (Washington) Tales of the Alhambra—Jesse's (Edward) Scenes and Occupations of Country Life—Leigh Hunt's Essays, with portrait and introduction by Edmund Ollier—Mallory's, Sir Thos. Mort d'Arthur, the Stories of King Arthur and of the Knights of the Round Table; edited by B. Montgomery Ranking—Pascal's Provincial Letters; a new translation, with historical introduction and notes by T. M'Crie, D.D., LL.D.—Pope's Complete Poetical Works—Rochefoucald's Maxims and Moral Reflections, with notes and introductory essay by Sainte-Beuve—St. Pierre's Paul and Virginia, and the Indian Cottage; edited, with Life, by the Rev. E. Clarke—Lamb's Essays of Elia; both series complete in one volume. Handsomely bound. Reduced to 1s. each. If sent by Post 3d. each extra.

Essays—Scientific, Political, and Speculative. (Second Series.) By HERBERT SPENCER. (Published at 12s.) Demy 8vo, 362 pp., 3s. 6d. P. 6d. A rare opportunity.

Matter and Motion. By N. A. NICHOLSON, M.A., Trinity College, Oxford. 48 pp., demy 8vo, 3d. P. 1d.

The Year Book of Facts for 1880. Containing the principal discoveries in Geology, Dynamics, Geography, etc., with the Speech of the President at the British Association Congress of that year, with Index. 210 pp., 7d. P. 3½d.

Practical Remarks on State Vaccination, addressed to the Smallpox and Vaccination Committee of the Epidemiological Society. By EDWARD J. HUGHES, M.D., Medical Officer to the Holywell Union. 32 pp., demy 8vo, 1d. P. ½d.

The Crimea and Transcaucasia; being the narrative of a journey in the Kouban, in Gouria, Georgia, Armenia, Ossety, Imeritia, Swannety, and Mingrelia, and in the Tauric Range. By Commander J. P. TELFER, R.N. With two fine Maps and numerous Illustrations; two vols. in one, splendidly bound in cloth, gilt edges, royal 8vo, 600 pp. (Published at £1 16s.) A handsome presentation book, 5s.

An Essay on Classification. By LOUIS AGASSIZ. 8vo. Pp. vii. and 381. Cloth. (Published at 12s.) Reduced to 3s. P. 6d.

Light, and its Influence on Life and Health. By Dr. FORBES WINSLOW. 301 pp. 1s. P. 4d.

Human Longevity; and the amount of life upon the globe.—By P. Flourens, Professor of Comparative Physiology, Paris. Translated by Charles Martel. Boards, 1s. P. 2½d.

The Meteoric Theory of Saturn's Rings, considered with reference to the Solar Motion in Space. With illustrations. Paper wrapper, crown 8vo, 1d. P. ½d.

The Human Mind. A System of Mental Philosophy. By J. G. Murphy, LL.D. Cloth, crown 8vo, 350 pp., 2s. P. 5d.

The Modern Practice of Physic, exhibiting the symptoms, causes, prognostics, morbid appearances and treatment of the diseases of all climates. By R. Thomas, M.D. Eleventh edition, revised by A. Frampton, Physician London Hospital. In 2 vols., royal 8vo, 564 pp. and 756 pp. This work contains a great number of recipes and prescriptions for all kinds of diseases, each given in both Latin and English. With a copious index and table of contents. 6s.

The Finding of the Book. An essay on the origin of the Dogma of Infallibility. By John Robertson. This is the important work which provoked the famous heresy prosecution. Published at 2s. Post free 1s.

The Irish Problem and how to solve it. An historical and critical review of the legislation and events that have led to Irish difficulties, including suggestions for practical remedies. Cloth, demy 8vo, 410 pp. This work is only just issued, and brings the History of the Irish Question up to the present time, and contains in addition to Compensation for Disturbance Bill, several Acts of Parliament, including the Coercion Bill of the present year. 2s. P. 9d.

The Rights and Duties of Property. With a plan for paying off the National Debt, dealing with the Science of Political Economy, the Land Question, etc., etc. Cloth, 260 pp. 6d. P. 3d.

Satan: His existence disproved, and the notions of Battles in Heaven and of Fallen Angels shown to have originated in Astronomical Phænomena. 1d. P. ½d.

Intervention and Non-Intervention on the Foreign Policy of Great Britain, from 1790 to 1865. By A. G. Stapleton. Demy 8vo. 300 pp. 2s. P. 6d.

Reply to Bishop Watson's attack on the "Age of Reason." By Thomas Paine. 1d. P. ½d.

Splendid Steel Portraits of **Lord Brougham, John Bright** and **Richard Cobden.** 24 by 18. 1s. each; or the three for 2s. 6d.

The Pentateuch and Book of Joshua in Contrast with the Moral Sense of our Age. Published at 6s. 6d. in parts. By the late Thomas Scott. In 1 vol. complete. 2s. P. 5d.

Christianity in the Nineteenth Century. A Religious and Philosophical Survey of the Immediate Past. By Etienne Chastel, Professor of Ecclesiastical History at the University of Geneva. Translated by J. Beard. Cloth, crown 8vo, 236 pp., 1s. P. 3½d.

The History of Christianity. By E. N. BOUZIQUE. Translated by J. BEARD. In three vols., nearly 400 pp. in each, crown 8vo, cloth. 5s.

Children's Ailments: how to distinguish and how to treat them. A manual of nursery medicine, addressed to mothers and nurses and to all who are interested in caring for the little ones. By WILLIAM BOOTH, L.R.C.P. Ed., etc., etc. This extremely useful little work, published at 2s., gives the symptoms and modes of treatment of nearly 100 ailments, instructions for the general management of young children, and 47 prescriptions with a table of doses for all diseases. 3d. P. 1d.

The Anti-Papal Library.—"How did we come by the Reformation?" by J. R. Beard; "The Dragonnades of Louis XIV., or the barbarous atrocities of Romanism under Pope Innocent XI.," by E. A. Bouzique; "Mary Alacoque and the Worship of the Sacred Heart of Jesus, presented in their real character," by Louis Asseline; "Coalition of the Thermal and Mineral Waters of France against the Sacred Waters of Lourdes and La Salette." These pamphlets, written by eminent advanced writers and translated by the celebrated Unitarian, J. R. Beard, are full of information concerning the frauds and impostures of the Romish Church. Published at 4d. and 6d. each. The four post free for 4d. Also in the same series—"Confession in the Church of Rome: what it is and what it does." By the noted writer, M. Morin; translated by J. R. Beard. Published at 1s. 80 pp. 3d. P. 1d.

Rudiments of Geology. By SAMUEL SHARP, F.S.A., F.G.S. Introductory, Stratigraphical and Palæontological; with exhaustive Table of Classification of Geological Formation. Cloth, 6d. P. 2d.

The Story of the Ashantee Campaign. By WINWOOD READE, the *Times* Correspondent (author of the "Outcast"). With colored map, cloth, crown 8vo, gilt, 440 pp., 2s. 6d. P. 5d.

Ludwig Borne. Recollections of a Revolutionist, by HEINRICH HEINE; Abridged and Translated by T. S. EGAN. 2s. P. 3½d.

English Fragments, from the German of HEINRICH HEINE. Translated by S. NORRIS. Cloth, 1s. 6d. P. 2½d.

Health Lectures for the People.—Causes Reducing the Effects of Sanitary Reform—Clothing—Good Nursing, and its Necessity in the Treatment of Disease—The Loss of Wealth by Loss of Health—How a Tenant may Make his Cottage Healthy and Comfortable—Defective Drainage as a Cause of Disease—The House Water, its work of purification—Personal and Household Arrangements in Relation to Health—Health and Recreation in Childhood—Consumption—Sick Nursing among the Poor. The whole of these by eminent authorities. The twelve, post free, 1s.

Science Lectures for the People.—The Functions of the Brain—The Birds of the Globe—Insectivorous Plants—The Modern History of Gunpowder—Edison and some of his Inventions—The Sun—On Certain of the Phænomena connected with Solution and

Crystallisation—Mental Evolution—The Aborigines of Tasmania—Suspected Relations between the Sun and Planets—Palestine in its Physical Aspects—The Relation of Structure to Function in Animal Organisms. The whole of these by the best living scientists. The twelve, post free, 1s.

Our Hereditary Legislators.—Six Letters on the House of Lords, by "Verax," reprinted from the "Manchester Weekly Times." 32 pp. Post free, 1½d.

The Irish Land Act: will England demand it?—Illustrated by Tales of My Tenants. By an Anglo-Irish Tenant Farmer. 175 pp. 6d. P. 2½d.

Free Sale of Tenant Right, with fair but strict terms by mutual agreement between Landlord and Tenant.—A practical settlement of the Land Question in Ireland. By J. G. V. Porter, Esq. Paper covers, 84 pp. Post Free, 4d.

EDUCATIONAL.

FROM LIST B.

Elementary Chemistry. By Rev. H. MARTYN HART, B.A. 1s. P. 3½d.

A Compendium of English History. From the Earliest Times to A.D. 1872. With copious quotations on leading events and Constitutional History, with Appendices. By HERBERT R. CLINTON. 358 pp. Published at 7s. 6d. 2s. 6d. P. 5d.

First Book of English Grammar. By JOHN HUGH HAWLEY. Third edition, Cloth, 3d. P. 1d.

Latin Grammar. By L. DIREY. Pp. 179. Neatly bound. (Published at 4s.) 6d. P. 2d.

English Grammar. By L. DIREY and A. FOGGO. Pp. 136. (Published at 3s.) 6d. P. 2½d.

The Life of Cicero. By CONYERS MIDDLETON, D.D. Complete in one volume, with copious index and steel frontispiece. Demy 8vo, 760 pp. 2s. 6d. P. 9½d. Very cheap.

Facts and Figures, Important Events in History, Geography, Literature, Biography, Ecclesiastical History, etc., etc. Arranged in classified chronological order. Post free, 6d.

Elements of Chemistry, Theoretical and Practical, including the most recent discoveries and applications of the science to medicine and pharmacy, to agriculture, and to manufacture. Illustrated by 230 woodcuts, with copious index. Second edition. By SIR ROBERT KANE, M.D., M.R.I.A., President of Queen's College, Cork. Cloth, royal 8vo, 1069 pp. Price, 3s. 6d.

Bale's Anatomy and Physiology of Man. Students' edition. Profusely illustrated (published at 10s. 6d.), for 3s. 6d. P. 5d. And the same work, School edition (published at 7s. 6d), for 2s. 6d. P. 4½d.

Parker's Compendium of Natural and Experimental Philosophy, Mechanics, Hydrostatics, Acoustics, Astronomy, etc., etc. Post 8vo, profusely illustrated, 400 pp. 1s. 6d. P. 3½d.

The Elements of Agricultural Chemistry and Geology. By the late Professor J. F. W. JOHNSTON and C. A. CAMERON, Prof. Chemistry, R.C.S., etc., etc. Post 8vo., 500 pp., tenth edition. 2s. P. 4½d.

Elements of Astronomy, for Academies and High Schools. By ELIAS LOOMIS, LL.D. Well illustrated, crown 8vo. 2s. 6d. P. 4d.

Crabbe's Technical Dictionary of all the Terms used in the Arts and Sciences. Post 8vo, 600 pp., 2s. P. 5d.

The Child's Ladder of Knowledge. By G. J. HOLYOAKE. Illustrated (published at 8d.), post free 4d.

The Students' Chemistry. Being the Seventh Edition of Household Chemistry, or the Science of Home Life. By ALBERT J. BERNAYS, Ph.D., F.C.S. 347 pp., well illustrated, 1s. 6d. P. 4½d. This book is one of the best standard authorities.

Brief Notes on Chemistry; with Tables on the Metallic and Non-Metallic Elements, and **Concise Tables for Chemical Analysis.** By W. GROOME, M.A., etc., Head Master of the Beds. Middle Class School. Both these works, extremely useful to students, are bound in limp cloth, demy 8vo. The two 6d. P. 1½d. Also by the same author,

A Concise Treatise on Music, Musical Harmony, and Thorough Bass. Illustrated, limp cloth, 30 pp., demy 8vo, 3d. P. 1d.

One Thousand Geometrical Tests. Comprising exercises in Mensuration, Euclid, Practical Geometry, and Trigonometry; specially adapted by a novel arrangement for examination purposes, but suited also for general use in schools. By THOMAS S. CAYZER, Head Master of Queen Elizabeth Hospital, Bristol. 82 pp., cloth, demy 8vo, 6d. P. 2d.

Hallam's Constitutional History of England. Pp. 970. 3s. 9d. P. 8d.

Hallam's Europe during the Middle Ages. 720 pp. 2s. 8d. P. 6d.

Volney's Lectures on History. Post-free, 6d.

The Philosophy and History of Civilisation. By ALEXANDER ALISON. Cloth, Royal 8vo, 478 pp., 2s. P. 7d.

The Child's Reading Book. By G. J. HOLYOAKE. Illustrated, 1d.

History of Civilisation in the Fifth Century. Translated from the French of A. Frédéric Ozanam by ASHLEY C. GLYNN. B.A. 2 vols. in one, 470 pp., an excellent work, 2s. 6d. P. 6½d.

The Principles of Language Exemplified in a Practical English Grammar. With copious exercises. By J. Crane. 264 pp. 6d. P. 3d.

HALL OF SCIENCE MANUALS.

I.—Light, Heat, and Sound. By Annie Besant. In three parts, 6d. each. Illustrated. Bound in limp cloth, 1s. 6d.; cloth, 2s.

The whole of the late Thomas Scott's publications still in print can be supplied. Catalogues sent on application.

THE

NATIONAL REFORMER.

Journal of Radicalism and Freethought.

EDITED BY

CHARLES BRADLAUGH and ANNIE BESANT.

Weekly—Price Twopence.

Post free to any part of Great Britain, Europe, Egypt, the United States, and the whole of British America, 10s. 10d. New Zealand, Australia, British African Colonies, South America, West Indies, Ceylon, and China, *viâ* United States, 13s. India, Japan, and China, *viâ* Brindisi, 15s. 2d. per annum.

With its large and constantly-increasing circulation, The National Reformer—which is constantly reviewing works on Theology, Philosophy, Politics, and Sociology—is an admirable Advertising Medium especially for Publishers.

SCALE OF CHARGES FOR ADVERTISEMENTS.

First Thirty Words	£0	1	6
Every additional Ten, or part of Ten Words	0	0	6
Quarter Column	0	12	6
Half a Column	1	0	0
Column	1	14	0
Page	3	0	0

Special Arrangements may be made for repeated insertions.

www.ingramcontent.com/pod-product-compliance
Lightning Source LLC
LaVergne TN
LVHW010217110826
845151LV00004B/1114

* 9 7 8 1 4 2 5 5 2 7 0 4 4 *